artWorks

For as long as there has been art, there has been discussion about art. Over the past two centuries, as ideas and movements have succeeded each other with dizzying speed and the debate between various aesthetics has turned increasingly vivid, art criticism and theory have taken on an unprecedented relevance to the development of art itself.

ARTWORKS restores to print the most significant writings about art—whether letters and essays by the artists themselves, memoirs and polemics by those who lived with them in the thick of creation, or illuminating studies by some of our most prominent scholars and critics. Many of these works have long been unavailable in English, but they merit republication because the truths they convey remain valid and important. The list is eclectic because art is eclectic; taken as a whole, these titles reflect the history of art in all its color and variation, but they are bound together by a concern for their importance as primary documents.

These are writings that address art as being of both the eye and the mind, that recognize and celebrate the constant flux in which creation has occurred. And as such, they are crucial to any understanding or criticism of art today.

AVAILABLE IN ARTWORKS

Apollinaire on Art: Essays and Reviews, 1902–1918
edited and introduced by LeRoy C. Breunig
with a new foreword by Roger Shattuck

Futurist Manifestos
edited by Umbro Apollonio
with a new afterword by Richard Humphreys

Surrealism and Painting
André Breton
with a new introduction by Mark Polizzotti

Selected Letters, 1813–1863
Eugène Delacroix
edited and translated by Jean Stewart
with an introduction by John Russell

My Galleries and Painters
D.-H. Kahnweiler, with Francis Crémieux
with an introduction by John Russell and new material

Memoir of an Art Gallery
Julien Levy
with a new introduction by Ingrid Schaffner

Stieglitz: A Memoir / Biography
Sue Davidson Lowe
with a new foreword by the author
and a new preface by Anne E. Havinga

Letters to His Son Lucien
Camille Pissarro
edited and with an introduction by John Rewald
with a new afterword by Barbara Stern Shapiro

The Innocent Eye: On Modern Literature and the Arts
Roger Shattuck

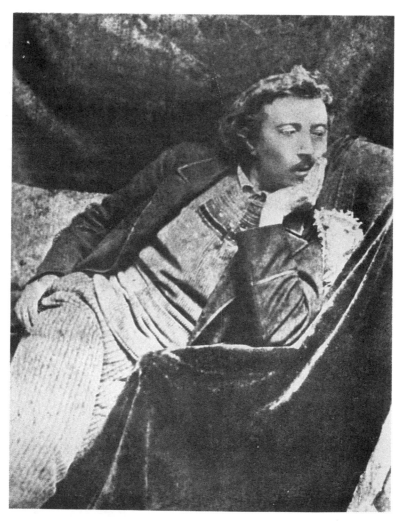

Photograph of Gauguin, 1888
(*from Mmle. Annie Joly-Segalen*)

Letters

to his Wife and Friends

❦

PAUL GAUGUIN

edited and with a preface by Maurice Malingue

translated by Henry J. Stenning

artWorks

MFA PUBLICATIONS

a division of the Museum of Fine Arts, Boston

MFA PUBLICATIONS
a division of the Museum of Fine Arts, Boston
465 Huntington Avenue
Boston, Massachusetts 02115
www.mfa-publications.org

For a complete listing of MFA Publications, please contact the publisher at the above address, or call 617 369 3438.

ISBN 0-87846-665-7
Library of Congress Control Number: 2003108585

Available through D.A.P. / Distributed Art Publishers
155 Sixth Avenue
New York, New York 10013
Tel.: 212 627 1999 · Fax: 212 627 9484

FIRST ARTWORKS EDITION, 2003
Printed and bound in the United States of America

" What have I done

to be so unhappy?"

PAUL GAUGUIN

PREFACE

ON THE 8TH MAY, 1903, at Atuana, a village of Dominique, an islet of the Marquesas group, Paul Gauguin lay, inert, prostrated by two successive swoons, no longer conscious of morning or evening, day or night. Towards eleven o'clock on that morning, Pastor Vernier, summoned hastily, entered the native hut in which the painter lived and found him lifeless, one leg hanging out of bed, but still warm. And then Tioka, the faithful old Marquisan, who accompanied the pastor, threw himself on the body of his white friend, crying in despair : " Gauguin is dead, we are lost."

*   *   *

For some little time, Paul Gauguin had realised that his diseased heart could not beat much longer. Had he not written to Daniel de Monfreid : " I suffer with my heart : My heart is attacked." He well knew its weakness, resulting from the poverty in which he had been struggling for fifteen years, the privations he had endured, and the troubles which had overwhelmed him. He had not been treated for the syphilis with which he was affected, the sequence of a deplorable night of love before his departure for Tahiti, and it had poisoned his system; but how could he have paid for a doctor and procured remedies when he lacked the money to buy food? Incapable of standing up, he could see his swollen legs covered with enormous red, angry eczema sores, which tormented him horribly.

Not a word of complaint escaped him. To keep silent, he summoned the pride of his ancestors—the remote Borgias of Aragon —from whom he claimed descent. But as the new century dawned, although he exerted enormous will-power, and while he had begged for only two years of health to reach a certain maturity in his art, he knew he was finished.

Had his life then ended only in failure? " I am a great artist, and I know it," he would say to his wife, and in order to give unfettered expression to his pictorial vision—as a free man—he had

had the prodigious courage to renounce all that life holds dear: a position on the Bourse, wife, love, children, home. He had raised up a barrier of indifference between the world and himself as regards everything not appertaining to his art—which is not to say that he was incapable of emotion. But nobody, except Daniel de Monfreid, had ever understood his confidence in his genius, his pride, his apparent scepticism, his self-styled egoism. What was it to him that his own life appeared to the world as a failure, and that he was finishing it in suffering and misfortune? He knew the value of his example, the importance of his message and, putting painting first, he regretted nothing. Following his star, he had never abandoned the struggle, despite his mental and physical torments, his distresses, his ghastly solitude. " What bothers me the most," he confessed, " is not so much poverty as the continual obstacles to my art, which I cannot practise as I feel it, and as I could were it not for the poverty which ties my hands."

And now, he was beaten by this poverty and illness. Although it was the opinion of Pastor Vernier and the writer, Victor Segalen, who was present in Papeete at the sale of the painter's effects, and later visited Atuana, as well as of the doctors who studied the symptoms of his disease, that Paul Gauguin died of a heart attack, I say, for my part, that he died of starvation and despair.

*   *   *

Paul Gauguin died of starvation and despair. Such is the tragedy which emerges from this correspondence which we have collected, without unfortunately, being able to include the letters addressed by the artist to Daniel de Monfreid, and published by Victor Segalen, who used initials instead of the names of persons mentioned.

To-day, with the exception of Judith Gérard, Paul-Emile Colin and Léon Fauché, the last survivor of the 1889 Exhibition of the Impressionist and Synthetic Group of Painters, both friends and enemies of Gauguin have in their turn disappeared, and although the living may claim consideration we owe nothing but truth to the dead. I have, therefore, omitted no word and no name from these letters—save that of a young Dane, Miss de M . . . —nor any accusation made by the painter against those he held responsible for the wretched conditions in which he lived in Tahiti.

The first letters, those of Mme. Heegaard, the mother of a friend of his wife, reveal a genial Gauguin, delighted with the married state and at having carried away from Denmark a pearl as precious as Mette Sophie Gad. In all these letters he gives the impression of being enamoured of this healthy, strong, open-minded, tall and handsome girl of twenty-four, as well as physically aroused by the contours of her firm, well modelled body. Affectionate husband, loving father, tenderly describing his first baby : " White as a swan, strong as Hercules," Gauguin glided through the happiest days of his life.

But the happiness of extraordinary persons never lasts long. The employee of Bertin's Bank became the impressionist painter, Paul Gauguin, whose pictures found no buyers. In December, 1884 —two years after this metamorphosis—Mette had decided to return to Denmark, and Gauguin was selling tilt for a living. He sent regular reports to Messrs. Dillies & Co. of Roubaix, his employers, on the course of business, which was, of course, not good; exerting himself although detached from everything alien to his art, not to omit the slightest detail likely to assist the firm in coping with competition.

With the doggedness which characterised him, he was to be for several months the remarkable agent for tilt that was unsaleable because of its high price; persevering with customers, amenable towards his employers, until wearied at length with percentages, measurements and invoices, he was to abandon family, tilt and Denmark.

In August, 1885, there begin the letters to " My dear Mette," which were to continue until 1897 and certainly constitute the most extraordinary records of love, suffering and bitterness towards the only woman whom Gauguin really loved and respected, and also the most overwhelming indictments in the trial of Mette Gauguin, who can now be charged with incomprehension of the artist, indifference towards the man, and with having as a wife failed the father of her five children.

Let me explain. We may concede that, of middle-class family and education, attracted by Parisian life and Gauguin's business position—had he not fourteen pairs of trousers—Mette, in contrast with wives of innumerable artists, found it difficult to contemplate poverty for herself and her children. But it is certain that, once definitely separated from her husband, she contrived a modest but

nevertheless agreeable existence, and although she detested painting
—(" This lousy painting that you have often enough insulted," he
once said to her), she carried off to Copenhagen and disposed
piecemeal of her husband's collection of the works of Cézanne,
Degas and others; and was never without Impressionist, Breton or
Tahitian canvases, despatched by Gauguin, Emile Schuffenecker or
Daniel de Monfreid, which canvases she sold for her own benefit.[1]

Her self-esteem, as a Dane married to a Frenchman living in
Paris, but afterwards obliged to return alone and eke out a laborious
and mediocre existence in her own country, had suffered a severe
shock, and I believe she never forgave Gauguin this change in social
position. It is probable that Mette, the daughter of an official,
brought up with some degree of mental freedom but in the observ-
ance of somewhat rigid moral principles, never could understand
how a father of five children could throw up a comfortable position
without bothering what was to become of his family.

It is obvious that her womanly susceptibility was bitterly
wounded when the man in whom she had put her trust showed no
hesitation in choosing between her and his painting. Her humiliation
was the more painful when she had to endure the reproaches of
her relatives and the sarcasm of her brothers and sisters, in regard
to the translation work to which she applied herself in order to
live.

And so at no time, even in the most tragic circumstances—
when the unhappy man announced that he had had to post up bills
to obtain the wherewithal to care for his sick son Clovis; that he
had spat blood; tried to commit suicide—did she make a gesture of
consolation, nor intimate that he could still count on her love. On
the contrary, she never replied to his requests, sometimes let two
months pass without writing him a line and constantly reminded
him of her pecuniary needs. When Gauguin complained of receiving no word from his children on the occasion of his birthday, she
cynically replied: "You have no money, don't expect them." To
his justified grievances, she retorted that she prized her peace of

Note 1. In June, 1896, Gauguin stated: " My collection had been bought
for 15,000 Francs (on the admission of my brother-in-law, who
bought it); plus not a few of my old canvases, plus the canvases
and pottery. I estimate the lot would realise 30,000 Francs. In
addition I have sent 4,000 Francs at various times. From these
sales, I have had only 600 Francs. And I have always lived
wretchedly."

mind above everything, and went on to say: "Why weep, our two lives are sundered."

Had she ever loved him? Gauguin seems to have answered this question in anticipation of her reply: "Your letters are as they used to be in our life together: anything but an exchange of ideas and emotions." Her letters in fact, are banal, correct and very detached. She always ended them with a frigid, "Your wife Mette," which tormented and enervated the artist, causing him to pass a sleepless night whenever one was received. Moreover, she never tried to see him again, and on the two occasions when they did meet, her chief anxiety was to avoid a fresh maternity.

It was a long time before the severity which Mette Gauguin displayed towards her husband modified the tender feelings which he bore her. He plunged into casual amours at Pont-Aven, set up house in Paris with a Javanese, and in Tahiti bedevilled hussies invaded his bed every night; but his most secret thoughts were of her who was his wife, and whom he never ceased to love. It is certain that this separation, desired by Gauguin at the time, was not intended to be permanent. From time to time he assured Mette that, when success came, they would resume their life together and that he would be able to assure her an existence worthy of the name she bore. He would build it up like a picture: after the years of trial, husband and wife surrounded by their children, "flesh of their flesh," entering upon an era of peace and happiness. The words he uses are of an affecting banality. "You will rest, and as for me, I will work . . . your faithful lover and husband." When he is in despair he exclaims sadly: "I am loved if I love, I am written to if I write," but he immediately showers a thousand endearments on his wife, and never ceases to confide in her. He contemplates with perfect lucidity the sickening, disgusting life he is leading, and thus extols the happiness to which he aspires: "Whatever people may invent, they will never discover anything better than a united family."

This perfect egoist—as so many people have deemed him—is a father who suffered keenly in living apart from his children. Obviously, he could have had them with him if he wanted to. He renounced his paternal duties deliberately, because constrained to do so by the demands of his art. The presence of his children would have imposed on him paternal obligations, and he would thus have lost a part of the limited time so necessary for the flowering of his art. And nothing could avail to deflect him from his painting.

He jokes about the illegitimate children he scatters about the world; a daughter in Paris, a boy Emil and more daughters in Tahiti and in La Dominique, but his legitimate children, " flesh of our flesh," as he reminds Mette so seasonably, are never out of his thoughts. He would have liked to direct their education, form their minds, feel they were French; instead of this, his wife tore them from him, and made them Danes in heart and soul. He found it particularly painful to believe, according to certain allusions from Mette, that his children might one day blush for the name they bore. This idea obsessed him for a long time.

He was devoted to little Clovis and his daughter Aline, with her innocent expression, in whom he saw reflected his own sensitiveness, and who understood him better than Emil, Jean and Pola. For this sweet, submissive child, who alone realised that her father, despite his poverty, was a great painter, he compiled, in 1893, a notebook which he dedicated to her between a bad reproduction of Corot and an eulogistic chronicle of Jean Dolent:

This Notebook is dedicated to my daughter Aline.

Scattered incoherent notes like dreams, like Life—all made up of scraps.

These two children, of delicate health, were doomed to die young, Aline in 1897, at 18, and Clovis in 1900, at 21 years of age.

Other letters are addressed to " Dear Schuff," once in the service of Bertin, where he made Gauguin's acquaintance. He, too, forsook the Bank for painting. Emile Schuffenecker took a studio first in the Rue Boulard, afterwards in the Rue Durand-Clary, and spent several hours every day entertaining his friends. They were always certain to find a bed there and something to eat. Married to a charming and pretty woman, who in those early days was not disturbed by a lively household, the " worthy Schuff " opened wide his doors and, amid the smoke of cigarettes, long discussions on art, destined to revolutionize painting, took place every evening and were often prolonged far into the night.

This friend, through good and ill report, welcomed Gauguin, whenever the painter, not knowing where else to turn, found his way to the house. He never refused a request for money.

Although he was not enamoured of Gauguin's Breton works, Schuffenecker remained an impressionist all his life. He admired his friend and recognised his genius and on his account deliberately sacrificed his peace of mind. But the visits of geniuses are rarely a source of quiet, which Schuffenecker was not long in finding out, especially between 1888 and 1891, when Gauguin often showed the basest ingratitude. Nevertheless, nothing ever wore out his patience or his friendship.

With Emile Bernard it was somewhat different. This young man of twenty, well-informed, zealous, mystic, with a remarkable talent for painting, whom Schuffenecker met on a road in Brittany, looked up to Gauguin much as Rimbaud looked up to Verlaine. And tragedy, albeit of a different kind, was in store for both painter and poet.

Gauguin's meeting with Bernard, in August, 1888, in the sitting room of the pension Gloanec, at Pont-Aven, was the collision which precipitated the synthesis, which Gauguin would sometimes ironically write " Saintaise because it rhymed with foutaise "[1] but the importance of which was at once realised by Gauguin with his extremely acute perceptions. Between the four walls of a little room in the pension Gloanec, Bernard rapidly painted for his new friend, from memory, so as to cut out the useless complication of forms and tones, a magnificent canvas, *Breton women in a meadow*, representing Breton women in black dresses, seated in a green and yellow meadow; and Gauguin, enchanted by this method, which consisted in reducing all forms to their essential lines and the colours to all the tones of the palette—a method which he tried to imitate without being perfectly successful—painted in his turn for Bernard the *Vision after the Sermon*, upon a red instead of a yellow green background, and in which he avoided shadows as well as the modelling in the heads.

But Bernard was only twenty, while Gauguin was over forty. The former lived in a perpetual gushing of art forms, designs, water-colours, oils, stained-glass windows, frescos—preoccupied entirely with lines and new creations; the latter, while admitting his poverty, sought to escape from it, and accepted everything that his connexions could do in order to evade it. He was thus naturally not disposed to deny the paternity of pictorial symbolism which Albert Aurier attributed exclusively to him on seeing the *Vision after the Sermon*, a paternity which exasperated Bernard to such an

---

[1] " Foutaise " and " Saintaise " impossible to translate. Personal invention of the poet.

extent that his personal and artistic life was thereby profoundly disturbed.

In his letters to Bernard, in which he never deviated from his position of the elder, Gauguin freely discusses the efforts he made to attain to his mastery, often gives him very valuable advice, and encourages him to persevere in his endeavours, in spite of the hostility of his family, who neither admitted nor understood his vocation. It is true that the famous elder had another reason for being benevolent: he wanted and at the same time respected his friend's sister, Madeleine Bernard, a young girl of exquisite sensibility and noble character, whom he even meditated abducting so violent was his desire.

Letter after letter reveals the solitary life of Paul Gauguin, with his hopes and disappointments, the life that he dreamed of as peaceful and industrious in the South Sea Islands, the isles of Paradise, where all is beauty, kindness and light—and that made him so wretched.

The actual facts can be stated in a few words. Gauguin wanted 2,400 francs a year upon which to live in Tahiti. He has himself stated that, when he succumbed to the spell of the South Seas in 1895 and set off for the second time, he had obtained the promise of certain picture dealers to guarantee him regular sales, not one of which was ever kept. While awaiting the first remittances, he reckoned to live for two years on loans to be granted by the proprietor of the Café des Variétés, 2,600 francs : the painter Maufra 300 francs: Dosbourg a frame-maker, 600 francs: Talboum, 800 francs, of which he had received no more than 600 francs by 1897.

The budget which he had carefully prepared was completely disorganised, and, from April, 1896, his letters to Monfreid are again full of his financial worries: " The longer I go on, the deeper I sink," he rightly said; but he was sinking because the majority of the amateurs and dealers with whom he was in touch, either directly or through the agency of Daniel de Monfreid, scented the artist's financial value, and made every effort to obtain his canvases as cheaply as possible in order to do a good stroke of business.

The dealer Vollard[1] was one of those chiefly responsible for Gauguin's poverty. He obtained for 2,000 francs a fine picture

[1] Vollard never comes but when he already has a buyer and 25% commission is not enough for him; he cares not a damn for anything but success. Gauguin, 22nd February, 1899.

which he had already sold to an amateur for 10,000 francs, and bought for 150 or 200 francs pictures which he disposed of for 1,000 francs, whilst remitting money very irregularly to the painter. By 1900, Ambrose Vollard had stocked away in the famous cellar below his shop in Rue Lafitte, a number of Gauguin's pictures, which he kept in the expectation of making large profits.

These facts, which demonstrate clearly the exploitation of the artist, would not have to be recorded, had Théo van Gogh lived. It may be said that with the death of Théo van Gogh, whom Vincent had interested in his welfare, Gauguin saw his sole chance of success vanish, for Théo would soon have found customers for his painter, without seeking to defraud him.

*   *   *

With impared digestion, excessively impressionable, exhausted by sleepless nights, sometimes remaining in a crouched position for twenty hours out of the twenty four, literally " killed," as he himself described it, Paul Gauguin, " the savage," " the barbarian," from time to time recovered sufficient lucidity and strength to seize his brushes and express his vision of primitive beauty and humanity by depicting a race in which he divined the origins of the world.

These works composed with surprising virtuosity, in which the design aims at expressing the form, in which the alternate use of powerful scales of warm and cold tones, blue, red, orange, yellow, violet, impart to the subjects reproduced an arresting significance: that of death and life—these works abounding in simplification, brutality and reflection restored the monumental quality to painting. And Gauguin's art was the parent of modern art.

Brittany, Martinique, the South Sea islands—these magical lands —could not appease the sufferings of Paul Gauguin, the solitary. But these letters, published now[1] for the first time, restore him to us to-day, stripped of legend, a veritable God of painting, taking his rightful place among the Immortals.

Maurice Malingue.

[1] Published by Bernard Grasset, Paris, in 1946.

Bust of Mette Gauguin by Paul Gauguin
(*permission of Home House Trustees*)

FOREWORD

As it is impossible to publish at present the general correspondence of Paul Gauguin—the letters to Daniel de Monfreid edited by Victor Segalen in 1918 being excluded from the present collection for private reasons—I have tried to collect all I could of the letters addressed by the painter to his wife and his friends.

Consequently, my enquiries have led me to the few survivors of those who knew Paul Gauguin, either in 1888, or during his last sojourn in France, from 1893 to 1895.

I have met Marie le Pape, the pretty servant maid at the Gloanec pension, who saw nothing in Gauguin but an artist who wished to paint her nude, Madame Judith Gérard, daughter-in-law of the musician Molard, whose ardent youth captivated Gauguin, Léon Fauché, "the man of Nancy" of the Volpini exhibition, at whose residence Gauguin etched the famous portrait of Stéphane Mallarmé.

I was cordially welcomed by everyone, who, in memory of Gauguin, did their best to recall this remote epoch of their existence, or placed at my disposal letters which they still possessed.

A large numbers of letters have also been communicated to me by the families of their addressees or their successors, as well as by collectors of autographs. But this correspondence reveals gaps which it is impossible at the moment for me to fill. Many letters have been destroyed by Gauguin's friends, others are scattered either in France or abroad, where I have been unable to trace them. In any event, *Gauguin's Letters to his Wife and his Friends*, comprise, independently of those received by Daniel de Monfried, a correspondence the study of which is essential for an understanding of the man and the painter.

I am indebted to Mme. Jeanne Schuffenecker, daughter of Emile Schuffenecker, for sending me some letters addressed to her father and to Messrs. Dillies & Co., of Roubaix, Gauguin's employers.

Thanks to these documents, I have been able to clear up many obscure points in the relations between Gauguin and his wife. Emile Bernard's widow has authorised me to publish the important records collected by Emile Bernard in his studio on the Quai de Bourbon. I am indebted to M. Alfred Dupont for the letters addressed to Arsène Alexandre, Charles Morice and the Colonial officials. To Dominique Denis for those to his father Maurice Denis. The letters to Stéphane Mallarmé were discovered at Valvins, by Professor Henry Mondor, of the Académie Française. Thanks to the famous bookseller, Marcel Lecomte, I became acquainted with letters and postcards addressed to Madame Rachilde. Marcel Guérin communicated to me the letters to Félix Bracquemond. The Gouzer family those to their relative Dr. Gouzer. M. J. Williame, notary of Châtauroux, acquainted me with the letters addressed to his uncle, the art critic Albert Aurier and the Library of Art and History of the University of Paris allowed me to inspect the important correspondence of the painter with his wife.

In addition to the persons above mentioned, I am also indebted for valuable information to André Fontainas, François Cadoret, Mayor of Riec-sur-Belon, Robert Le Gloanec, the painter Emile Compard, the engraver Paul Emile Colin, Clement Altarriba, Michel Ange Bernard, Jean Loize and the comte de la Rochefoucauld, as well as the widow of Maurice Denis.

Marcel Guiot has kindly lent me photographs of unpublished works of Gaugin.

I have added a few notes designed to elucidate events already so remote, to which the painter alludes.

On the other hand, I have not corrected grammatical errors which Gauguin sometimes makes, while refraining from adding thereto the famous intolerable *sic*[1].

Moreover, these mistakes are the rare signs of fatigue which escape Gauguin. Whatever the incidents which marked his life, lowered his health or depressed his spirits, the painter's writing is never straggling. On the contrary, it seems that the more Gauguin decayed physically, the steadier became his hand in writing. Thus

---

[1] No attempt has been made to reproduce these errors, whether of grammar or punctuation, in this translation.

at Copenhagen, as at Pont-Aven, Martinique, Tahiti and Dominique, the artist's caligraphy is slightly sloping, always regular and distinguished.

Now and then he decorated his letters with a sketch, while as to paper, his slender resources would not allow him to be exacting. He bought packets of white sheets or lined paper from tobacconists or stationers, of a poor quality which has not worn well.

M. M.

PAUL GAUGUIN: LETTERS

1.

TO MRS. HEEGAARD[1]   Paris, 9 February, 1873.

Dear Madam,

The kind letter you have been good enough to send me congratulating me on the choice I have made in asking for Mette's hand, tells me that you also love her. Good friends are rare and I am happy to bestow this title on you, to which I attach much importance.

I am sure that Miss Mette[2] will find many admirers in France, the strength of her character combined with her loyal feelings attracting everybody's esteem, so I count myself very happy at her choice.

Rest assured that in carrying off from Denmark so precious a pearl, I will do everything possible, and even impossible, so that she will not regret leaving all her friends, whom she will love, in spite of that, as in the past. I look forward to greeting you on your arrival in Paris, and in the meantime, remain with all good wishes,

PAUL GAUGUIN.

Give my affectionate greetings to Miss Louise[3].

---

[1] Early in the year 1873, Mr. Heegaard, a Copenhagen manufacturer, invited Mette Sophie Gad, his daughter Marie's best friend, to visit France with her. It was during this trip that Mette became acquainted with Paul Gauguin, at the boarding house kept by the sculptor Aubé's wife.

[2] Mette Sophie Gad, born 7th September, 1850, at Vestero, See of Alborg, in Denmark. Daughter of a civic officer, Théodore Gad, and of Emilie Lund, she became at seventeen governess to the children of the politician Estrup, then Prime Minister. Pretty, intelligent, frank of speech, but rational in her ideas of life, Mette married Gauguin on the 22nd November, 1873, in the Town Hall of the 9th Arrondissement, in the Rue Drouot. The religious ceremony was celebrated the same day in the Lutheran Church in the Rue Chauchat.

[3] Louise Heegaard, Marie's sister.

2.

TO MRS. HEEGAARD.   Paris, 25 April, 1874.

My dear Madam,

Nothing reminds us more of friends than the seasons in which we first knew them. Spring is here; I am thinking of you and wondering if you can manage to come and see us this year: you really must have a little holiday! A warm welcome awaits you here, and I should like to know what you think of Mette: she has grown so handsome, although a trifle thin—she walks now as if her knee had never bitten the dust. You are quite right—husbands are the best doctors.

We have spent a delightful winter, some might say, a little severe, but it has been very nice in our little flat. Mette told me you are sometimes vexed at her silence—forgive the poor little woman, for she has suffered somewhat, and you know that she does not support illness with quite the courage of a Christian martyr; and then she keeps up a correspondence with her family, which occupies a little of her time. I will try to let you feel no difference by writing to you in her stead, but it is impossible to cope with her sudden attack of high spirits for despite . . . of a delightful enough . . . remains always . . . boring and disagreeable husband.[1]

Let me turn my eyes towards Denmark, and I catch a glimpse of two rather apathetic young girls who do not often reply to the letters we write them; and yet we were fond of them; we are still fond of them; we made a little fuss of them. I did not think I had touched their heart-strings, but I had hoped for a little loving remembrance.

Mette does not feel able to give you a sketch of the fashions, whilst, as for me, I have no idea how ladies are dressed, provided they are not ill dressed. I believe hats are extravagant this year, and that costumes will enrich the dressmakers and ruin the husbands. *Le Printemps,* your favourite shop, is the centre of curiosity and everybody is going there to see the man with the fork.

Q.   Who is the man with the fork?

R.   Nothing more than a man attacked by the betting mania; he betted he would stick a fork in his throat; his friends at breakfast challenged him, and he has won twice over, as the fork slipped out

---

[1] The missing words cannot be deciphered, the paper having been torn.

of his fingers and is at present in his stomach (a fact): we know the doctor who is attending him.

If you come to Paris you will go to the *Français,* where they are performing a play called the *Sphinx;* Mlle. Croirette dies every day in an alarming manner and has scored a marvellous success. I forbear giving you a description of the play, as you will read all about it in the papers.

Fritz[1] is in Paris at the moment, we introduced him yesterday to Madame Arosa. I believe he intends to stop here a month and to paint in a French studio. Madame Arosa is to introduce him to-day to a painter, and he is delighted.

Our poor Ingeborg will have to do without him for some time. Fortunately, the little widow did not come to Arosa's[2] yesterday, for if she had, poor Fritz would have been struck all of a heap by her provocative eyes and the simple and natural grace we know so well—but Ingeborg need not be jealous: I will watch out for her.

In spite of all my grievances, remember me to those young ladies.

My regards to Mr. Heegaard.

Yours very sincerely,

PAUL GAUGUIN.

3.

TO MRS. HEEGAARD   Paris, 8 July, 1874

I add a few words to Mette's letter to forestall your reproaches of ingratitude and indolence.

Both of us are grieved at your stay in Denmark, much too long in my opinion. I see clearly that I shall have to stay for a few years where I am, before I can slip off for a little trip to Copenhagen. I am one of those whom Fate condemns to stay at home; I have

---

[1] Fritz Thaulow, Norwegian painter, who became Gauguin's brother-in-law through marrying his wife's sister, Ingeborg Gad, from whom he was subsequently divorced.

[2] Gustave Arosa was Paul Gauguin's guardian. An amateur of art and literature, and possessing an excellent collection of pictures, Arosa entertained a great deal at his Saint Cloud property. By frequenting this house, Gauguin's artistic tastes were undoubtedly developed. It was through Calzado, Arosa's son-in-law, that Gauguin was offered a post in Bertin's Bank.

had more than my share of travelling and now I am obliged to keep my nose to the grindstone. We jog along comfortably enough, but we do need a few friends close handy; Bichette is always moving about: she is now at Vichy, later she goes to Switzerland. However, we don't feel her absence very much, for when she is in Paris, she never has time to see us. The Spaniards, as well as her numerous friends, take up all her time, which I quite understand—our house is so small and so empty of flatterers.

We saw Adolphe on two or three occasions; he must be quite near Rio de Janeiro by this time. Mette has just received a letter from him, which was posted in Lisbon . He is utterly worn out, and I hope the voyage will restore him.

We should, of course, be pleased to see your young Amser, but as to guiding him, I do not know what to do. As you know, I am not clear myself as to what constitutes virtue and vice. Mette could certainly give him good advice, but I doubt whether he would listen to it.

Please convey to Mr. Heegaard my regrets for my inability to serve him, as there is no business to be done here.

Regards to your two charming daughters. I am still waiting to hear from the little Marie, to whom I wrote some time ago, hoping for a reply.

Pending your visit to our little flat, I remain,

Your affectionate friend,

PAUL GAUGUIN.

4.

TO MRS. HEEGAARD.   Paris, 12 September, 1874.

My dear Madam,

While I must send you thanks for your cordial letter, I have a bone to pick with you. What do you mean by setting off on your travels without stopping in Paris, your favourite city, and where you have sincere friends. Mette would have been so happy to see you and show you her baby.

He is really pretty : this is not merely what his mother and father think, it is what everybody says. White as a swan, strong as Hercules. I do not know whether he is good-tempered, probably not, as his father is so morose. I cannot believe but that you will come and see this little phenomenon on your return journey. Mette is not yet up and she tortures herself trying to imagine diseases that science cannot cure. Poor Mette has been very lonely; her mother would have been very useful at this time. The Arosas went sea-bathing at a little place in Brittany; they came back on Wednesday. Marguerite was looking well; I think the sea air must have done her good, counteracting anæmia, the particular blight of this century and of Paris.

Madame Fonignet must be furious at having received no news of the birth of our boy, but I fancy everything between her and us is over.

I forgot to tell you his name. It is Emil,[1] so you see, you guessed very nearly right. As to his godfather, we are still waiting. M. Fritz never finds it easy to make up his mind, and although he promised us to come at the beginning of the winter, I am pretty sure he will change his mind. I should, however, like to make the acquaintance of some of my family; it is wretched not being able to travel.

Oh! ungrateful Marie, your letters are undiscoverable. I have ransacked my drawer without being able to find anything. I suppose it is the language difficulty, you are afraid of being teased. Women! we always love you far too much.

Come to Paris, dear Madam, we want to see you here soon. My regards to everybody. I venture to send kisses to the two young ladies, and keep a tender place for you in the heart of your friend,

PAUL GAUGUIN.

5.

TO MRS. HEEGAARD. No date, September, 1874.

Dear Mrs. Heegaard,

I received your letter after some little delay, owing to the different routes it took. Mrs. Fonignet sent it on to me by post. I am very grateful for your interest in me; I have not been able to give your message to the Arosa family, nor shall I be able to do so until next Sunday. As to Pepito, the rascal is treating himself to trips to Spain; he is going to escort his aunt to Madrid. I hope it will do him good, as the poor fellow's health is always a little shaky.

1 Emil Gauguin, born at Paris in September, 1874.

I am relying on your care to restore to my Mette her good health, and perhaps the air of the garden will give her some of the strength she needs. You can understand my keen desire to have her home again, and you must not be angry with me if I soon carry off from you, a friend whom you love dearly.

France cannot be more smiling, so do come again to exchange a little greeting. I hope to see you before long, and this time we will try to spare you the tedium of the Fonignet household. How did you find your little Marie ? I think she was a little sorry to leave her friends, but happy to return to her family—joy and sorrow, as you see, sometimes go together.

I know you would like me to come to Copenhagen and I am most grateful for the welcome you would give me, but, in all the circumstances, it is impossible. That I shall go one day, perhaps, I dare not hope. However, if Mrs. Gad can come next year to see her children, she will find a good husband and a loving son—I am sure of being both.

My regards to your two daughters and to Mr. Heegaard. Kiss my Mette, and I send you my heartfelt greetings.

Always yours,
PAUL GAUGUIN.

6.

TO MESSRS. DILLIES & CO.[1]

Copenhagen (beginning of December, 1884.)

. . . He requires samples of each material, with the terms written below for identification. Kindly send him about two yards of each kind, including the small size . . . and trappings for horses. I believe this last article is very good in Northern countries. These last to be sent to Mr. Hermann Thaulow, Christiania.

As I have already informed you, my brother-in-law enjoys ample credit. In Norway pharmacies are a Government concession. He also owns a mine, for which a French Company is offering 500,000 francs. You can easily take up references, as my brother-in-law is well known in Christiania.

[1] Previous letters to Dillies & Co. have not been found.

If therefore you have confidence, it would be most useful, indeed almost a necessity, for us to have in stock a sufficient supply of material and so avoid the continual despatch of small lots. You know how forgetful people are in business, and a customer who has to wait may change his mind . . .

I want to know if as regards Norway, which is Scandinavian but not Danish, you will let me have a commission.

If one of these gentlemen is going to Paris, I would like him to call on Mr. Thomeseau, 1, Rue d'Amboin, where I was employed, and who would give the necessary references.

Has the cloth ordered for Christiania been sent?

Awaiting your reply, I am,

Yours faithfully,

P. GAUGUIN.

7.

TO MESSRS. DILLIES & CO.

105, Gambe Kongevej,

Copenhagen.

End December, 1884.

Gentlemen,

Do not think I have been idle, but the festivities from Christmas until New Year's Day make it almost impossible to do any business. I was informed at the Customs that the duty was 33 oere per lb., which increases the price by 92 centimes per yard, and this comes very dear in a country where they prefer things cheap and nasty. This is particularly idiotic because hemp cloth pays O.12, cotton cloth O.K. 16 oere, and yours being considered as an *unknown* material. I am taking steps to have it classified as in the former class. On your part, you might write in German explaining that your cloth is like other hemp cloth, recovered like others, with a material, the only difference being that your recovering is by a special process which you have patented. Be good enough to do so at once, as all this delay prevents business from starting. I have made enquiries of the big steamship company, and have been told that royal authority is required to change the supplier. I will get in touch with the present supplier, who is a big merchant here, but not a manufacturer, and it is possible considerable business will result.

I have to go about things very cautiously to avoid making a

false move, which would shut the door on me. I am still waiting for the trappings and a stock of cloth from which to supply retailers. As soon as I receive these, I will go to Jutland to see the head of the Company, who happens to be a friend of my family. He has already replied once that he will not try anything new, but depend upon me, I now have the means to persuade him to change his mind.

I have an appointment with the chief physician of the hospital to discuss the small waterproof cloth : any business in that quarter will not amount to much, but would be useful as a recommendation. Kindly take urgent steps to send us in Norway and also here, the necessary material to be available after the April stocktakings.

With every wish not to be tiresome, I am compelled to broach the question of advances. I mentioned this in my last letter.[1] I have to pay 220 crowns for the patent, which makes a hole in my slender purse, and I ask you bluntly if you could not alter your decision.

Please go into the matter again and let me hear from you; I trouble you only because in order to obtain the necessary introductions, I have to mix much in society and am embarrassed by lack of money. Copenhagen is not like Paris : business men are not received until enquiries have been made and references taken up.

Awaiting your reply.

Yours faithfully,
P. GAUGUIN.

8.

TO MR. CELLOT.　　　　Copenhagen, 105, Gamle Kongevej,
Friday, 2 January, 1885.

Special Factory of
Tilt and Imperishable Cloths.
Dillies & Co., Roubaix.
P. Gauguin—Agent.

My dear Cellot,

Although I am usually far from inquisitive, this time I am constrained to ask you for a lot of information about the business you offer me. I am very frank, and cannot promise you miracles.

---

[1] In August, 1884, the Gauguin family left Rouen for Copenhagen, where Mette thought she could earn money by giving French lessons. On his part, Gauguin had obtained the agency for Denmark of a Tilt Manufactory which made waterproof and imperishable cloth, Messrs. Dillies & Co., for whom he worked bravely until May, 1885.

Copenhagen is not a bit like Paris, where any intelligent man may put up a sound business proposition, and be sure that it will be examined. Here, where nearly everybody knows everybody else, one cannot offer even ingots of gold for sale, without first being introduced as a person of great responsibility, etc.

Fortunately, I have valuable contacts here, such as will within a short time introduce me everywhere; I have, however, to learn the language, to which I am applying myself industriously. All these inconveniences will persist for some time, but will end soon, especially if I can settle the question of money, which is absolutely wearing me out, and which I cannot see the end of unless I can get help and support. A difficult thing when one is abroad and the father of a family and obliged to show a bold front to the world, etc. . . . Having said this, I come to the information I want.

1.   To represent a firm, especially in Denmark, there must be a firm in the first place : are you a manufacturer ? Then, once the customers are found, could I depend upon regular supplies without increase of price ?

2.   Does your patent cover all Europe ?

For a long time varnish has been made which preserves metal from oxydization, so long as the metal is not exposed to rust; ships' hulls are in this category. Yours is the best, you say; I hope so, although in business one tries sometimes to persuade when one is not oversure. However, we'll let that go.

As to nets—for cod fishing—Being a sailor I can tell you that the problem was solved a long time ago, by tanning the nets to preserve them from rotting, and the fact that the nets never wear out all at once. They get torn and the tears are repaired as they happen, so that a net is in great part renewed by repairs. Your varnish will never prevent it from tearing.

3.   I do not keep a shop here, but have the agency for one or more firms.

If I insist on this point, it is because in this country, where everyone is extremely inquisitive, concealment of any kind is bound to be injurious. If, as I intend to do, I offer your varnish to a big naval contractor, he will not fail to make the most meticulous inquiries in Paris about the manufacturer, even if I make out the invoice.

4.   I have no capital, but in order to work at all, I must have a small stock of your products in hand, and as I sell them, I will

remit the proceeds. This involves your having great confidence in me (perhaps you haven't) but I assume you have. It would also mean a preliminary expenditure on your part of a considerable amount.

I write this hastily and tersely, but you will see what I mean, so please answer my questions and don't be offended at my insistence. My tendency is always to be too trustful and, for this reason, in spite of my intelligence, I shall always be a tenth rate business man. However, it is not mistrust which inspires my present enquiries, but a desire to know exactly where I stand.

If we come to an arrangement, I will write to my Norwegian brother-in-law, a live wire who is looking after our tilt on a fifty-fifty basis. He, better than anyone else, will know how to stick your varnish on the Norwegians. It is easier to do business with these people, who are so different from the Danes. They are really interested in new things, and quite ready to be the first to try them. Don't talk to me about conservative peoples : a republic may not be the ideal method of government, but what a spirit of initiative it gives to young men !

Cordial greetings,

PAUL   GAUGUIN.

I cannot sell anything without having a definite patent, required for French articles, and which costs 340 francs ! ! I confess to my shame that I haven't got the money.

9.

TO MESSRS. DILLIES & CO.   Copenhagen, 7 January, 1885.

After several interviews with the Customs people, I have at last got them to agree that your tilt will be classed *as* cloth, provided that you send a large piece, one end being left uncovered with your patented preparation, so that they can tell exactly of what material it is composed. I assume you can let me have this.

Your tarpaulin for the Railway arrived about a month ago,

and was put to the test without delay. The officials find it very well made and easy to handle; they told me that up to the present the tests are favourable but they must be continued for several months before they can come to a decision. I have seen the cloth they use at the moment. It is a cloth of double thickness, which makes it very awkward to fold; on the other hand, yours seems to them very thin by comparison. I said to them that their cloth was so heavy because the waterproofing process was almost nil, and it is this preparation which renders it almost completely weatherproof, and lighter in weight although not quite so strong. Kindly let me know if I am right and say if your cloth is thick enough. Their covers cost them 111 francs 10 centimes. I believe yours would be much about the same price. If this is so, we may fairly hope to do good business with the Railways six months hence, provided your tilt wears as well as the heavier stuff, which will be ascertained in due course. Most of those I have seen on the carriages are in a pretty bad state.

Yours faithfully,
P. GAUGUIN.

10.

TO MESSRS. DILLIES & CO.   Copenhagen, 13 January, 1885.

I have to acknowledge receipt of your letter of the 10th inst. I did not know of this new arrangement of my brother-in-law with Mr. Carl Mort.[1] However, I can vouch for his respectability, as I know who this gentleman is. He comes of a very good Danish family and has an excellent reputation, carrying on agency business in Norway. My brother-in-law may have taken him on to help in the retail trade. I have written to him for all necessary information on the matter. I may not hear from him immediately, as he is travelling in the chief towns of Norway as agent for our business. I feel confident that in a few months' time we shall see results.

In your last letter you intimated you wanted to see some results in Denmark, but please remember that I have been here

---

[1] He was referring to Mr. Carl de Morgemtorne.

only a short time and I cannot force the pace. A certain diplomacy has to be exercised and many inquiries have to be made, before one finds out which is the right door to try. I get about in the business world and I have already interested many useful people. Here, everything is done very bureaucratically, and before any business will be considered by a Company, a written request must be made, which has to be vouched for as far as possible, and backed up with samples.

I have none of your circulars in German, which means I have to give many verbal explanations, which takes time. I am more than ever convinced of a certain degree of success. I am in touch with the Jutland Company; there you have a formidable competitor. For a long time Russia has supplied them with tilt which gives them every satisfaction. Find out what Russia is doing, and if possible, supply me with arguments against their products. Generally speaking, you may take it as a fact, that in the North the waterproofing process is not by way of impregnation, neither is it exactly by way of recovering a cloth. They use three layers of cloth—the middle layer is prepared with—X—and inserted between two layers of untreated cloth. This results in a heavy product, of which the surface is supple and the inside resistant.

I am very sorry I cannot persuade you to alter your decision about an advance, as this holds me up at every moment. I cannot take a cab and the days are now very short, so that I am always up against this everlasting question of money. There is a great difference between too little and unnecessary expenditure. I am obliged to dine with many persons who might be useful to me, and I shall also have to receive people, and am stopped by lack of money.

In a few days I shall have to take out of the Customs the material of which you advise me; how am I to settle the bill? All this is a worry and impedes my freedom of action. An acceptable man in whom an important firm has confidence must maintain a certain standard. Placed too low, I am a bad representative, but established on a suitable rung of the ladder, I assure you, I can bring off some good business, and yours will not have been placed in bad hands.

Yours faithfully,

P. GAUGUIN.

Landscape with cattle
Oil 1885 (*Private collection*)

11.

TO EMILE SCHUFFENECKER.[1] Copenhagen, 14 January, 1885.

My dear Schuffenecker,

I have had a letter from Guillaumin;[2] it appears that you wanted to buy one of his exhibited pictures, but that it was already reserved. Why don't you go to him and choose another; I believe you will be glad to have one of his works, while I should be pleased to hear of a sale for this poor but highly talented artist.

As for myself, it seems to me at the moment that I am mad, and yet the more I brood at night in bed, the more I think I am right. For a long time philosophers have reasoned about phenomena which appear to us supernatural, and of which, however we have the *sensation*. Everything is there, in this word— Raphael and others, people in whom sensation was formulated before the mind started to operate, which enabled them, while pursuing their studies, to keep this feeling intact, and to remain artists. And for me the great artist is synonymous with the greatest intelligence; he is the vehicle of the most delicate, the most invisible emotions of the brain.

Look around at the immense creation of nature and you will find laws, unlike in their aspects and yet alike in their effect, which generate all human emotions. Look at a great spider, a tree trunk in a forest—both arouse strong feeling, without your knowing why. Why is it you shrink from touching a rat, and many similar things: no amount of reasoning can conjure away these feelings. All our five senses reach the brain *directly*, affected by a multiplicity of

---

[1] Emile Schuffenecker, born at Fresne-Saint-Mames (Haute Saône). This excellent impressionist painter first exhibited at the Salon of 1877 and was in 1880 one of the founders of the Independent Salon. Employed by the broker Bertin, he formed a friendship with Gauguin, whose talent he later admired without being influenced by it. Although father of a family, he several times received Gauguin when the latter was penniless and often assisted him as far as his modest means would allow. It was at his home that the artists of the impressionist and synthetic group would gather to discuss their theories and also to dine. "Give me something to eat," said Emile Bernard to him, "and I will recite poetry."

[2] Armand Guillaumin (1849-1927), impressionist painter. Employed in the Department of Bridges and Roads of the city of Paris, he devoted himself entirely to painting in 1891, when a bond of the Crédit Foncier brought him a Prize of 100,000 francs. He made famous the village of Crozant (Creuse), where he took up his abode.

things, and which no education can destroy. Whence I conclude there are lines that are noble and lines that are false. The straight line reaches to infinity, the curve limits creation, without reckoning the fatality in numbers. Have the figures 3 and 7 been sufficiently discussed? Colours although less numerous than lines, are still more explicative by virtue of their potent influence on the eye. There are noble sounds, others that are vulgar; peaceful and consoling harmonies, others that provoke by their audacity. You will find in graphology, the traits of candid men and those of liars; why should not lines and colours reveal also the more or less grand character of the artist. Look at Cézanne, the misunderstood, an essentially mystic Eastern nature (he looks like an old man of the Levant). In his methods, he affects a mystery and the heavy tranquillity of a dreamer; his colours are grave like the character of orientals; a man of the South, he spends whole days on the mountain top reading Virgil and looking at the sky. So his horizons are lofty, his blues most intense, and with him red has an amazing vibration. Virgil has more than one meaning and can be interpreted as one likes; the literature of his pictures has a parabolic meaning with two conclusions; his backgrounds are equally imaginative and realistic. To sum up: when we look at one of his pictures, we exclaim "Strange." But he is a mystic, even in drawing.

The farther I go into this question—the translation of thought into a medium other than literature—the more I am convinced of my theory—we shall see who is right. If I am wrong, why does not all your Academy, which knows all the methods used by the old masters, paint masterpieces? Because it is impossible to create a nature, an intelligence, a heart. The young Raphael knew all these things intuitively and in his pictures there are harmonies of line which cannot be accounted for; they are the veiled reflection of the innermost recesses of the man's mind. Look at the details—even in the landscape of a Raphael picture, you will find the same emotion as in a head. Purity pervades the whole. A landscape of Carolus Durand[1] is as raffish as a portrait. (I cannot explain it but I have this feeling.)

Here I am tormented more than ever by art, and neither my

---

[1] Calorus-Durand, painter (1838-1917), created a sensation at the 1865 Salon with the *Assassine,* the realism of which influenced both Courbet and the Spanish masters. A fashionable portrait painter, his art rapidly became conventional.

money worries nor my quest for business can turn me aside from it. You tell me that I should do well to join your Society of Independents; shall I tell you what would happen? You are a hundred strong : tomorrow you will be 200. Artist tradesmen are two thirds intriguers; in a short time you will be assuming the importance of Gervex[1] and others, and what shall we, the dreamers, the unappreciated, do? You have had a favourable press this year; next year they will stir up all the mud to fling at you, so as to appear respectable.

Go on working, *freely and furiously*,[2] you will make progress and sooner or later your worth will be recognised, if you have any. Above all, don't perspire over a picture. A strong emotion can be translated immediately: dream on it and seek its simplest form.

The equilateral triangle is the most firmly based and the perfect triangle. A long triangle is more elegant. We say, lines to the right advance: those to the left, retreat. The right hand strikes, the left defends. A long neck is graceful but heads on shoulders more thoughtful. But I am running away with myself and talking all kinds of rot. Your friend Courtois is more reasonable but his painting is so stupid. Why are willows with hanging branches called weeping? Is it because drooping lines are sad? And is the sycamore sad because it is found in cemeteries; no, it is the colour that is sad.

As to business, I am always at the same point, the start. I shall not see the result, if there is one, for six months. Meanwhile, I am penniless, up to the neck in squalor—which is why I console myself in dreaming.

Gradually we shall extricate ourselves; my wife and I give lessons in French: you will laugh, me, lessons in French!

I wish you better luck than ours. Regards to your wife.

P. GAUGUIN.

---

1 Henri Gervex (1852-1929), realist painter, one of whose best canvases inspired by a de Musset poem, was refused by the 1878 Salon for alleged immorality. The police then prohibited its public exhibition.

2 " You have known for a long time what it is I wish to establish : the right to dare everything," wrote Gauguin to Daniel de Monfreid in October, 1902.

12.

TO CARL DE MORGEMTORNE.   Copenhagen,

Undated, January, 1885

To Mr. Carl de Morgemtorne.

I am the general agent for Scandinavia for Messrs. Dillies, and desiring to enlist your support for this business, I am writing to offer you a share of my commission for business done in Norway, viz.:

Four per cent. of the price, ex rail Roubaix, for small transactions.

Two per cent. for large transactions at a reduced price.

Kindly let me know if you are in agreement.

Yours, etc.,

PAUL GAUGUIN.

13.

TO MESSRS. DILLIES & CO.   Copenhagen,

Undated, end of January, 1885.

1. I have received a reply from Norway about Mr. Carl: you can rely upon his diligence in attending to our business. He is an old insurance agent, and at present a commercial traveller. My brother-in-law having a Government pharmacy, cannot openly engage in another business, so he has taken a friend into his service, this Mr. Carl, to obviate any complaints. This is all to the good, as both have influential connections.

2. I have seen the Chief Surgeon of the Hospital and we have tested your excellent small waterproofs in every way, but they are not exactly suitable for hospitals; these gentlemen are quite indifferent to expense, wishing only to obtain the best article. They use a very flexible rubber material made with all possible care for the special purpose of the hospitals and which can be washed without fear of contamination. The Surgeon was very friendly but he could not assume such a responsibility towards his patients as to make a change. Your cloth, being impregnated only instead of being recovered, has the drawback of a rough surface. What they have is very dear but it must be admitted, perfect.

I have received a reply from Jutland, which is dubious enough, but they are prepared to make a trial. Kindly send immediately a sample like that you sent here, but as strong as possible, to try and improve on their product. I strongly urge you not to charge for it.

They are at present suffering from heavy snowfalls, and it is to your advantage for your products to be tested in cold weather, as their large cloths are stiffer in the handling than yours. I anxiously await a sample of trappings to show to an important saddler with whom I am in negotiations: without a sample, one talks to little purpose.

I have just received your letter and am glad to learn you have sent samples. But one comparison is hardly enough—I wanted to offer them retail. I hope you have sent the old tilt ordered to Norway.

Yours faithfully,

P. GAUGUIN.

14.

TO MESSRS. DILLIES & CO.   Copenhagen,
                                          Undated, beginning February, 1885.

I hasten to reply to yours of the 29th January, 1885.

I am a little surprised to hear that my brother-in-law has refused to accept the parcel despatched. I say a little, as my brother-in-law is at the moment ill in bed, and in addition, he has asked Mr. Carl to attend entirely to this business, not because he is loth to promote it on my account, but because he is absolutely prevented from appearing even as a principal. His pharmacy business, as I have told you before, which is rather an important one, is held under Government and he does not want to incur the reproach of spending even a minute in any other concern. In this connection I send you the letter I have received from Mr. Carl de Morgenturne, which will show that an hour's interview is worth months of correspondence, and that letters invariably create mis-understanding. I hope soon to proceed to Norway to put things in order; nothing but the expense of the journey delays me. I ought to mention here, something which I am sure you will appreciate. In Copenhagen as in Christiania you do not find, as may happen in

Paris or London, unreliable agents likely to run off with the goods. People here do business entirely on reputation and credit. That is why I am pleased to observe that you show less mistrust towards them, while preserving your usual caution. You may send goods on trust to Mr. Carl de Morgemtorne without risk. I have told him that I had the management of this business, but to facilitate matters, you should get into direct touch with him. On all Norwegian busi-ness, you would have to credit him with 4 per cent. and 2 per cent. and me with 6 per cent. and 3 per cent., as I bear the risk of loss at the rate of 10 per cent. and 5 per cent. If all this seems reasonable and you agree, kindly write to Mr. Carl confirming these conditions, and send him at the same time, details of prices and leaflets in German. He is an energetic man who enjoys a considerable reputation in Norway, and may be relied on to do his best.

You know better than anyone, that to introduce a novelty, perseverance and a certain expenditure are necessary at the start

What headway am I making with the Companies? I cannot say exactly, except that I have to proceed slowly and these gentlemen will not be hurried. I shall not receive a favourable reply until later.

One question: When your red tilt is folded, the crease shows up lighter than the rest. This looks as though it is a crack, which it is not. Could this be remedied?

Yours faithfully,

P. GAUGUIN.

15.

TO MESSRS. DILLIES & CO.

Copenhagen, 5, Gamle Kongevej, 105, 8 February, 1885.

I have only just received your parcel of tilt samples. This parcel went the round of Copenhagen, being addressed Kongevej instead of *Gamle* Kongevej. Be good enough in future to address to Copenhagen V. This letter indicates the district, the town being divided into four parts, North, South, East and West.

I have not, up till now, been able to employ myself fully, as I have not enough samples to show to the various firms. At the end of the week, I go to Norway to put business there on a proper footing, and make all necessary arrangement with Mr. Carl. He is not entirely satisfied with 4 per cent., but after all, it is I who took the risk of starting the foreign agency, it is I who have incurred and will often still incur travelling expenses; and as, moreover, I am liable for losses, I think I may conscientiously retain an interest larger than that of my agent. However, the terms might be modified, and if it is necessary to stimulate Mr. Carl's interest, I will do so at the last moment. I am not at all inclined to be mean, and shall act for the best. On your part, grease the wheels of business, and all will go slowly but well. As to your parcel, it arrived in good condition, but what a pity the varnish was not quite dry. The paper had stuck to a large number of the articles, and I had to wash and dry them to make them presentable to customers. It would be desirable, if your resources permit, for you to have a quantity of perfectly dried material in stock. This is of capital importance at the start, particularly here, where a different method is employed. It appears to me that the preparation is inside, that is between two folds of cloth. The surface looks more attractive. Could you pass your dry cloth between two cylinders? That would improve its appearance, giving it a better polish, without lessening its suppleness and impermeability.

Yours faithfully,
P. GAUGUIN.

16.

TO CARL DE MORGEMTORNE.

Copenhagen, 12 February, 1885.

I duly received your letter and if I have not replied earlier it is because I expected to go to Norway at any moment; unfortunately, I had to postpone my journey. You should have received a letter from Messrs. Dillies, to whom I wrote that we were almost in agreement. Do not be surprised if the terms I communicated to you were on the low side. In any case they are the same as those offered to Hermann. He must have made a mistake in mentioning 5 per cent. to you, as I offered him 4 per cent.

My own commission is small and I have had considerable trouble in arranging to come abroad and I went into the matter very carefully before deciding to leave my country and embark on this venture. As you rightly surmise, I have a certain amount of responsibility. I would actually prefer to give you 5 per cent., if you would agree to bear 5 per cent. of losses in the case of defaulters, which is something you could avoid in large measure, by your knowledge of buyers. Remember that in a matter like this, the exploitation of a patented article, it is only the beginning that is difficult; later the demand will grow of itself into considerable dimensions, without any special exertion on your part.

All orders coming from Norway will be placed to your credit. With the Railways alone we should be able to do 30,000 francs a year, so considerable is the wear and tear. In France a company like the West uses 400,000 francs worth of tarpaulins per annum. As you see, the commission may well reach a considerable figure. Have you any contacts with Sweden? If so, you may be able to do something there. When I come to Christiania we can discuss this, and I am sure you will find me accommodating, whatever you may have thought to the contrary at the start.

Yours sincerely,

P. GAUGUIN.

17.

TO MESSRS. DILLIES & CO.　　Copenhagen, 17 February, 1885.

Kindly make up 5 pieces to the following measurements: —

4 ells by 13 ells and 3 inches　　4

4　„　6　　„　　„　　1

Quality A. Northern Railway. They want one strap at each corner.

I quote the above measures as they are those used in Denmark. I think an ell is 2 feet, that is, 66 centimetres.

I should be glad if you would execute this order promptly. Make out the invoice and address to Mr. Heegaard, 37, Havergade, Gvenlages, whose order I took according to your price list.

Yours faithfully,

P. GAUGUIN.

18.

TO MESSRS. DILLIES & CO.   Copenhagen, 26 February, 1885.

Herewith the name of a merchant of repute who has examined your tilt and is very pleased with it. In spite of all the information I have given him about prices, he desires to ascertain the net cost by purchasing six lengths and making up the covers himself, having facilities for that purpose, and he asks me to inform you that he would like 20 yards of your tilt, of the superior quality.

He is of opinion that if unbleached tilt is shown to the Customs, the duty would be only 12 oere per lb. Immediate despatch is essential, because he sells to Sweden, and is going there in a week's time, when he will at once proceed to get orders. Most of the tilt he sells is Belgian or German and appears to me pretty bad—yours should have a good chance. Please be good enough, then, to do what is necessary to send the tilt asked for at once (green). Send the invoice to me, which I will get paid, but send the goods to his address, with Port and Customs duties for his account. We ought to be doing good business with this merchant in the future; please give me therefore your lowest quotations.

Further, I have heard from Jutland that your samples arrived in good condition and appear better than they have been using. This, from a man who was sceptical, is satisfactory as far as it goes; let us hope the tests will prove equally satisfactory. I am very hopeful about this, the more so as the tilt will be looked after by a technical friend of mine. Given these conditions, the promise for the future is excellent.

My application to the Navy has been submitted to the Minister, after having been recommended at a high level. The Secretary also, has promised to keep an eye on the matter. This is all useful, but we must not build castles in the air. Their custom is to prepare it themselves in the shops, naturally with old fashioned methods, and old habits need a lot of conquering.

Yours faithfully,

P. GAUGUIN.

19.

TO MESSRS. DILLIES & CO.

Copenhagen, Undated, March, 1885.

I have been visited by an Admiral, a distant relation who is in charge of the provisioning of the Arsenal. He ordered 125 yards of tilt, *A. Black, Superior Quality,* and he led me to think that this will lead to big things.

We will try, he told me, to make you not regret leaving your country. He wants me to deliver the goods direct to him at the Arsenal without going through the Customs. Kindly therefore despatch at once to me. I will pay Customs duty and obtain repayment at the Arsenal.

So as to be on the safe side, I quoted him a high price, totalling 523 francs 20. I will adjust matters when I receive the cloth from Moller. So please make out an invoice to Chefen for Orlogsvaerftets Regnskabsvaesen, with price left blank and signed. I will collect the money when delivering the goods. It would be very kind if you would let me keep this money on account, but if this course does not meet with your approval, *rest assured I will send the amount without delay.*[1]

Kindly also inform me if I must adhere to the price of 3 francs per metre; with Customs duties, we are above the German price. I know your cloth is of superior quality, but if we quoted the same price, we could get hold of all the business in a short time.

20.

TO MESSRS. DILLIES & CO.   Copenhagen, 17 April, 1885.

I received notice of the receipt of the parcel for the Navy on the 15th April, but did not obtain delivery until to-day. Transport charges were 15 shellings. You see the journey took more than 10 days: in short, we may say the whole transaction took a month. I have paid the Customs 12 oere per pound, which will be the charge henceforth.

---

[1] Gauguin pocketed advances, and when he left Denmark his account was in debit. Messrs. Dillies made several requests for this money.

I have to-day seen the Manager of the Jutland Railway, to whom I was recommended by Mr. Estrup, President of the Council. I was very well received and in three months (they won't be hurried) he has promised to go into the matter carefully. He did not conceal from me that, in the interests of economy, they are now making their carriages covered, to avoid the necessity of tarpaulins. You say in your letter that I seem discouraged. This is not quite true, but I own I am tired of all these visits and interviews which promise so much but offer no glimpse of earnings until later. It all takes so long by correspondence. . . .

I have been nearly run off my feet with the Seithland people: they are not precisely accommodating. To-day I have spent five and a half hours, backwards and forwards between the Arsenal and the Customs. It must be owned that if I should earn anything with your agency I shall not be robbing anyone.

I omitted to tell you that I invoiced these goods to the Navy below the price I previously quoted them. I have added charges to the cost of goods. Kindly place this total of 400 francs to my debit, which I will retain with your kind permission, and credit me with 40 francs plus 6 francs 40 . . . .[1] for the Heegaard order.

As soon as you have succeeded in making a non-inflammable sample, please send me one, large enough to be tested. Also samples to be left in offices, which are a good advertisement. I think a few lines in the newspapers would do no harm: everybody reads the advertisements here, as they do in England.

Yours faithfully,

P. GAUGUIN.

21.

TO SCHENHEYDER. Copenhagen, 17 April, 1885.
To Commander Schenheyder,
The Arsenal.

I beg to advise you that I have to-day despatched to the Arsenal, the consignment of 128 metres of tilt ordered. Unless

---

[1] . . . . Words and figures indecipherable.

otherwise informed, I will hand you the invoice on Tuesday, accompanied by your written order, which I believe will be in accordance with your wishes.

The invoice with Customs duty and carriage will amount to 345 crowns. There is a small difference in your favour compared with my quoted price, as the Customs subsequently agreed on a lower rate of duty.

Yours faithfully,

P. GAUGUIN.

22.

TO EMILE SCHUFFENECKER.   51, Norregade, Copenhagen,

24 May, 1885.

Fabrique spéciale de
Toiles imperméables
et impourrissables.
DILLIES & CO., Roubaix.
P. GAUGUIN—Représentant.

My dear Schuffenecker,

You wrote to my wife, but I reply. What do you want by way of assurance? Nothing much, but in any case, set your mind at rest. No one regards you as an egoist, and it is well known with whom you are annoyed about your charges. But there is nothing to be done about all this!

I smiled at your idea of going to Durand-Ruel,[1] for the good man can hardly keep himself above water, and as for the trifle he has been able to do for the Pissarros and others—it is not out of friendship, but because he is involved for almost a million and he is afraid that the Impressionist painters are depreciating their goods by selling at any price they can get. You know quite well that this

---

[1] Paul Durand-Ruel (1831-1922), famous picture dealer. After taking up Corot, Courbet, Theadore Rousseau, Daubigny, Diaz, etc., he discovered the Impressionists, for whom he nearly ruined himself several times, but whose success he eventually assured both in France and in the United States. The Durand-Ruel gallery founded by his father in 1833, is now managed by the grandsons of the great dealer, Messrs. Pierre and Charles Durand-Ruel.

infernal Jesuit does not care a straw about me in my poverty. *Bertaux*! Why, it is entirely owing to him that I am in the soup, for I should never have made the break, if he had not promised to support me for a year, a promise he has not kept—he must curtail his expenses owing to the critical state of affairs, must make a position for himself, etc. Which means I cannot ask anything of him now.

Here I have been undermined by certain Protestant bigots, who know I am an infidel and consequently would like to see me down. The Jesuits are as St. John compared with the Protestant devotees, to begin with the Countess de Moltke, who agreed to pay the boarding school fees for my son Emil, only suddenly to stop doing so for religious reasons. There is nothing to be said. Many French pupils have not materialised for the same reason. As for myself, I am beginning to be fed up with it all, and think of cutting the painter and coming to Paris to work, as an operative in Bouillot's[1] studio—this would be for a mere pittance, but I should be free. Duty! Let anyone put himself in my place. I have done the best I can, and I yield before the utter impossibility of carrying on. Thanks once again for all your interest in us: there are not many who respect a man when he is sliding into beggary!

If you see Guillaumin, tell him a letter from him just now would give me pleasure; always when I receive a letter from France I breathe again. Six months of absolute silence have gone by. I am completely isolated. Of course, in the eyes of the family, I am a monster not to be earning money in an age when only the success-ful are respected.

Our little Paul[2] is in bed with pneumonia, which brought him to death's door, but happily the crisis is past. All this has made me very cheerful.

My wife sends all good wishes to yours. She is not too pleasant at the moment. Poverty has completely soured her, she is wounded

---

[1] Bouillot, sculptor, whom Gauguin had known when he lived at 79, rue des Fourneaux, in 1877, and who taught him the craft. Directed by the figure-carver, he modelled a bust of his wife, which Bouillot executed in marble; and later, carved that of his son Emil without supervision.

[2] Paul Gauguin, born in Paris, December, 1883, the artist's youngest son, known as Pola Gauguin. He wrote *Paul Gauguin mon père*, which was published in France in 1938. An English translation was published by Cassell.

especially in her vanity (in this country where everybody knows everybody else), and I am the target for all kinds of reproaches. Of course, it is because of my painting that I am not an eminent stockbroker, etc., etc.

Best wishes to you both.

PAUL GAUGUIN.

Do write me all about the Exhibition—that is what distracts me most of all. And has yours at the Tuileries been held?

I suggest an exchange. Take one of my pictures to Sinbad the Sailor and send me a copy of the *Barque de Don Juan* of Delacroix, if not too dear. I assure you I live only when I withdraw to an artistic city of the mind. Have you noticed that this man had the temperament of the wild beasts—which is why he painted them so well. Delacroix's drawings always remind me of the lithe and sinewy movements of the tiger. You cannot tell where the muscles are attached in this superb animal, and the turn of a paw suggests the impossible, even when real. In the same way, Delacroix's arms and shoulders always turn back in a wholly impossible and irrational manner, but always express the reality of passion.

The draperies twist and twine like a spotted snake enraged. Be that as it may and think what you will of it, his Don Juan's boat is the breath of a powerful monster and I should like to refresh myself by a sight of it. All those famished people alone on the terrifying ocean, having only one dread—to be the next to draw the unlucky number from the hat. Everything shrinks in the face of hunger. There is nothing but painting, no still-life deception. The boat is a toy, which has been built in no shipyard. Mr. Delacroix is no sailor, but what a poet! To my mind he did well not to imitate Jerome in archaeological exactitude.

And to think that Mr. Wolff[1] has written in the *Figaro* that not one of Delacroix's pictures was a masterpiece—always incomplete, he says. Now that he is dead, he becomes a genius, but his pictures are not perfect. Look at Bastien Lepage[2]; here is a painstaking man, conscientiously probing nature in his studio. Mr.

[1] Albert Wolff, journalist and art critic, who waged violent warfare against the impressionist painters in the *Figaro*.

[2] Bastien Lepage (1848-1884), a painter of peasant life and portraitist. He was regarded for a time as the rising hope of the realist school.

Wolff is far from suspecting that Delacroix is not only a great draughtsman of figures, but a pioneer to boot, that his stroke is a means of emphasising an idea. However, these things cannot be explained.

I have had no works exhibited here. One day I will tell you how the exhibition was closed at the end of five days, by official instructions, how serious criticisms in my favour were suppressed in the newspapers. Of all the dirty intrigues! All the old academical clique were trembling as if they were dealing with a Rochefort in art, flattering enough for the artist, but disastrous in the result.

In Copenhagen I had to get a frame made by a joiner, as the frame-makers would lose all their other customers if they made a frame for me—and this in the 19th century! But if we are of no account, why all this uproar? We shall have no more painters, and the public and my painting will fall into inanition, smothered in ridicule and pity. Granted one has an imperfect talent, but a talent nevertheless—and to find doors slammed everywhere! We must confess that we are the martyrs of painting. Tush! Human stupidity is almost as strong as the vanity of mortals!

23.

TO HIS WIFE.   Paris, 9 August, 1885.

My dear Mette,

I write you a few lines only: Messrs. Dillies continue to pester me, and I do not know what to reply as I cannot let them into family secrets; and moreover, they would not understand, no frank and honest man being able to imagine such things. They have just learnt that the two pieces of tilt which Hermann ordered and which were sent in December last, have been refused.

Suppose for a moment that your brother-in-law, once his enthusiasm had evaporated, discovered that, as a pharmacist, he could not handle anything else—is this a reason for leaving in the lurch one from whom he had ordered something? Let him settle, at least for the goods ordered before he abandoned the affair.

Now that your sister has succeeded in pushing me out, I need not remain any longer for this reason,[1] and there is no question of the family honour.

Write to your sister Pylle that all this is extremely harmful to you, and that Hermann must settle all the business with the customers. Whatever happens, Hermann should write fully to these people, in German, if he likes, but write he must.

I have enough worries without having all credit in my own country destroyed by the fault of others. Does it not occur to you that I have need of my reputation for integrity here, now that I have to start all over again? To clear up other people's muddles, and to keep starting all over again is, I confess, quite beyond me.

I have not yet received my packing case, and I want it in order to arrange the sale of what it contains. Winter is coming and I shall be without my tools.

Reply to me and write at once to Norway. I want an answer that will dispose of the matter once and for all.

Kisses to all the family.

PAUL GAUGUIN.

24.

TO HIS WIFE.   Paris, 19 August, 1885.

My dear Mette,

I see from your letter that you are still away, from which I conclude that friends are caring a little about you, and in the midst of all my vexations, it is something to know that you are not altogether neglected. As soon as you have a reply from Hermann, let me know, as I have not as yet sent any word to Dillies; my position in regard to the firm has become so false owing to the events in Norway, that I cannot give them all the facts, and I am waiting to report a satisfactory conclusion to the whole business.

You ask me what I am doing this winter. I hardly know myself, everything depends upon the resources at my disposal. Nothing can be started with nothing. I have no money, no house, no furniture—only a promise of work from Bouillot if he has any. If

---

[1] Exasperated by his wife's lack of understanding and by the hostility shown by her family, having abandoned all hope of improving his material situation, Gauguin left for Paris in June, 1885, taking with him his son Clovis. They lodged in cul-de-sac Fremin.

Martinique Women   Pen drawings
1887   (*Collection Maurice Malingue*)

he has, I shall rent a little studio from him and work and sleep there. I shall buy whatever food I can afford. If I sell some pictures, I shall go next summer to an out of the way spot in Brittany to paint pictures and live economically. Brittany is still the cheapest place for living. When I get over the worst, if business looks up, and my talents get suitably rewarded, I shall think of settling down somewhere.

On your part, try to make me known in Denmark. This, if you succeed, should benefit you as much as me, and is the surest means of bringing us together again.[1]

I still have no news of the packing case. You might make enquiries in Copenhagen. It must have been properly addressed, otherwise I should not have received advice that it was on its way. I cannot think what has happened. I have no linen. My pictures were advertised at a dealer's, and I may miss sales owing to their non-arrival. I do not know if you have put my personal belongings in. In any case, I shall want them this winter—except the hat; I have no mind to buy new clothes. Do you think of making me a smock out of the remaining material; this would be most useful for working in.

As to the big order, perhaps these gentlemen are mistaken, and it is only sail-cloth.

In any case, I know nothing of it and Colonel Tisman ought to know—did you see Colonel Tustrup when you were with your cousin in Jutland? And do ascertain if the Navy people are satisfied with their supplies. This is worth looking into, and might lead to big business.

Kiss all the children.

Isn't Falstett foolish to get married.

PAUL GAUGUIN.

1 What happened was the opposite. Gauguin, in fact, was incensed at seeing his wife continually demanding canvases which she sold fairly well without ever sending him money. Thus in 1896 he wrote to Daniel de Monfreid: "My advice to prepare my future by selling in Denmark only benefited my wife without any chance for me to enjoy the fruits. I am certain that the canvases despatched by Schuffenecker will be quickly sold and that my wife will clamour for others; this is what I want—when my wife has sold the canvases, write her that, according to my strict orders, you will send her 3 canvases only in return for an advance payment of 400 francs, which is a third of the value sent previously. I want (in short) one third of the sale of my pictures, and as I have no confidence, I want it in advance. (Let this be understood.)

25.

TO HIS WIFE. Dieppe, 19 September, 1885.

My dear Mette,

Since my last letter, I have been travelling. I have arrived here at Dieppe,[1] where I stay two or three days, before spending about three weeks in London, you know where. As you must have seen in the Copenhagen newspapers, the Spanish business has grown confused and this of course, assists the little development we are seeking. It is then only a question of time and I have not failed to take steps to renew the friendships formed. For the future therefore the business is almost certain. But as for the present!

Schuffenecker writes me that Mr. Bouillot regrets he has no work for me, as Mercier thrust on him a figure carver for the work on which I counted. I see in all this some dirty work which I dare not unravel. Have you written Mrs. Bouillot? I know your desire is to see me on the Bourse.

I confess your present silence seems to me extraordinary—a month has gone by without a word from you. I am still awaiting an answer about the Norwegian business before replying to Messrs. Dillies. You have the children with you, don't forget, and their health cannot be a matter of indifference to the absent one. Try then to write more often and always address letters care of Schuffenecker, where I shall be in three or four days' time. I have no notion what I shall attempt when I return to Paris, without money and without furniture and above all, without work.

Dillies' business grows day by day in France and Belgium. At the Antwerp Exhibition their tilt carried off the medal far and away above all others.

The packing case has at last arrived, after being detained in the Customs; when I return I will see what is in it. They read the address as rue Boulevard. Your indecipherable writing again. In despatching cases you must take the utmost care, or you will have

---

[1] Nothing is known about this visit of Gauguin to Dieppe nor of his stay of three weeks in London, referred to in this letter. Jacques Emile Blanche, who stayed in Dieppe in 1885 with Fritz Thaulow, mentions in a book the painter's presence, the extravagance of his attire and a certain wild air, which impressed his father, Dr. Blanche, famous alienist, as signs of megalomania.

no end of a bother. I am now suffering from violent rheumatic pains in the shoulder, another of the delightful mementoes I have brought away from Denmark—but why bewail the past! If only this were all, I should congratulate myself on having quitted it so cheaply. Unfortunately, I expect anything from your country and your family.

As you know I have a sort of instinct which enables me to divine what is happening, and I am sure that at this moment your dear sister is up to her tricks. The blow dealt me was a violent one, but I can stand up against it, especially at the moment, when I have some trumps in my pack, brought from London.

Kiss all the children for me.

PAUL GAUGUIN.

c/o M. Schuffenecker, 29, rue Boulard.

26.

TO HIS WIFE.   Paris, Undated, beginning of October, 1885.

My dear Mette,

My sister[1] has just brought Clovis back to me, regretting that she cannot have him any longer; as I cannot get any work from Bouillot and painting is under a cloud, I have to think what to do for both of us. I am therefore seeking a modest position on the Bourse; and it is a great pity I have no bedding here. I must try and get this for the child's sake. I do not know yet how I am going to buy it. I have looked over the things you have sent me; there are a lot of them. I suppose it isn't your intention to give my fur coat to your brother? *I had hoped you would have sent it to me,* as well as the shirts and collars I asked for.

Try to get translations otherwise than through your sister so that you may establish an independent connection and then you might be able to continue translation *even in France*—if one day there is an escape—and you could thus aid the household a little. See Falstett's friend. Weeping gets us nowhere, we must think of the

---

[1] Marie Gauguin, born at Paris in 1847, had married a Chilean business man, Juan Uribe.

future. I might receive 600 francs[1] in a few days from the sale of a Pissarro and a Renoir; as soon as I have them, I will send you 200 francs.

At the moment, I have only my summer trousers, which are well worn, and moreover make me look ridiculous in this wintry weather. It is very important I dress decently for the Bourse and I had hoped you would have packed my winter trousers in the case, but you have not sent a single pair. You must make up another parcel containing my winter outfit, and if you can, a counterpane and a quilt.

I must rent a small flat, and I shall have to hire two beds, one for Clovis and one for me. You know what this costs, and it is foolish to buy new things when one has an abundance of them in Denmark. Size up the position and put your best foot foremost. You can send the parcel carriage forward, but address it clearly to Favre, 19, rue Perdonnet, where I am from now on. As soon as I get a position on the Bourse and find I am able to live, I will send you a little money. And do what you can to keep our valuables together, the furniture as well as my Pissarro pictures. This is all very disjointed, but I have so much to fluster me—to find work, money and a flat and to fetch Clovis, who for the next eight days is staying with Mr. Jobbé-Duval.[2] He returned from the country in splendid health: strange how the air of France improves him. He looks better every day, with sparkling eyes and a brilliant complexion. Your country does not suit the children. I forgot to suggest that you should give the carrier specific instructions to despatch from Copenhagen direct to Paris; otherwise, your parcel will go via Cologne and will be shipwrecked in the Customs.

Include in the parcel, my fencing things.

Write me soon.

PAUL GAUGUIN.

I send you the decision giving the sole agency. Messrs. Dillies have written to Bjorn. Try to get him to reply.

[1] With his profits from speculating on the Bourse, Gauguin had made a collection of impressionist paintings, comprising works of Pissarro, Monet, Renoir, Guillaumin, Sisley and Cézanne, which, in 1885, he valued at more than 15,000 francs.

[2] Jobbé-Duval, pupil of Ingres, and member of the neo-classical school. He worked on the frescoes of the Church of Saint Supplice in 1859. He owned the pavilion which Gauguin had rented in the Rue Carcel in 1879.

27.

TO HIS WIFE.   Paris, 13 October, 1885.

My dear Mette,

I have your letter which crossed my last. I do not know which way to turn. The sale on which I counted has slipped through my fingers and I have rented a small flat, 10, rue Cail, next to Sinbad. Within the next five or six days I must furnish it somehow to shelter Clovis and me and I have no money. In short, business is dead for everyone at the moment; which is why I am making enquiries now about a position on the Bourse, in the hope of finding one in a month or two's time—which will probably be badly paid and devoid of prospects.

There is nothing for it but to hold out until better times in painting, as Bouillot has no work. As to Clovis, he goes to school next door, and when I am not here, the concierge, who is a good sort, looks after him, sometimes in her own flat, sometimes the Sailor. You need not be anxious about him. If you can send him a jersey, so much the better, for he could do with it.

Send me some bedding, coverlets only—not the bed itself: one can get wooden beds for almost nothing at the stores.[1] But send all this without delay, and make sure the carrier understands what he has to do.

I haven't many sheets.

I am very rushed this morning and must stop.

                              PAUL GAUGUIN.

28.

TO HIS WIFE.   Paris, Undated, 20 October, 1885.

My dear Mette,

I was very disappointed with the packing case which I received on the 9th and for which I paid 15 francs on delivery here—it weighed 15 kilogrammes. I thought it would have contained the bedding but no. You should have put the piece of fur in the pockets for my overcoat collar. Clovis is at present sleeping on a little bed

---

[1] L'Hôtel des Ventes rue Drouot

I have hired, and I, on a mattress with my travelling rug. You know how expensive bedding is. Two mattresses at least and a pillow for Clovis—blankets and quilts do not weigh much and would not cost more to send than the carriage on the last case. You can get a large parcel skilfully made up without a case at all, using packing canvas and trussing it with straw. Immediately, for we are freezing in the night and *I have not a penny to buy bedding.*

You might also put in a little linen, two pairs of sheets, pillow-cases. Send it like the last packing case, per steamer to Havre, which is the quickest and surest way. Pack my box of crayons in the middle of all this.

I will write you at greater length soon; at the moment, I am too worried and exasperated by this bedding question.

The way you look after children in Denmark, you must be at your wits end with little Paul who catches cold so easily; as soon as I have the wherewithal to buy homeopathic remedies I will send you some, to stave off a cold whenever the symptoms appear. Aconite at once, and then mercury. As for yourself, that is another matter. Worry has a great effect on your constitution, and the best medicine would be a little peace of mind and that you don't seem to want. You excite yourself needlessly over nothing, and all the more so, when there is really something serious the matter. What can we do about it!

In your own country, where you could properly expect help and protection, those best able to serve you, have been of no assistance to you. Do not fret about Clovis. Children of his age do not know what suffering is, provided they are loved a little, and as to food, this is not difficult, especially as the best morsels are kept for him. With an egg and a little rice he makes a good meal especially when there is an apple for dessert. Sinbad who has not a penny himself finds means, however, to help me a little at the moment. Do not give way to dreaming, especially as the most tried of the two is myself, living in one room without furniture and with four bare walls to cheer us up.

Your husband,

PAUL GAUGUIN,

10, r. Cail.

29.

TO HIS WIFE.   Paris, 2 November, 1855.

My dear Mette,

I do not know what is happening to you, you wrote two letters in succession, and then suddenly dead silence. I am still waiting for the *weuen* circular translation. Have you sent off the things I asked for? I feel their want pretty severely at present. Clovis has no woollen vest to put on, otherwise he is well enough. I am always on tenter-hooks about the sale of pictures and I have all my work cut out these days to keep us alive. I have found nothing yet on the Bourse, there is so little business doing and so few vacancies.

I see from the papers that Danish politics are a little agitated at this moment and that your dear Estrupp has been a target; it is true they have foolishly missed him. You ought to know that nothing is to be expected from this quarter; the ruling class is so little progressive while the nobility is a shadow of its former self and imagines that it owes no duties towards the weak, while always demanding respect and servility.

I have received the stockings for Clovis; he now has something to put his feet into for some time. He is very good and plays quite alone in his little corner without bothering me; he sometimes asks where his mother is and when she will come. You will find he has none but good memories of you; let us hope the others will not be brought up in ignorance of their native language and their wretched father[1]—it will take me a long time to swallow that!

I dined Thursday with the Jobbés; the old chap is as lively as ever and asked me to send you his kind regards. I spent a very miserable day this Sunday, the sky being overcast as it so often is in Denmark; fortunately the Sailor, my neighbour, came this evening with his sweetheart to dine at the house.

It is a welcome refuge for him from domestic irritations, as he often quarrels with his father.

Write me soon what you are doing. Have you plenty of pupils? What about Bjorn?

A kiss from Clovis.   PAUL GAUGUIN.

---

[1] Gauguin had a preference for Aline and Clovis, whose sensibility he divined. He always reproached his wife with making Emile, Jean and Pola, Danes in language and education.

30.

TO HIS WIFE.   Paris, Undated, end November, 1885.

My dear Mette,

I answer by return of post, so that you can reply forthwith as to the sale of the pictures, about which I am very uneasy. I left the pictures in Denmark, and at the rate they are going off, one day I shall have nothing left. I am anxious about my two Cézannés, which are rare of their kind, as he finished but few, and one day they will be very valuable.

Sell rather the sketch by Degas, as only he, it must be confessed, sells very readily, and it should fetch much more than 200 crowns. I leave you a free hand since *you are in need* and, in default of money from me, you have now a resource here; but the sale of the Manet and the Miss Cassett, must be stopped—or one day I shall have nothing.

The important thing is to push mine.

Do not worry about Clovis; he has all he wants, except little vests under his shirt. It is extremely cold at this moment, and I feel keenly the need of a mattress and quilts. Who knows, I may have them one day. You have only given me three pairs of sheets, which means that I cannot replace them as they go to the wash, one pair for Clovis and a pair for me. And my linen shirts?

I am in a hurry to catch the post.

Goodbye for the present.

P. GAUGUIN.

I have received no news of Elizabeth Moller; moreover, I don't want to see any *Danish women* here.

31.

TO HIS WIFE.   Paris, Undated, about 20 December, 1885.

My dear Mette,

I would point out that your letters always arrive a month after mine, so that you never reply to my questions. I asked you for the translation of the *weuen* document; every day I am bothered for it and these gentry even ask if I have a situation and when I hope to repay their advances. Thus I require the translation and to know if Bjorn expects to do any business in tilt.

I recommended you to exhibit something for Christmas, and to make arrangements for this with Phillipsen; *quid?* Your wonderful sister-in-law whom you seem to commiserate seems to be a humbug. She knew I was here without money, and did not even offer me hospitality in her fine flat until I got out of difficulties. As I did not visit her, she decided the other day to come and see how I was, bringing me the child's garments which the Danish woman had left with her eight days before. Her only sign of interest was to find the floor unpolished, as if I was going to polish it! I was not painting, but had just finished a portrait of a man which, of course, she found frightful in its impressionism.

When announcing her departure for America she bade me tell her where Clovis was in case I was not here, so that she might come and say goodbye, which meant in plain English; don't send him to me, he is not wanted.

Don't bother about Marie then, I beg of you; she pays her debts in words instead of actions, more so now than ever. As for me, the situation never varies. It is winter and I cannot paint without a model; business is worse than ever in France. I have been promised a post as advertising manager[1] with 200 francs per month, but it has not yet materialised. For the last month it has been cold here, not to mention the snow, and I am sleeping on a plank wrapped up in my travelling rug; the worries of the day are balanced by the insomnia of the night.

I have been pursued by annoyances all the week: after telling someone on the Bourse that Cellot[2] was a ponce and a sharper, the thing got round, which impelled this gentleman, ill-advised by Esteleta (swashbuckler of the worst type) to send me his second. After discussions, we arranged for a duel by pistols because Cellot was alleged to have palpitation of the heart; but at the last moment Cellot backed out, not wanting to fight an Ishmael like me.

[1] Of a firm specialising in railway advertising, Gauguin received his contract on the 26th February, 1866, but declined the post.

[2] This Cellot is the same man to whom Gauguin wrote on 2nd January about business affairs which might have been the cause of the difference.

I need Emil's birth certificate, *which must be sent by return of post.*

I thought Mrs. Adler was to buy the *Snow Scene.*

Kiss the children for me.

Your husband,

PAUL.

Emil should write me every month in French, I see that you no longer speak the language at home.

32.

TO HIS WIFE.   Paris, 29 December, 1885.

My dear Mette,

I have at last received the bedding which is some comfort, as it freezes hard every day. I have also received your letter with the translation, but, unfortunately, without the birth certificate, so that I had to pay 2 francs 60 to get one at the Town Hall, besides delaying me.

I am scarcely surprised at the refusal of my pictures in the midst of the Christmas daubs and it does not upset me, but if one does not send one cannot say anything. The malevolence must be recorded, that is all, and it must not be kept secret. If you could even get it into the paper, it would be publicity and one day we shall see who was right.

In March we are going to hold a very comprehensive exhibition[1] including the new impressionists who have talent. All the schools and studios have been discussing it for some years and this exhibition is likely to make a great stir; perhaps it will prove the turning of the tide—we shall see. Picture dealing is completely dead here now and it is quite impossible to sell paintings, especially the orthodox. What used to sell for 1,500 to 2,000 francs at the dealers now fetches 100 francs with a 50 franc frame. It is a great point in our favour, *but for the future.*

---

[1] The eighth and last exhibition of painting of the Company of Painters, Sculptors and Engravers was held at 1, rue Lafitte, from 15th May to 15th June, 1886. The presence of Gauguin had, as in the fifth and sixth exhibitions of 1880 and 1881, alienated Claude Monet.

You are always the same, not looking where you are going, falling and hurting yourself. According to your letter, you seem to have spent Christmas alone, and it looks as if your family haven't much use for you. What has happened to these people, alleged to be so hospitable, and this family which you lauded to the skies to me—all unworthy as I was to tie their shoe strings? Perhaps one day you will be able to tell whether a door is open or shut. Anyhow, recriminations are worse than useless; after all, to do ourselves justice, we haven't stolen anything from them. As to being reunited one day, I don't think about it, as I cannot see how it can be done. Without funds, I cannot summon the energy to give you the comfortable life you need.

Kind thoughts to the children.

> Your husband,
> PAUL GAUGUIN,
>> 10, R. Cail.

33.

TO HIS WIFE.   Paris, 2 January, 1886.

My dear Mette,

The Dillies people have written me that they intend to wind up their business in Denmark, about which they wish to hear nothing more. They are dunning me for repayment of the advances. They want the agent to send them the three pieces of tilt that were in the house. You wrote me that Bjorn took them: does he intend to buy them? Have you been to the Navy Office to ask if they were satisfied with their trials? See to this as quickly as possible and try to make Bjorn write them. You realise what an embarrassment it is for me with these gentlemen. In France they are manufacturing 1,000 metres per day. Try and settle up this business better than the Norwegian one. I will pay them the balance one of these days, out of my salary, when I have one. Yesterday was New Year's Day and Clovis sends you his wishes for a happy new year. Thank Emil for the nice letters he sends me.

> Your husband,
>> PAUL.

They complain about no word from Copenhagen.

Just as I was sending my letter, I received one from you fretting about Clovis. He is much better and at this moment is playing happily, cutting up newspapers. I am glad that you have got over your fall and that work gives you some satisfaction. You are wrong to think I am discouraged; I am penniless, it is true, but I hope to earn money some day; enough to be free and have peace of mind. Do not be grieved if you cannot assist me, I want nothing from you and if I got you to send me a little bedding, it is because that of all the furniture I left behind[1] I took only the minimum of what I required.

34.

TO HIS WIFE.   Paris, 27 February, 1886.

My dear Mette,

I have your letter which gives such a doleful picture that I will try to agree with you, but I must confess that your plight does not look so pitiful to me. You are in a pretty, comfortably furnished house, with the children around you, engaged on a laborious task but one which pleases you: you see people, and as you enjoy the company of women and of your own people, you ought to be satisfied sometimes. You are enjoying the amenities of marriage without being bothered by a husband. What more do you want, except a little more money, like many others.

Whereas I have been turned out of my house and am living in one room with a bed, a table, no firing and seeing nobody. Clovis is a hero; when we sit down together at table in the evening with a crust of bread and a relish, he forgets how greedy he used to be; he says nothing, asks for nothing, not even to play and goes quietly to bed. Such is his daily life; he is quite adult, he grows every day, but is not very well, always has headaches and a certain pallor which worries me.[2]

[1] In October, 1884, Mette Gauguin had despatched from Rouen to Copenhagen the furniture, bedding, linen and pictures, leaving nothing in France. It may be surmised that henceforth she intended to live in Denmark.

[2] Of delicate health, Clovis Gauguin was to die in June, 1900, aged 21, of blood poisoning following an operation on the hip. As Gauguin was no longer in correspondence with his wife after the death of his daughter Aline, and it seems that neither Monfreid nor Schuffenecker advised him of his son's premature death, the painter could never have known this new calamity.

You are quite wrong to think I am angry. I have succeeded in hardening myself and feel nothing more than disgust at all that has happened. If the children are forgetting me to-day I am quite indifferent even to that. Moreover, I envisage no possibility of ever seeing them again. Would to God that death claimed all of us. It would be the best gift he could bestow on us.

The future in store for them is not exactly rosy but to bring them up to become educated workers or beggars is an utterly false calculation.

Do not worry about forgiveness of your faults, I have forgotten all that long ago; even your sister who acted most wickedly and stupidly then, now seems to me a woman like other women. I was always wrong to believe in decency.

All is forgotten, Good-bye.

PAUL GAUGUIN.

35.

TO HIS WIFE.   Paris, about 25 April, 1886.

My dear Mette,

Every day I have been meaning to write you. What would you, time passes with so little alteration of bad luck that I see myself sinking deeper into the mire and becoming inert and almost insensible. They are talking of war here; it is a door of escape for which I hope but don't believe in. I should welcome the coming of that day, and would not fail to seize the opportunity of taking part.

I have not sent you Clovis's boots; at the last moment I found a way to stretch the leg so that the foot could be got in. By putting wool in the toe, it will do. I have been unable to see him[1] since New Year's Day, as I owe the school a whole term's fees and I am supposed to be travelling. Winter this year is more severe than ever, and it is now freezing, specially for my comfort. Water is coming through the walls and the pains in my shoulder are starting again.

You do not mention the swelling in your breast; by now you ought to know whether it is serious. Your last letter is strange

---

[1] Clovis was then at school at Antony (Seine).

with your suicides and your love, which has just sprouted as if by magic; however, love at a distance doesn't cost much. It is with you as with me; now that you are no longer there, I feel I go on loving you, and you will see that in ten years we shall be compelled to see each other again, if we have to burn the place down.

Pay attention to one thing which may be important; I see from your letters you are forgetting how to write French, and apart from the Danish idioms that you use, you also make numerous spelling mistakes, which you used not to do.

So your dear baby takes after you ? So much the better. And how is his delightful little character developing? Now not one of the children need speak French. Your family must be satisfied with winning all along the line.

There you all are, all Danes!

Love and kisses to all of you.

PAUL GAUGUIN.

P.S. Necessity knows no law, and sometimes forces men out of their social confines. When the little one sickened with small pox, I had twenty centimes in my pocket and for three days we had been eating dry bread on credit.

Distracted, I thought of offering my services to a billposting firm as a bill poster at the depôts. My gentlemanly appearance made the manager laugh. But I told him quite seriously that I had a sick child and that I wanted work. I have therefore been posting bills for 5 francs a day. Meanwhile Clovis was in bed with fever, and in the evening I went home to look after him. This occupation lasted three weeks, and to-day I have been engaged by the Manager of the Company as Inspector and Secretary of the Board at 200 francs a month. It seems they think I'm intelligent, and in a year's time I shall have a better position. They are now engaged in negotiations to start an agency in Madrid, of which they will put me in charge, at a salary of 300 francs a month, plus lodging and 20 per cent. commission. The Company is wealthy and for 30 years has been engaged in an expanding business. See what a fine future is opening for me! The present is still hard, but things are looking up, and a distinct improvement on the past.

Your Danish self-esteem will be shocked to have a husband who is a bill poster. But what would you; not everyone has ability.

Don't worry about the little one, he gets better and better, and I do not contemplate sending him back to you; on the contrary, as I get more bills to post, I think of sending for the other children. You know I have the right to do so.

You ask me to reply as placidly as you write, so I have gone very calmly through all your letters which tell me quite coolly and reasonably enough that you have loved me, but that you are only a mother and not a wife, etc. . . . these are very pleasant memories for me but they have the great drawback of leaving me no illusion about the future, so you mustn't be surprised if one day, when my position has improved, I find a woman who will be something more to me than a mother, etc. . . .

I realise that you regard me as devoid of all attraction, which is an incentive for me to prove the reverse. Perhaps it will be easier in Spain. Meanwhile go on as you are doing, looking the world in the face, full of your duties, your conscience clear, for there is only one crime, adultery. Apart from that, everything is right. It is not just for you to be turned out of your home, but quite in order that I should be turned out of mine, so don't take it to heart if I set up another. And in the latter I shall be able to post bills. We all blush in our own way.

Regards to your family,

Your husband,

PAUL GAUGUIN.

As for my friends who gossip and who are not yours, let me tell you that all this tittle-tattle comes from people who are not French, consequently *your friends*.

36.

TO HIS WIFE.   Paris, 24 May, 1886.

My dear Mette,

More than two months have gone by and you have given no sign of life. It was I who wrote the last letter.

You sulk to gratify your self-esteem; what matters one pettiness more or less, and good God, if you think you are doing well, go on, it is a course that does you honour. A truce to compliments. At our Exhibition[1] I saw again some worthy Danes, Krojer, Dolhmann, Lund, etc. . . . They always come to see if there is anything good to pick up from us. I blew up Krojer who did not know whether he was on his head or his heels. I saw in the Salon the famous Brandès, who pretended not to recognise me. However, he was less interested in the painting and me than in the fashionable ladies moving about the official fane.

Clovis is at present at school in the country; quite well (it seems) for I have not dared to go and see him, not having the wherewithal to pay next month's fees.

Yesterday I saw the Jobbés, who send you their kindest regards.

I have seen my sister, to whom you write such long letters. To console me she shouts everywhere from the housetops that I am a wretch, that I left Bertin for painting, that this poor woman, without a roof, without furniture, without support has been abandoned by this dreadful painter.

I believe in fact that the mob is always right, that you are angels and I an atrocious scamp, but I make proper amends, I grovel at your feet, as the end approaches, it is my duty to pull myself together.

How is little Paul?

I kiss you,

PAUL GAUGUIN.

37.

TO HIS WIFE.   Undated, Paris, May, 1886.

My dear Mette,

What a long time I have been without news of you and the children; I know you are very busy translating Zola's book, his worst book from every point of view.

Last Sunday I saw the Jobbés, who also complained of receiving no word from you since the last letter that Mother Jobbé wrote you. This does not concern me. The Heegaards must have paid their

---

[1] The eighth exhibition of painting, 1, rue Lafitte, of the 15th May to 15th June, where Gauguin exhibited 19 impressionist canvases, including *Cows Resting*, *Willows*, *The Church*, *View of Rouen*, *Still Life With Apples*.

Portrait of the Sculptor Aubé
Oil (*Musée de Beaux Arts, Petit Palais, Paris*)

usual visit to Paris; this I know from Marie who told me she had a call from Mrs. Heegaard. Unfortunately or otherwise, she was not at home that day.

To go back to the beginning, I think you are right in doing a little translation there in spite of the small returns at the start. Danes pay so badly as a rule that this does not surprise me. What I would not advise you to do is to attempt to explain slang terms; it is better to translate them by an equivalent in the Danish language and even leave some of the words in the original French.

In your last letter no mention was made of little Aline, I thought she was to come to Copenhagen with your sister Pylle. How is she? Is her hair growing? I urge you to have it cropped a little as this makes it grow better later on. Perhaps you prefer the opposite. In that event my advice will not be taken.

Clovis is still at his little school in the country, and will also be there next month, Marie having decided to pay the fees for the month.

And so your sister is to become a Minister's[1] lady? It would seem that the hour approaches when she will be able to display herself in all the effulgence of her virtue.

PAUL GAUGUIN.

38.

TO HIS WIFE. Undated, Paris, end of May, 1886.

Dear Mette,

I have received the photos of the two children. Little Paul is recognisable, but I confess I am amazed at the change in Jean, so much so that at first I thought someone else must have posed. However, he appears to be developing like the others in height and breadth. Before I see him again there will be many more changes. I am glad you have got through the winter passably, it is quite enough for one to suffer hunger.

My best course would be to slip away to Brittany and live in a boarding house for 60 francs a month, where I could work.

[1] George Brandès (1842-1927), famous Danish literary critic, born in Copenhagen, who had married one of Mette Gauguin's sisters, and whom the painter later accused of having exploited his wife's distress to buy from her cheaply canvases of his impressionist collection.

Our exhibition put impressionism on the map, and I have had considerable success Braquemond,[1] the etcher, bought from me with enthusiasm a picture for 250 francs and has put me in touch with a ceramist who intends to make artistic vases. Delighted with my carving he has asked me to execute, at my convenience, during the winter, pottery work to be sold on a fifty-fifty basis. This might turn out to be a profitable sideline. Aubé used to work for him, these pots kept him alive, and that is something.

In any case, this is only for this winter, and I am most anxious to paint some pictures in Brittany. If you could sell my Manet locally, I could pay Clovis's fees for some months, otherwise I am at the end of my tether. I have been offered a berth as labourer on a plantation in the South Seas, but this would be to abandon all my hopes for the future, which I dare not do when I feel that with patience and a little help art can still bring me some sunshine.

I have received from Emil a letter in dreadful French, one day none of the children will be able even to speak it. You hold the trump cards, everything belongs to you and I have nothing to say.

The purport of your letter is extremely interesting, it amounts to this " I am well enough here, so are my children—you are wrong, Clovis and you have nothing. I want nothing better than to remain good friends, otherwise I stay quiet in my corner." Oh! you women, you have a philosophy of your own. Anyhow, *Vea victis.*

Hermann has gone mad. So much the happier for him. Someone looks after him.

Goodbye for the present.

PAUL GAUGUIN.

39.

TO HIS WIFE.   Undated, Paris, early June, 1886.

My dear Mette,

On Thursday next, the 12th, I shall be packing up my things and as I cannot say where I shall be after then, having no fixed abode, please write henceforth care of Schuffenecker, 29, rue Boulard. I will go there from time to time to see if anything has turned up.

---

[1] Felix Bracquemond (1833-1914), painter and etcher, one of the best aquafortists of the 19th century.

I want to go to Brittany where I can live cheaply, but I cannot contrive to collect the cash for my support. However, we won't discuss this again. Some time ago I saw Bouillot, who has work for a year; another one who finds it easier to make promises than to keep them.

He has not given a moment's thought to my existence, and this winter I must work at carving and pottery. He told me that Mrs. Bouillot owed you a letter for a long time but that she is too lazy to write and that you must not be cross with her.

I have little news to give you since my last letter of not long since and to which you have not replied.

I sent you however some lines to cheer you up, I know that you love literature as being the finest manifestation of human intelligence. And I'll bet you don't cheer up, although you have every reason for doing so, now that you are surrounded by those you love in the midst of all that recalls your sweet infancy, and are respected as you deserve to be. What could I ever offer you in this dirty country, La France, in comparison?—a participation in poverty and labour, which are things not to be shared like good fortune. I am back from Schuffenecker, who is always a good fellow, and who admits to me that I have caused him to make progress. Unfortunately, he is increasingly worried by his wife who, far from being a companion to him, is developing into a real harpy. Strange how marriage succeeds: either it leads to ruin or to suicide. But *Piping Hot*[1] tones down the truth.

By the way, I have not told you that on more than one occasion I encountered Miss de M . . . tripping along the pavement of the Boulevard des Italiens at about five o'clock in the afternoon. On my life, she was really elegant and her complexion and sparkling eyes, as well as something in her walk said a world of things. Let us think no evil of our neighbour, but there are limits to the freedom that a foreign lady may use in Paris. If a Frenchwoman allowed herself the tenth part in Copenhagen, your excellent Danish women would be less discreet than I am.

After all these matters concern me very little and if I mention them it is because (in spite of me) she used to be one of your best friends.

Kiss the children.

PAUL GAUGUIN.

[1] Title of Zola's novel, *Pot Bouille*.

40.

TO FELIX BRACQUEMOND.

Undated, Paris, about 15 June, 1886

Dear Mr. Bracquemond,

I will come and see you on Wednesday to bid farewell to you and Madame. If Mr. Chapelet[1] can manage it, he will come with me. I leave Paris on Thursday evening to practise art in a corner of Brittany.

Until we meet.

PAUL GAUGUIN.

41.

TO HIS WIFE.   Undated, Pont-Aven, end June, 1886

Gauguin, Painter,
  c/o Mme. Gloanec,
    Pont-Aven (Finistère).

My dear Mette,

I managed to find the money for my journey to Brittany, and am living here on credit[2]. There are scarcely any French here—all foreigners, 1 Dane, 2 Danish women, Hagborg's brother and a lot of Americans. My painting arouses much discussion, and I must say finds a pretty favourable welcome among the Americans. This is some hope for the *future*. True I make many rough sketches and you would hardly recognise my painting. I hope to pull through this season; and if you can get a little money for the Monet would you send it to me. What a pity we did not take up our abode in Brittany formerly; at the pension we pay 65 francs a month for board and lodging. And one can soon grow fat on the food. There is a house which could be had for 800 francs with stables, coach-

---

[1] Chapelet, famous ceramist (" an artist equal to the Chinese," Bracquemond said of him) at whose studio Gauguin carried out the finishing of all his ceramic works.

[2] Gauguin once said that misery only had turned his steps towards Brittany. In reality, he learned from the painter Jobbé-Duval, who had stayed at Marie-Jeanne Gloanec's pension at Pont-Aven, since 1860, that living there was very cheap, and that, occasionally, Marie-Jeanne might be able to give him credit. In order to be quiet, he lodged in an attic on the second floor.

house, studio and garden. I am sure that a family with 300 francs a month could live very happily.

You imagine we are isolated. Not in the least. There are painters winter and summer, English, American, and others. If later I can obtain a small, but *certain* and continuous sale for my pictures, I will establish myself here the whole year.

In your last letter you spoke of being ill in bed, but you do not say what the illness is. You must not let things slide. But what would you do if you had no roof over your head? Everything is relative in this world, and you should consider yourself happy compared with others. Emil is enjoying himself on holiday, the others are in the country. My little Clovis remains at school during the holidays, and I have not been able to have him home. Let us hope that next winter will be better, in any case it should be less uncertain. I will kill myself rather than live by begging as last winter.

I shall take a little studio near Vaugirard church, where I will work at modelling as Aubé used to do. Bracquemond, who befriends me because of my talent, has put this trade in my way and told me that it may become profitable.

Let us hope that I shall show as much talent in carving as in painting which I shall carry on, however, at the same time.

Kisses for the children,

PAUL GAUGUIN.

Send me a photo of little Aline if you can get one taken.

42.

TO HIS WIFE.   Undated, Pont-Aven, July, 1886.

My dear Mette,

I received your letter to-day on returning from work, what is this you tell me? that you have a tumour in the breast—truly there is no end to bad luck. In any case, as you have a cousin who is a good doctor, ask him seriously if it is cancer, and above all do not shrink from an operation before it gets worse. Later you will repent having hesitated. I realise it is terrible to be hacked and hewed about, especially for a nature like yours that dreads illness. it is easier to be lulled into false security. If I could be operated on for you, I would gladly suffer it, in spite of all the ill you have done me and which I shall not forget. In any event, write and keep me informed; I shall now be uneasy all the time I am here.

If you are too unwell to do so, get a friend to send me a few words.

I confess I should prefer to have a photo of little Aline taken alone, as the effect is lost in groups, but just as you like.

I am doing a lot of work here to some purpose; people respect me as the best painter in Pont-Aven[1]; true this does not put a penny in my pocket. But perhaps it is an augury for the future. In any event, it gives me a respectable reputation and everybody here (American, English, Swedish, French) is anxious to have my opinion, which I am foolish enough to give because eventually people make use of us without proper recognition.

I shan't get fat at this trade; I weigh now less than you. I am as thin as a rake, but on the other hand I am feeling better. The more my troubles accumulate, the more my energies are stimulated, without encouraging me. I do not know where I am going, and I am living here on credit. Money worries discourage me utterly and I should much like to see the end of them.

However, we must resign ourselves to it and let come what will, and perhaps one day, when my art has hit everybody in the eye, some Good Samaritan will rescue me from the gutter.

But we must not stir up all this bitterness, and since I am here for three months to recuperate, let us take advantage of the quietude.

Clovis is at boarding school at Antony (Seine). You have no need to write, I hear about him through Schuffenecker who goes to see him, as it is a convenient journey. Is Falstet still at Copenhagen? Kisses for the children and send me your news.

PAUL GAUGUIN.

July, '86.

---

[1] In this summer of 1886 there were gathered at Pont-Aven, where Gauguin stayed for the first time, Charles Laval, Jourdan, H. Delavallé, then Granchi, Puygodeau, Grouchy-Taylor, Piccolo-Franchi, Sylvain Depeige, Dal Médico, and among American sympathisers, O'Connor. Emile Bernard, carrying a letter of introduction from Schuffenecker, arrived on the 15th August and did not leave Pont-Aven for Paris until the 28th September. Gauguin and Bernard did not see much of each other at this time but nevertheless exchanged ideas. "There is also here" (in the Gloanec pension), wrote Bernard to his parents on the 19th August, "an impressionist named Gauguin, a big fellow of 36, who sketches and paints very well." Gauguin admired Bernard's pictorial daring, whilst the latter recognised the former's talent.

43.

TO HIS WIFE.   Undated, Pont-Aven, end September, 1886.

My dear Mette,
I have been expecting a letter from you every day with Aline's photo, which you promised. Naturally, there is always the fear that you are ill with cancer; and if you are ill, you ought to arrange for some one to write to me.

I had news of Clovis the other day; he seems to like his school more and more, comporting himself like an old-timer. I miss him sadly, and if I had the money, I would have brought him here with me. The poor little chap will have had no holiday, but we cannot do what we like in this world.

The evenings at Pont-Aven drag out when one is alone and work is finished[1]. I have no news of Marie and don't even know where she is; thus total silence envelops me; it must be confessed that this is not diverting. The days follow each other so monotonously that I have nothing to tell you that you do not know already.

In a month I shall be back in Paris, unfortunately to look for work. Let us hope that the modelling I hope to do in ceramics will keep Clovis and me.

You are longing for the winter for the lessons to start again and yet you are far from well. As long as you are not ill in bed! It is strange how I am bearing up against all this strain, I have never been so active; when I do fall it will probably be a sudden collapse. After all, it will be no evil and there need be no regrets.

Kisses for all my family.

PAUL GAUGUIN.

44.

TO HIS WIFE.   Undated, Pont-Aven, November, 1886.

Dear Mette,
I shall leave for Paris on the 13th of this month, when you will have to write me to 257, rue Lecourbe. Schuffenecker has just

---

[1] After dinner, Gauguin and his friends would gather in the dining room of the inn and discuss painting until midnight. Marie-Jeanne Gloanec would have to shoo them off to their bedrooms upstairs so that she and her maids could go to bed, their Breton beds being installed in the dining room.

rented me a small hovel there. I have received little Aline's portrait. She seems to be growing like you.

You appear to be putting on flesh, it is obvious you are happy. So much the better.

Emil has written me, he seems content and happy. But, good God, how childish his letters are for his age. I write in haste in the midst of packing up my works. Many studies.

Love and kisses.

PAUL GAUGUIN.

45.

TO HIS WIFE.   Paris, 26 December, 1886.

My dear Mette,

I have your second letter, this is to say that the first reached me.

But since my arrival in Paris the life I lead is far from gay. I confess I can find nothing to write about. I have been subsisting, God knows how, upon the 350 Frs. from the sale of my little Jongkind. On top of this I have had to pay the boarding school fees for Clovis, who is with me at this moment, without shoes for his feet and without any toy for Christmas. However, one gets used to everything. I have just spent 27 days happily in hospital;[1] unhappily I have come out. Always these damnable colds I catch in winter; I thought this time I was escaping but no! this confounded body of iron collapsed. Can you imagine how cheerfully I spent the long nights in hospital brooding over the solitude which is my environment. I accumulated there so much bitterness that really if you were to come just now (you wanted to see Clovis for an hour or so) I doubt whether I could receive you except spitefully.

You have a home and rye bread almost certainly every day; cherish it. It is a paradise compared with . . .

Ask Schuffenecker what painters think of my painting—probably *nothing*. The man who has nothing is done.

I am engaged in making art pottery.[2] Schuffenecker says they

---

[1] The name of this hospital is unknown.

[2] The ceramics executed by Gauguin are undoubtedly works of art, but they have had no influence on the evolution of modern ceramics. They are much sought after to-day by collectors and art museums.

are masterpieces and so does the maker, but they are probably too artistic to be sold. However, he says that if this idea could ever be introduced into an exhibition of the industrial arts, it would have an amazing success. I hope the Devil was listening. In the meantime, my wardrobe is in the pawnshop, and I cannot even pay calls.

Yes, I have not seen my sister for a long time. I have been in hospital, and the only time I saw her on my arrival in Paris, she made a scene exclaiming (which she also does from the housetops) that for eight years I have been unwilling to work at anything except my painting. However, Juan[1] needs for a commission and banking agency he is starting, some one who understands banking, who can be relied on not to rob him, and who can take his place during his trips to Europe. Such a clerk cannot be found in Panama; inferior employees get 2,000 francs. Marie has me in mind for such a post.

Enough of the subject, it disgusts me. She has not been able to find time to see Clovis for six months.

And your sister? is she getting married again; I should say now is the time.

Your husband,

PAUL.

Say all nice things to Miss Engelmann, that intelligent young person I like so much. She is just made for living with me. Your self esteem (the Northern vanity) is fed by the proximity of one with an inferiority complex. If you have a few vests to spare, send them to me, I implore you.

46.

TO FELIX BRACQUEMOND.   Undated, Paris, January, 1887.

Dear Mr. Bracquemond,

Thanks for all you have done, which must at times have been a nuisance to you. You once very truly said: it is not difficult to practise art, the thing is to sell it!

Let us hope we shall be successful in pottery, but when?

We must talk about Durand-Ruel, his affairs are more complicated than himself.

Kind regards.

PAUL GAUGUIN.

[1] Brother-in-law.

47.

TO HIS WIFE.   Paris, March, 1887.

My dear Mette,

By a vessel sailing on the 10th of next month I embark for America. I cannot go on any longer living this tedious and enervating life, and I want to put all to the test, in order to have a clear conscience. Will you make arrangements to bring Clovis home?

I will send you shortly a power of attorney to deal with any legacy from my uncle,[1] should he die during my absence.

Why tarry so long without writing me; I should have thought I was entitled to hear from you from time to time. My letters are not very cheerful, but what do you expect, I have had to suffer almost beyond the limits of endurance. Ask Schuffenecker who has seen me at work, whether I deserve all this! Before leaving for the unknown, I should at least like to hear from you if I cannot embrace you. All this time I have been deluded by business which promised a fortune in the future, and is now postponed to the Greek Kalends. There is a suggestion of bringing me into partnership for big business in Madagascar; one day perhaps the clouds will break.

Tenderest love and kisses. Write me soon.

PAUL.

48.

TO HIS WIFE.   Undated, Paris, early April, 1887.

My dear Mette,

I awaited your letter with impatience, as I depart from St. Nazaire on the 10th, so you see I have no time to lose. You seem to have misunderstood my letter about Clovis. You have to find *someone* to take charge of him on the journey. I have *just* enough to pay my fare and shall arrive in America penniless. What I shall do there I do not yet know myself. You need no telling that without

---

[1] Isidore Gauguin, brother of Clovis Gauguin, the painter's father, lived at 7, rue Endelle, Orleans. Gauguin spent a great part of his infancy in Uncle Zizi's house.

the sinews of war, things are very difficult but I want above all to flee from Paris, which is a desert for a poor man.

My reputation as an artist grows every day but meanwhile I sometimes go three days without eating, which not only destroys my health but saps my energy. This latter I want to recover, and I am going to Panama where I will live like a native. I know of an islet in the Pacific (Tobago) a league from Panama; it is almost uninhabited, free and fertile. I will take my paints and my brushes and rejuvenate myself far from the haunts of men.

I shall still be suffering from the absence of my family but I shall have cast off this disgusting beggary. Don't worry about my health, the climate is excellent, and one can live on fish and fruit which are to be had for the taking.

Side by side this I am playing with another idea, which may turn out well. Some time ago a splendid business proposition was made to me. Knowing my energy and my intelligence (and particularly my integrity) it was suggested that I proceed to Madagascar for one year as a partner to carry on a business established there. Unfortunately the person they sent there has returned with sufficient fortune and wants to be quit of business. So my sleeping partners, instead of continuing that business, want to do something fresh on a large scale; they have promised to let me know in Panama when they will be ready. The last words they addressed to me were: " Sir, to-day men of your stamp are rare, and we are looking for them no matter where."

Perhaps this proposition will come off, in any case I will ascertain if Juan would like to have a branch in Madagascar. According to all the information I have been able to pick up, one can always make a fortune quickly and live comfortably at the same time. Ask Sophus who has travelled if it is not a good country for business.

It would be an excellent thing for us because Bourbon island is only a three days journey and is now quite civilised with schools, etc. It is more important than Copenhagen . . . I do not think that you would want to rejoin me, but I could see you from time to time while keeping an eye on the business. But all this at present is very much in the air.

At the moment I am somewhat of an invalid and am nursing myself. If you want an idea of the life I have led, ask Schuffenecker, who has helped me a little, he who has so little himself.

And all this wretchedness, deprived of affection, my life broken beyond hope of repair. For you said that you loved me: do you remember your attitude towards me, during the last days we were together? To-day you believe you have changed for the better, and I would fain hope so. If, one day after many trials I succeed (we should have to be reunited), will you bring to the domestic hearth the hell and the discords of yesterday? Is it love that you promise or rather hate, all the bitterness of these last tormented years. I know that you are good at heart, and not ignoble, moreover I put some faith in reason.

You are having Clovis; this child needs love, he will not be able to endure the slight affection you and your family have for him; he is sensitive and intelligent and will say nothing but he will suffer. With affection you will be able to do all you want with him; otherwise you will make him obstinate. If people speak badly of his father he will feel it cruelly. It is a delicate plant that I am confiding to you. I cannot go to see him not having paid his term fees lately; but to-day my heart and mind are steeled against all suffering.

I notice with regret that you are taking morphia, it will get you into a pretty mess, it leads no-where, and deprives you of all moral force. I know it is hard to endure headaches, but it is better to fight against them. Take a little less tea instead of opiates.

When you are inclined, write me to Panama, Juan M. Uribe, to be forwarded.

Meanwhile reply about Clovis by return of post. In my absence Schuffenecker will be my substitute for many things.

If I could only embrace you before I leave.

A kiss for all,

PAUL (who loves you still)
It is foolish, but like that.

49.

TO HIS WIFE.   Undated, Paris, early April, 1887.

I have postponed sending this letter, in order to have the power of attorney, for which I have had to wait, when you receive this letter I shall be on the way.

My dear Mette,

You will find enclosed a power of attorney authorising you to act in my name in the event of a legacy. My uncle is very old and has been very poorly this winter. His last letter was harrowing, my situation disturbs him profoundly. If he should die any money you use should be for the children; I think you are too sensible to use it for yourself; little as it may be, it would be a powerful lever to set us on our feet and facilitate our reunion: I cannot, however, at the moment, see any immediate prospect of this; courage again, you will want it to support all your burdens. You have no need to ask me to help you; if I do not do so, it is owing to utter impossibility, and not to vindictiveness. I recall bitterly the words uttered by your brother in tones as patronising as contemptuous. " You cannot live together, and we will do our best to help you." Frankly, when one cannot do anything it is better to keep silence than to make promises. Do you really think that after two years, applying myself diligently, I should not have become capable of giving French lessons?

Your somewhat short letter enables me to divine many things that you do not admit namely, that the affection of your relatives has not proved a satisfactory substitute for that of your husband, and that you feel as if I were really wicked and had abandoned you for ever. Many would have done so in my place without any compunction since your family fostered the breaking up of our marriage.

To go back to our first topic: I make a bid for fortune with my worldly possessions on my back and nothing in my pocket and I feel keenly my inability to send you any money. All my art pottery remain to be sold and I have left instructions for you to have the proceeds. I hope you will have them soon, and that this will enable you to await my return. I keep back nothing for myself and this I do gladly. You must not reproach me for these two years of neglect; you must remember that since 1873 I have cost your family practically nothing and that these two years are the consequence of a blow from which few could recover.

And what would you say if I became mad like Hermann after losing his fortune: Your sister Ingeborg, the pride of the family, what has happened to her? She has not married again and is not likely to, now.

You yourself have brought back to Denmark your honour

intact, you work harder than the others, and they turn the cold shoulder to you. I no longer feel any resentment towards you, and you can look anybody in the face, now that you deserve friendship and protection.

I hope we shall be reunited one of these days but I assure you there *must not then be any of your relatives between us;* or, instead of being good and loving towards you I shall become a ferocious beast.

Clovis remains at school until he is fetched away. Consult Schuffenecker who will look after my affairs in Paris. I leave Saturday, 9th April.

I kiss you fondly a thousand times as I love you.

PAUL GAUGUIN.

J. N. Uribe. Panama—for M. Gauguin.

50.

TO HIS WIFE.   Undated, Panama, end April, 1887.

My dear Mette,

Here I am in Panama[1] in excellent health as always. The voyage was tough; bad weather and third-class passengers packed like sheep, but a man can put up with this.

I have seen Juan this morning who is the same as ever, except that when Marie is not beside him, he is more accessible in money matters (a question of vanity). In 8 days time we shall be on our island of Tobago, living like savages—and I assure you theirs is not the unhappiest lot.

There is no need to be anxious about employment here. By taking a little trouble one can find work in three days.

When I am quite settled in Tobago and easy in my mind, I will write you at length.

Send me a few lines. How did you find Clovis?

I send you a thousand kisses,

PAUL GAUGUIN.

Your brother was really stupid not to go to St. Thomas; life in the Antilles (Martinique, etc.) is delightfully easy and agreeable.

---

[1] Gauguin had resolved to leave for Panama, where he reckoned two could " live on nothing " in peaceful labour.

51.

Undated,
Panama, end April, 1887.

TO EMILE SCHUFFENECKER.

Panama Canal Company,
Workshops and Transport Dept.
My dear Schuffenecker,

Here I am settled in the wrong island! With the cutting of the Isthmus life has become impossible even in the most deserted places. The Indians of the hills are not tilling the ground or doing anything, neither will they part with an inch of land. Martinique is a fine country where life is cheap and easy. We ought to have stayed there; we should have been working by now, with half the passage money in our pockets. Nothing is to be got out of my brother-in-law. In short, in all this we have been stupid and unlucky. This won't do at all, we must repair our errors, and I intend (by working on the Canal for two months) to save a little money to take us to Martinique. If Portier has been clever enough to sell something for me, *send me the proceeds quickly* so that I can clear out of here.

I will write you shortly my impressions of the country. Our address :

M. Liesse (Public Works Company) Steamship Agency, Colon. (to be forwarded to M. Laval[1].)

We are both very well in health (Laval[1] always a little frail but I never felt stronger). Despite this, every precaution must be taken, I am told some are swept off in two or three days.

Regards to all who think of me.

Yours, etc.,

PAUL GAUGUIN.

Send any money in bank notes, to avoid loss in exchange.

[1] The painter Charles Laval, his disciple, accompanied Gauguin on this voyage. Admirable artist though he was, he was so strongly influenced by his friend that some of his canvases have had his signature scraped off by unscrupulous dealers and today bear that of Gauguin. His work has thus almost completely disappeared. The Paris Museum of Modern Art has a self portrait of the painter presented by Emile Bernard. Laval died of consumption in 1894.

52.

TO HIS WIFE.   Undated, Panama, early May, 1887.

My dear Mette,

I have many things to tell you, but I can't get them sorted out. Our voyage out was as lousy as it could be, and we are, as they say, in the soup. Devil take all the people who give the wrong information. We called· at Guadeloupe and at Martinique, superb country where there is something for an artist to do and where life is cheap and easy and people affable. We ought to have gone there; it would have cost half the fare and we should not have lost time. Unfortunately we went to Panama. My fool of a brother-in-law is there with a shop that looks anything but prosperous; he hardly spent five shillings on our reception, in short, he was as stingy as could be. In a rage, I diddled him out of a 35 franc coat, which was worth 15 second hand. Another annoyance, the cheapest hotel is 15 francs a day, that is 30 francs for the two of us, so we have spent 400 francs without having been able to do anything. These idiots of Colombians, since the cutting of the canal, will not let you have a yard of land at less than 6 francs a yard. It is totally uncultivated and weeds grow everywhere, yet it is impossible to build a hut and live on fruits without people mobbing you as a thief. Just because I pissed in a dirty hole full of broken bottles and filth, they made me walk right across Panama for nearly two hours, escorted by two gendarmes and finally made me pay a piastre. Impossible to refuse. I badly wanted to kick the gendarme, but here justice is summary, they follow you at 5 paces, and if you move they let you have a bullet in the head.

Anyhow the folly was committed; we must repair it. To-morrow I am going to swing a pickaxe in the isthmus for cutting the canal in return for 150 piastres a month, and when I have saved 150 piastres, that is 600 francs (which will take two months), I will leave for Martinique.

Laval is differently placed; he can earn fair money for some time painting portraits, which is quite well paid here, 500 francs, as much as one wants (there is no competition), but they must be done in a special way and very badly, a thing I could not do.

Don't grumble about your work. Every day I have to break the earth from half past five in the morning until six in the evening

Pottery by Gauguin   (*Private collection*)

under the tropical sun and in the rain. At night devoured by mosquitos.

As to the mortality, it is not so terrible as it is said to be in Europe; among the negroes who do the worst jobs the mortality is 9 in 12, the others only about half.

To go back to Martinique—this would be an enchanting life. If I could only sell in France about 8,000 francs of pictures we, that is, all the family could live as happily as possible and I believe it would be possible even to give lessons. The people are so genial and gay. (True, it is a French colony).

Write me a good long letter.

PAUL GAUGUIN.

M. Liesse (Agent Public Works Company) Steamship Company, Colon (For M. Gauguin).

53.

TO HIS WIFE.   Saint-Pierre, 20 June, 1887.

My dear Mette,

This time I write you from Martinique, where I hope to stay awhile. For a long time I have had bad luck and I cannot do what I want. I worked 15 days for the Company when order came from Paris to suspend much of the work and that same day 90 employees were dismissed, including me, of course, as a newcomer. I packed my traps and came here. Which was not a bad thing. Laval has just had an attack of yellow fever, which I fortunately cut short by homeopathy. So all's well that ends well.

We are at present lodging in a negro hut, and it is a paradise, alongside the Isthmus. Below us is the sea fringed with coco trees, above are all sorts of fruit trees and we are 25 minutes from the town.

Negroes and negresses are milling around all day murmuring their creole songs and perpetually chattering. Don't think it is monotonous, on the contrary it is most varied. I cannot tell you how enthusiastic I am about life in the French colonies and I am sure you would feel the same. Nature most exuberant, climate warm but with cool intervals. With a little money there is every possibility of being very happy, but a certain amount is necessary. For instance, with thirty thousand francs, one can acquire at this moment a property which brings in 8 to 10,000 francs a year and live on the fat of the land. The only work is to supervise a few negroes for the gathering of fruit and vegetables which grow without any cultivation.

We have begun to work, and in a short time I hope to send you some interesting pictures. But in a few months' time, we shall be in need of money; this is the only cloud on the horizon. I am longing for your news and with all these changes I have not yet had any letters.

Here is another birthday (7th June) which I spent without a word from anyone.

I can tell you that a white man here has all his work cut out to keep his coat intact, for Potiphar's wives are not wanting. Nearly all are coloured from ebony to dusky white and they go as far as to work their charms on the fruit they give you to compel your embraces. The day before yesterday a young negress of 16 years old, damnably pretty, offered me a split guava squeezed at the end. I was about to eat it as the young girl left when a yellow lawyer standing by took the fruit out of my hand and threw it away: "You are European, sir, and don't know the customs of the country," he said to me, "you must not eat fruit without knowing where it comes from. This fruit has been bewitched; the negress crushed it on her breast and you would surely be at her disposal afterwards." I thought it was a joke. Not at all; this mulatto (who had nevertheless passed his examinations) believed in what he said. Now that I am warned I will not fall and you can sleep soundly, assured of my virtue.

I hope to see you here one day with the children; don't be alarmed, there are schools in Martinique and Europeans are treasured like white blackbirds.

Write me twice a month.

You cannot say that I have written you a naughty letter. Address to M. Victor Dominique, 30, rue Victor Hugo, to be forwarded to M. Gauguin, St. Pierre, Martinique.

54.

TO HIS WIFE.   Undated, Saint-Pierre, August, 1887.

My dear Mette,

I have been four months in Martinique and I have had no news of you and of my children. I have anxiously awaited each post and in my present state of health, this silence has brought on a relapse each time. What am I to think? Has anyone been ill? Or rather and most likely have you succumbed to bad advice? In Panama, it was imagined, I had only to stoop down in order to pick up gold by the bucketful; then suddenly, here I am at Martinique— thus a change of scene and the dream fades.

When I wrote you my last letter I was nearly dying; now I am up but I cannot walk any distance.

I am taking all steps here to get repatriated,[1] but do not know when I shall be returning, so it would be no good to write me now; your letter would arrive most likely when I was on the way home. Of all the afflictions you have caused me, this silence is the most painful and I shall reach France a prey to fever and suspense. If this is the road you are taking to make up for the hurtful past, you are going the wrong way. Truly, it may be said that with you I shall plumb the depths of vexations.

It were useless to relate all the misery of hunger I have to bear at this moment; it might probably give you pleasure; in the silence wherein you leave me it is permissible to presume anything, especially misfortune. Even if you were ill yourself, you could get someone to write.

Au revoir,

PAUL GAUGUIN.

55.

TO HIS WIFE.   Undated, Saint-Pierre, August, 1887.

My dear Mette,

Do not be too sad when you receive this letter; day by day we have to accustom ourselves more and more to misfortune. It seems that everything has crashed on me since I left Copenhagen; we can

---

[1] He had the same difficulties later at Tahiti and his request to the local authorities was refused.

expect nothing good when the family is broken up. I drag myself almost out of the grave and prop myself up on my mattress to write you. I received your tidings for the first time to-day, all your letters having gone astray.

During my stay at Colon, I was poisoned by the malarious swamps of the canal and I had just enough strength to hold out on the journey, but as soon as I reached Martinique I collapsed. In short, for the last month I have been down with dysentery and marsh fever. At this moment my body is a skeleton and I can hardly whisper; after being so low that I expected to die every night, I have at length taken a turn for the better, but I have suffered agonies in the stomach. The little that I eat gives me atrocious pains and it is an effort to write, as I am light headed. My last shillings have gone to the chemist and on doctor's visits. He says it is absolutely necessary for me to return to France, if I am not to be always ill with liver disease and fever.

Ah! my poor Mette, how I regret not being dead. This would solve everything. Your letters have given me pleasure as well as an anguish which now overwhelms me.

If at least we detested each other! (hatred nerves one) but you are beginning to feel the necessity of a husband just when it is impossible. And, poor Mette, worn out by work you ask me to help you.

How can I? At the moment I am in a Negro hut, exhausted, lying on a sea-weed mattress and without the wherewithal to return to France. I am writing to Schuffenecker to come to the rescue for the last time, as he has always done up to now. By this post I have good news of my art pottery. It seems to be successful and perhaps, I don't know, on my return I may find an opening. If only a little business can be done, it means a very good livelihood with 15 to 20 francs a day besides my painting. It does not do to count much on business for setting me on my feet, except by a miracle; I feel incapable of it.

I must end my letter as my head is swimming, and my face is covered with perspiration and I have shivers down my back. Good-bye for the present, dear wife, I kiss you and I love you (I ought to hate you when I look back and see the vile tempers which parted us). Since that day everything has gone from bad to worse.

A thousand kisses for the children, shall I ever see them again?

PAUL GAUGUIN.

As for Dillies, don't answer them, or if you do, tell them it is I they have to deal with, and that I have gone to work in Panama leaving no address.

56.

TO EMILE SCHUFFENECKER.   Martinique, 25/8/1887.

My dear Schuffenecker,

For the first time since I left Paris I have just received mail, all letters from my wife and from Sinbad, letters which have made the round of Panama. I was struck dumb at not having a single letter from you; what has happened in my absence, and is the proverb, the absent are always in the wrong, true?

I cannot understand what has tarnished our friendship. I still recall your words on my departure, telling me to return as quickly as possible—and that is exactly what I want to do but I cannot. Since I wrote you from Martinique one more misfortune has struck me: I have been mortally ill from dysentery, liver trouble and marsh fever—for eight days I rose only to eat and I am just a skeleton. I shall not in fact be any better until I am on the sea and in sight of my native land, and if I had the money for the voyage I would leave at the same time as this letter. Laval will remain for some time yet.

You will realize that my illness has swallowed up nearly everything in doctoring and medicine and we are on the brink of absolute penury. It is a great effort to be writing you these lines, as my head has become very weak, I have only a little strength in the intervals between delirium. Nervous crises almost every day and horrible shrieks, it is as if my chest were burning. Laval has received fairly good news from Paris about me. You know that a gentleman called to buy some pots from Chapelet. He was very enthusiastic about them and advertised them extensively in his circle, which should have produced sales. Moreover, I seem to have pleased him immensely; he would be willing, it appears, to put up 20 or 25,000 francs to buy a partnership for me with Chapelet. On these conditions we could do good business and I could count on my modest quota of daily bread. Moreover, there might be splendid results in the future. In these circumstances, it is urgent for me to return.

I implore you (unless something has happened of which I have no knowledge and which has estranged you) to do all that is possible to send me 250 or 300 francs immediately. Sell 40 of my pictures at 50 francs each, everything I possess, at any price; but I must get out of here, otherwise I shall die like a dog. I am in such a nervous state that all these anxieties prevent my recovery. My legs give way under me.

Go to it, Schuff, one strong pull and I assure you I shall be out of the wood. I have the feeling that ceramics will be my salvation (and I shall have my painting in addition). Best regards to your wife.

Sincerely,
PAUL GAUGUIN.

In any case write me a word of explanation.

57.

TO EMILE SCHUFFENECKER.

Undated, Martinique, September, 1887.

My dear Schuffenecker,

Thanks for your cheering letter which has only one defect, it did not contain the money for my return; my God, how everything has gone wrong on this voyage. I received your letter containing 56 francs almost at the same time, that is, three days before I received your letter dated June. Laval also received several letters including two letters of recommendation from Cottu equivalent to an order to provide good lodgings at Colon with a position in the Canal Company involving not too arduous work so as not to make us ill! These letters reached Colon eight days after our departure; nothing but ill luck.

To tell you frankly my situation here, I am still ill and will never be well in this climate, the arrival of every post brings on a relapse due to emotional shock. In spite of this I am limping along in an effort to make up for lost time and to make some good pictures. I shall bring back a dozen canvases, four of them with figures far superior to my Pont-Aven period.

Until the arrival of the 250 francs I have the 56 francs which you sent me, for the two of us to live on, i.e., for a month to a month and a half, for I cannot take the boat until 15 days after the arrival of that which brings letters.

You can realise our sufferings and how little strength the amount of food we can buy gives to a sick man anxious to get well again.

On top of all this I have had no letter from my wife since I have been here while I have written her two letters, including one telling her about my illness. What is happening to her? I suffer from insomnia every night because of this anxiety. If my wife should die at this moment I should be in a pickle about the children. At all costs I must return to France and I have no other means of travelling than the steamboat, which does not give credit.

You must be returning from your holidays with many good studies; I am sure that the opposition from J. P. Laurens will have put you in good spirits. However, you have only to sit tight. In spite of my physical weakness I have never done a painting so clear, so lucid (with plenty of imagination thrown in).

Do not be surprised if Lunès is pro-Pissarro, he is his cousin, we chatted together at the last exhibition, Pissarro, he and I; so he knows me well, but Pissarro did not trouble to speak well of me to him. When you see Sinbad the Sailor tell him that he lacks the finer sensibilities : he wrote telling me that if I go under it is my fault, and he does not know whether he would laugh or cry at my fate; that he is working modestly without asking anything of anybody (*a lie to start with*).

With most cordial greetings and love to the children.[1]

PAUL GAUGUIN.

58.

TO HIS WIFE.   Paris, 24//11/87.

Dear Mette,

It is possible that you do not realize how harmful your silence can be and that you find it quite natural not to have requested my address from Schuffenecker. Since you left Paris you have given no sign of life; Schuffenecker thinks you are cross with him because he scolded you a little when you called on him. And yet, who has been a true friend since our crash ? However, whatever that may be, I

---

[1] Miss Schuffenecker and her brother.

am delighted to have your news; to know that you are alive and
that the children are well.

I reached France somehow on a sailing boat[1] and the sea air
has strengthened me a little although my internal pains are still
unbearable.

Arriving in the middle of winter in the snow, I find the change
of climate a little hard. Fortunately for me Schuffenecker boards[2]
and lodges me during the convalescence I so sorely need. Business
in Paris goes from bad to worse; everybody regards war as the sole
means of extrication. It will have to come some day, and then there
will be plenty of vacancies, which will be very convenient for some
of us.

I do not know why, but in your letters there is always some
mental reservation on my account. You seem to think that if I am
not earning money it is because I do not choose to do so and that
I make no effort to get on my feet. If I came out of prison I should
find a situation more easily; what would you ? I cannot get myself
sentenced in order to interest the world in my fate. The duty of an
artist is to work in order to become strong; this duty I have ful-
filled and all I have brought back from the tropics arouses nothing
but admiration. Nevertheless, I do not arrive.

On my return a proposition was put to me by one of my
admirers who bought pottery from me. The idea was to enter into
partnership with Chapelet, which would have put me in the way of
a livelihood and perhaps have created a position in the future for
us all and in a sphere (the artistic sphere) which I understand very
well. At this moment M. Chapelet chooses to retire and live on his
savings ! Yet another thing that slips through my fingers.

I must find a situation where the work is sufficiently remunera-
tive to support life and to enable me to help you a little, as, for
example, the pottery moulding with Bouillot, but nothing can be
had from this quarter at present.

There are many things I cannot find here, including 2 frames

---

[1] Remembering his engagement as a pilot on the *Luzzitano* Gauguin worked
his passage as a member of the crew.

[2] On his return Gauguin lodged with Schuffenecker, who then lived in a
summer-house, 29, rue Boulard. But Gauguin's dictatorial character and
his habit of making himself at home everywhere, provoked violent scenes
with his host, and which culminated with the artist's departure, without,
however, rupturing the old friendship with the excellent " Schuff."

and a picture " *Snow Scene*." Tell me exactly what you took away, merely to satisfy me that I have not been robbed. Also send me the Manet unless you are able to sell it in Denmark—I will try to sell it here.

Have you heard from Marie since she left for Germany ?

Write me a long detailed letter and keep up your courage. We both have need of it.

A thousand kisses for the children, and my love.

PAUL GAUGUIN.

59.

TO HIS WIFE.[1]   Paris, 6/12/87.

Dear Mette,

Since my return there has been no great change in my affairs except that in a month's time I hope to have work in ceramics. If so, I shall earn enough to be able to send you a little, and if I have not done so up to the present it is because it has been flatly impossible.

And to tell the truth, when I left Copenhagen, I had reason to believe that you would be helped. Your brother maintained that I was in the way and I being absent, the family would be able to provide for you. Louise Heegaard also said that you should want for nothing so long as she was there. Which shows the gulf between speech and action.

To go back to the point, I believe that in a few days' time I shall be able to earn stated sums. I don't want you to lose courage, and I send you 100 francs which I have at this moment, not in excess of my wants, but which I do not actually need for the present, because Schuffenecker does not press for what I owe him, and he feeds me. I have sold a pot to a sculptor for 150 francs.

My health is not too good. I have put on weight, but from morning to night I have these unbearable internal pains and I have neither the time, the place, nor the money for proper attention. Besides what is physical torment compared with mental torment, and from this point of view your existence for three years has been

1 Accompanying this letter.

a paradise compared with mine. Although it may be difficult, it is not impossible that one day I shall be in the position *that I deserve.* To whom will you return and will your advisers, who are such bad payers, again tell you that your place is not by your husband's side.

Whatever may be invented, no one will hit on anything better than a united family, and for that a head cannot be dispensed with: I want that head to be the wife, but she should have all responsibility and the task of feeding the family.

You know the firm of Goupil, publisher and picture dealer; to-day this firm has become an impressionist stronghold. We are gradually being accepted and absorbed by his customers; here is one hope the more and I feel convinced that before very long I shall get going. Send me the Manet so that I can set about selling it.

In the classification of articles which you took away, I do not know what you mean by green trees; is it a fairly big canvas with the village of Pont-Aven in the background in bright sunshine and a little calf on the right?

Tell me, too,[1] if you took away the poems of Francis Coppé, and grandmother's book on London. I merely ask the question because I missed them in the removal, and not to scold you for carrying them off. If you have also taken away a pot which I made, take the utmost care of it for me. I will have it back again unless you are able to sell it (a good price would be 100 francs). I cannot find my certificate of service, what has become of it?

Re-read my letter attentively and answer me point by point.

If you see your relative the *great doctor* tell him my symptoms. Full-blooded, bilious temperament. I have had dysentery and liver trouble; before eating and two hours after, I have internal pains which terminate in flatulence. As I haven't the money to consult a doctor, I should like your relative if possible to advise me what course to adopt, hygienic measures in preference to medicine.

Now that I have finished with business, let us embrace and not abandon hope of an improvement in our position. My poor dear

---

[1] Flora Tristan, born in Paris the 7th April, 1803, daughter of a noble Hispaño-Peruvian, don Mariano de Tristan, and of a young Frenchwoman, Thérèe Lainé.   Journalist and novelist, apostle of feminism and revolutionary socialism, she led a most exciting life until her premature death in Bordeaux on the 14th November, 1844. Her chief works are: *Wanderings of a Parian, Mephis, Labour Union.* The book to which Gauguin referred is *London Walks,* Delloye, publisher, 1840.

Mette, I am very much afraid that after all these efforts and sufferings the financial situation is not healthy; I am very much afraid that we are no better off than when we started. I was delighted to see you in April, but could not fail to notice in you the same characteristics which would make our life together so difficult—the same rebellious instincts, stronger than ever, the same leaning to flattery rather than to truth. To cultivate pride and repel truth is the peculiarity of the small minded and mentally deficient.

Love and kisses,

PAUL GAUGUIN.

P.S. Does there happen to be an old Danish author whom you could translate into French. Laval's brother, who is a writer would correct the grammar, perhaps you could earn more money this way.

60.

TO HIS WIFE. Undated, Paris, February, 1888.

Dear Mette,

Your last letter said you were writing to-morrow! which is why I waited day after day before writing you. Since my return I have bestirred myself to find money and it is by no means easy. However I do foresee a better future now that I am beginning to be more favourably known in my art.

To come right to the point. Last Sunday some one at Goupil's was most enthusiastic about my pictures and eventually bought three of them for 900 francs and intends (he says) to take others from me.

My art pottery has also been shown to connoisseurs. Of course I have pressing debts, Clovis's boarding-school fees amounting to 250 francs among others. So you must pardon me if I do not send you more at this moment. On the eve of being launched I must make a supreme effort for my painting and I am going to Pont-Aven in Brittany for 6 months to paint.

I beg of you not to throw the handle after the axe but to strain every nerve to hold on for another year.

If Falstett is still in Copenhagen try to see him to ascertain if there is any way of inviting the impressionists to exhibit in Sweden as well as in Norway.

We are invited to Brussels, probably also to Glasgow. It would be greatly to our advantage to hold several exhibitions during the year '88. You must *understand that my interest is yours* and you must get it out of your head that painting is a trade only for the School of Fine Arts.

I know quite well that you do not believe in me unless I am selling pictures, but this is an opinion that must be concealed from the public. I quite understand that this lousy painting has been your ruin but since the harm is done you should accept the position and try to derive profit therefrom for the future.

This notion of making Emil a naval officer has knocked me flat. I will not mention it to my uncle, who, like me, would be dead against the idea. In the first place he could only be an officer in the French Service, where special training is required, which would probably differ from that given in Denmark. And I hardly imagine that you intend to make him a naturalised Dane!

I am opposed to the idea on principle, and I will write you more fully on this matter later. I must stop writing now, the pains are agonising, and my head is swimming.

PAUL GAUGUIN.

My congratulations to Mad. Brandins, I did not know the marriage had taken place. You were quite right not to let the little pot go for 10 francs, as I would not part with it here for less than 80 francs.

61.

TO HIS WIFE.   Paris, February, 1888.

Dear Mette,

I leave on Thursday for Pont-Aven, and I would like to answer your letter now that I am quiet. The country in winter is apparently not altogether favourable to my health, but I must work 7 or 8 months at a stretch, absorbing the character of the people and the country, which is essential for good painting. On this question, I see from your letter that you raise an impregnable wall, as competently as any purse-proud Philistine. There are two classes in society, one which has inherited wealth, enabling the individual member to live on his dividends, to buy a partnership or start in business on his own. The other class inheriting no wealth is to live on what? On the fruits of its toil. With some, prolonged assiduity in business or management brings in a more or less modest reward. With others the creative impulse (in the arts or literature) takes longer, it is true, to establish an independent and lucrative position. In what way do children suffer whose father is an artist and not an employee? Where are the employees who do not suffer financially, at least for a time?

And who form the finest part of the nation, living, fructifying, stimulating progress, enriching the country? The artists! You do not like art; what then do you like? Money? And when the artist is earning, you are with him. There is profit and loss in the game, and you ought not to share in the joy if you refuse to share in the pain. Why do you educate your children, since that is an immediate labour in view of an uncertain future? This brings me to Emil's case. Why an officer in the engineers? It is exactly the same thing as a naval officer, and the same question, to which you do not reply, remains to be answered.

Is he to be French or Danish? He should be, like his brothers, French. Moreover, the course he would take for the corps of engineers is the same as for an ordinary engineer. Once a qualified engineer I should be able, with the contacts I have, to put him in the way of earning an independent living. The more we progress the greater is the place which machinery will occupy in our lives and there will always be work for engineers.

Among the drawings you have sent me by the children, that of Aline's is the best, provided of course that she did it herself. I do not see why you should not encourage her along these lines. But no teacher! If she has the taste for it, let her copy what is in the house and after that let her make sketches from nature.

Your notion of seeing me at a watering-place in Denmark hardly amuses me from any point of view (1) The fare alone would keep me for three months in Brittany; (2) The work I should do in such a place, disturbed by the children, would not be as good as that which I should do here. Besides I have no summer clothes, which, in a bourgeois country, is a calamity; (3) Far apart from each other we find it almost impossible to reach a tolerable understanding, but down there it would be a repetition of the old boredom, quarrels, etc. And what would your family say? Think of it, you might have another child! (4) And the last reason. Since my departure, in order to conserve my moral energy, I have gradually suppressed my emotions. That side of my nature is absolutely dormant, and it would be dangerous for me to have my children by my side only to take leave of them after a short time. You must remember that two natures dwell within me: the Indian and the sensitive man. The sensitive being has disappeared and the Indian now goes straight ahead.

A long article recently appeared in the *Figaro* on the little revolution which took place in Norway and Sweden. Bjornson and Company have just published a book in which they claim for a woman the right to sleep with whomsoever she pleases. Marriage is suppressed and becomes no more than an association. Have you read it? What do they say about it in Denmark? See whether the book is translated into French: if not, you could not do better than translate it and send your translation to me, I would have it corrected and published. We might be able to squeeze an honest penny out of it.

Send me two or three flannel vests, I am without any, and this troubles me in the winter.

Love and kisses to all.

PAUL GAUGUIN.

c/o Mad. Gloenec, Pont-Aven (Finistère).

62.

TO HIS WIFE.   Pont-Aven, March, 1888.

Dear Mette,

I have just received the vests which you have sent me; thanks, they will do very well and I was badly wanting them. Since I have been here I have been in bed nearly all the time, I ought to have submitted to blistering for my liver trouble. I cannot get rid of all the bile that accumulates.

You tell me that you find it very difficult to write in your present state of mind. I understand it must be irksome for you to discuss things with me. Let me simplify matters. Send me about every three weeks one line: *The children and I are well.*

A new remedy has just been discovered for headaches, anti-pirine; this works a speedy cure, and you ought to use it. You bewail your solitary lot (and don't let me forget it either). I do not see it at all; you have the children near you, your compatriots, your sisters and your brothers, your house. What about me who am alone in a tavern bedroom from morning to night in absolute solitude. Not a soul with whom to exchange a thought. Assuming we could live as formerly you would be complaining at the end of eight days—but we are not doing so. I hope to be able to help you substantially in a year and I shall do so as soon as possible. But I see no prospect of resuming life in common under seven or eight years.

Let us hope that then I shall find in my children some compensation for my domestic disappointments. We two, being then old, may be able to understand each other better. Courage and patience.

Kiss the children for me.

PAUL GAUGUIN.

63.

TO EMILE SCHUFFENECKER.　　　Pont-Aven, 26 March, 1888.

My dear Schuff,

Thanks for the 50 francs you have sent me; although this does not solve the problem, I am a trifle easier at present.

For some days all trace of illness has disappeared, and I hope soon to be recovered. But good God, how melancholy everything is at the moment! No snow, but rain and hail. Impossible to work outdoors or within, as I cannot make use of models. Have you Huysmans' *Modern Art*?[1]

I have received an invitation to Sinbad's marriage. What would you? the poor fellow cannot keep afloat without a partnership and his marriage will bring him a little cash. All folly is excusable if pitiable.

---

[1] *Modern Art,* by J. K. Huysmans, is a collection of articles, and was published in 1883.

I have received an article by Fénéon,[1] Revue Independante, January. Passable as regards the artist, curious about his character. It seems that these gentlemen had to suffer like me and were little angels. So history is written.

Regards to everybody,

PAUL GAUGUIN.

64.

TO HIS WIFE.   Pont-Aven, About 15 June, 1888.

My dear Mette,

I have not written for a long time but the summer heat, like last year, has debilitated me. The hot weather has brought on the fever again, which has affected my head. I am in such a feverish state that I shrink each day from the moment of writing dreading to give you this news which would no doubt cause you to forget my address.

You blame me for letting a long time go by without replying to you. Reply to what? Your letters are as they used to be in our life together, anything but an exchange of ideas and emotions and I am beginning to be tired of writing without knowing how my letters will be taken. It happened to please you to join me[2] in the month of April, '87, and after I left you wrote me a warm letter. I will never believe that this letter was selfish. When I tried to make good in Panama your rare letters became icy and somebody who recently saw one (they can be shown like business letters without indiscretion) said to me on seeing how they end. "We beg to remain, yours faithfully."

You ask me to give you courage. What do you need it for except for encouragement in material matters. Are you shut up within the four walls of a tavern, are you deprived of a mother, of the sight of your children, of their chatter? What you mean is that if you had dividends coming in you would be the happiest of women.

---

[1] Felix Fénéon died in 1944. Agent for a big picture dealer, aesthete and anarchist. Fénéon was one of the most intelligent critics of art at the end of the 19th century. He was one of the first to defend the Impressionists.

[2] None of the biographies of Gauguin mention this meeting.

A group of painters outside Pension Gloanec at Pont Aven   1888
(*Private collection*)

Nobody to thwart your wishes, overwhelmed with attentions, spoilt, even courted.

Now and then I receive letters from people reputed to be intelligent, full of *sympathy, of admiration* for me, etc.

I was 40 on the 7th June and I have not yet received the tenth part of such birthday wishes from my family. When your son comes of age will you dare advise him to marry any one except a cook? Should he marry a lady she will have nothing to say to him outside conventional topics. Apart from twaddle, dress, tittle-tattle about neighbours, no conversation. If the son is more intelligent than his wife, he will get himself disliked. Only a cook will be proud of her husband, respect him and find it quite natural for the husband to paddle the canoe.

As you easily forget what you say and what you write, I send you a copy of your letter. See what it contains. Leaving out the news of the children, you can see how affectionate it is! Yet you demand affection from me and offer no return.

Copenhagen, 4 June

My dear Paul,

Although I am not sure that you are still at Pont-Aven, so long is it since I heard from you, I write you all the same as I want you to receive this on your birthday. You will see that we think of you here.

So the summer and the heat have come at last. Which means for me the season when I have nothing to do and when I earn nothing. Fortunately the children are invited to spend their holidays at the seaside. Clovis urgently needs this while it will do the others good. As for me I shall spend the summer no matter where or how so long as I spend nothing. But I have no intention of weeping. You seem to be bothering so little about what happens to us. I wrote you six weeks ago and you have not replied to me. Your last letters have been so little affectionate that I really don't know what to believe. Certainly you do nothing to give me a little courage and you ought not to find this very difficult. Anyhow, recriminations are useless, the object of this letter is only to say that I am far from forgetting you. Which may perhaps be all the same to you! The children are all well and are nice and well-behaved. Emil grows quieter and more reasonable. He is just back from spending his Whitsun holidays with his grandmother, and was very well-behaved.

Write me soon. I worry a lot about you.

Your wife,

METTE.

Thanks, I get along so, so. Until further order I am at Pont-Aven. In any case, I could not go away, as I owe two months board and lodging.

Your husband,

PAUL.

65.

TO EMILE SCHUFFENECKER.   Pont-Aven, June, 1888.

My dear Schuffenecker,

I am very late in answering you; as we get older, we get lazier and this state of despairing suspense is exceedingly enervating. However, it is a consolation to feel that friends do not forget you.

The Durand-Rual exhibition did not surprise me; he is pushing the goods at the back of the shop for all he is worth and if he can right himself it will always be a gain. Nor am I vexed that the Claude Monets are becoming dear; anyhow it will be one more example for the speculator who compares former prices with those of to-day.   And from this point of view, it is not excessive to ask 400 francs for a Gauguin in comparison with 3,000 for a Monet.

Your neighbour[1] ought to be proud of his medal and his mediocrity prize fits him like a glove! And chaffed by those who have no medal as well as by us fellows he can give himself airs— don't fret about all this, he laughs loudest who laughs last. Meanwhile times are hard.

I have written Van Gogh, I am always hoping he will be able to ease things for me. The Cézanne you ask of me is a pearl of great price, for which I have already refused 300 francs; I guard it as the apple of my eye and short of absolute necessity I will part with

[1] The painter Fernand Quignon, nicknamed at the time " the painter of black wheat."

it only after my last shirt; besides who is the fool[1] who would pay that; you give no clue as to his identity.

With affectionate regards to everybody,

PAUL GAUGUIN.

66.

TO EMILE SCHUFFENECKER.   Pont-Aven, 8 July, 1888.

My dear Schuffenecker,

Thanks for your cheery letter. You cannot expect to please everybody, even Miss Pouzin.[2] Set your mind at rest on this point. It is not the good artists who can injure you, but the bad ones. If satellites follow in the wake of a planet, the latter in its turn pulls them along in its movement.

I replied to Van Gogh[3] that I accepted his proposal, relying on Miss Pouzin to release me here so that I could slip away to the South. I have not heard from him, which surprises me, and have had bad news from Miss Pouzin, which is unpromising all round —a sign that good will come. You see how very optimistic I am.

I have relapses from time to time, which drive me back to bed, but on the whole I am on the road to recovery and I have got my strength back. Also I have done some *nudes,* which ought to please you. And not at all in the Degas[4] style. The last is a fight between two boys near the river, quite Japanese, by a Peruvian Indian. Very little finished, the lawn green and upper part white.

1 The fool was Schuffenecker who wanted to buy this Cézanne picture, one of Gauguin's impressionist collection, so as to render his friend a service.

2 Miss Pouzin, married to a banker, was studying painting under Schuffenecker's tuition.

3 Vincent Van Gogh, born 30th March, 1853, at Grost-Zundert in Holland. He had known Gauguin during the severe winter of 1886 and much admired his talent. Staying at Arles in 1886, and knowing his friend's poverty, he insisted on the latter joining him, in order to found the Studio of the South. Gauguin arrived at Vincent's lodgings, 2, place Lamartine, about the 20th October.

4 Edgar Degas (1834-1917). He held Gauguin in great esteem and defended him when the painter exhibited his first Tahiti canvases,

I am delighted to see that you have been able to resume work with better health.

With regards, etc.,

PAUL GO.

67.

TO EMILE SCHUFFENECKER.   Pont-Aven, 14 August, 1888.

My dear Schuff,

Thanks for having thought of me in sending your address, which I waited in order to write. You are now in your element since you need disputatious struggle to encourage you. A hint—don't paint too much direct from nature. Art is an abstraction! study nature then brood on it and treasure the creation which will result, which is the only way to ascend towards God—to create like our Divine Master.

Here is something as you like little dots. All the Americans have been raging against the impressionist, and I was forced to threaten to dot them on the crumpet, and now we have peace.

I may leave at any moment. I have started a pupil who will go far: the circle grows. Little Bernard is here[1] and has brought some interesting things from St. Briac. Here is someone who is not afraid to try anything.

My last works are on the right lines and I think you will find a new note, or rather the affirmation of my recent experiments or synthesis of one form and one colour, without either being the dominant. Courage then, and may God take you in his holy keeping by crowning your efforts.

---

[1] Emile Bernard (1868-1942). A precocious child, talented for drawing and painting, he was in the advance guard of modern painting, and certain canvases of 1886 and 1887, such as *My parents' house at Asnières*, and the *Head of a Man* of the Marcel Guerin collection, dating even before the decisive meeting with Gauguin, are of extraordinary boldness. He stayed in August and September at Pont-Aven with his sister Madeleine and his mother and, with Gauguin, created synthetism. The firm friendship which united them was ruptured in 1891 in consequence of numerous disagreements of which the chief was Gauguin's consecration as the chief of pictorial symbolism, while Bernard considered he was the initiator of his friend in the development of his art.

Are all of your family with you? If yes, my regards and child-like kisses.

Frater salute.

PAUL GAUGUIN.

Herewith a photograph done by an amateur (gratis).

68.

TO EMILE BERNARD. Pont-Aven, October, 1888.

My dear Emile,

Thanks for your letter which is interesting from two points of view. (1), That of the expansiveness which belongs to your age. There is time enough, to arrive, like me, at the stage when the heart is hardened (I only weep from joy or enthusiasm). (2) That of the second period which you are reaching (ethics of art) when execution obviously necessary as a stepping-stone, but not for the final aim, ceases to count. You hold all the trumps in your hand. With foot in stirrup betimes, you will arrive fully armed and in all the vigour of youth at the moment when the blocked road has been cleared in great part. You are extraordinarily gifted, and painting now, you will undoubtedly arrive, but at some other time, say ten years ago, you would not have found one person to admire you or look at you. So much the better for you.

In this connection Van Goch[1] has written a very curious thing to Vincent. I have, he says, seen Seurat[2] who has made some admirable studies representing a good workman relishing his titbit: Signac[3] is always rather cold: he seems to me like a traveller in little dots. They are to start a campaign (having the Independent Review as the chief organ of their propaganda) against us fellows.

[1] Theo Van Gogh, born in 1857, brother of Vincent Van Gogh. Manager of Goupil's gallery, rue Montmartre, he did yeoman service for the impressionists.

[2] George Seurat, born 2nd December, 1859, died 20th March, 1891. Creator of divisionism or pointillism, regarded as one of the fathers of cubism.

[3] Paul Signac, painter (1863-1935), friend and disciple of Seurat, one of the founders of the Independent Gallery.

Degas (Gauguin especially) Bernard, etc., would be made out to be worse than devils to be kept at arm's length like the plague. Behold *grosso modo* what was said. You can take it for granted but say nothing about it to Van Gogh, otherwise you will make me out to be indiscreet. I am more than pleased with the result of my Pont-Aven studies. Degas is buying from me that of the two Breton women at Avins. This is a handsome compliment to me: as you know I have the greatest confidence in Degas's judgment—besides, it is an excellent starting point commercially. All Degas's friends have confidence in him. Van Gogh hopes to sell all my pictures. If I have this luck I shall go to Martinique, I am positive that now I can do good work there. And if I can get hold of a substantial sum I will buy a house there and set up a studio where friends will find the wherewithal for life all to hand for almost nothing. I am inclined to agree with Vincent; the future is to the painters of the tropics, which have not yet been painted. (Novelty is essential to stimulate the stupid buying public.) In any case if you do not have to go on military service you can come here without fear, I have now so arranged matters that three can live very cheaply, and if your father stopped your allowance and you had nothing, you would find here an assured existence.

I have a commission for you. Ask Van Gogh to let you have the proceeds of the first picture of mine which he sells, and send me the following colours which I need. I do not like Vincent's colours, I prefer Tanguy's.[1]

Although silence is to be my part henceforth, do not forbid me to send my respects to Madame Bernard with all my good wishes for your charming sister.

Yours cordially,

PAUL GAUGUIN.

---

[1] Julien Tanguy (1825-1894), once a plasterer, " father Tanguy," who supplied colours to artists, set up as a picture dealer at 14, Rue Clauzel, Paris, and his little shop became a meeting place for Van Gogh, Gauguin, Emile Bernard, Lautrec, Pissarro and others. He was a great admirer of Cézanne, whose works he was the first to exhibit. Kind of heart and helped by " Mother Tanguy," he rendered great services to artists. When he died, Octave Mirbeau organised a sale at the Hotel Drouot for his widow's benefit.

69.

TO MADELEINE BERNARD.[1]   Pont-Aven, October, 1888.

Dear Sister,

If you want to go through life like most young girls, without aim, without reason, at the mercy of all the hazards of fortune good and bad, dependent on the world to which we sacrifice our all and which renders us so little in return, do not read what I am writing to you.

If, on the other hand, you want to *be someone*, to find happiness solely in your independence and your conscience, it is now time to think about these things and in three years to act.

First of all, you must regard yourself as Androgyne, without sex. By that I mean that heart and soul, in short all that is divine, must not be the slave of matter, that is of the body. The virtues of a woman are exactly the same as the virtues of a man and are the Christian virtues —duty towards one's fellows based on kindness, and always sacrifice, with conscience only for judge. You may raise an altar to your dignity and intelligence, but none other.

Lying and venality are vices, and, in the ordinary course of events, both men and women are addicted to them. All chains are the insignia of the lower orders, and if you do any slavish action, you flout divine laws. Do in a proud spirit all that would help you to win the right to be proud, and do your best to earn your own living, which is the pathway to that right. But crush all vanity, which is the hallmark of mediocrity, and, above all, the vanity of money.

When one day the puppet shall have given place to a living creature, all worth-while people will be found ready to support you. Do not be afraid. If you are in need of help, turn to us and say : "Brother, support me!" We artists also are in need of your defence, of your aid, and you can be persuasive. We should thus render each other mutual service—bring about an exchange of different qualities.

---

[1] Madeleine Bernard (1871-1895), of an exquisite and passionate nature, suffered much about her sixteenth year from her relatives' failure to understand her brother and herself. She was forbidden to correspond with Gauguin. Betrothed to Charles Laval, she died young at Cairo from consumption. In 1888, at Pont-Aven, Gauguin had been very much enamoured of Medeleine Bernard, whom he always called " Dear Sister."

I hope that both of you, mother and daughter, arrived safely and in good health. Be my mediator with your mother, and accept a fraternal kiss from your elder brother.

PAUL GAUGUIN.

Arles, 2, Place Lamartine, from 22 October.

70.

TO HIS WIFE.   Pont-Aven, October, 1888.

My dear Mette,

I am a little troubled about the children's health. It is their holidays and down there as here, sea-bathing is unwise at this season. And what has been happening to you all this time? Your silence is significant.

I have now recovered from my illness and am beginning to work. In a short while I shall leave for Arles near Marseilles. I have been invited to spend 6 months there with a painter who will board and lodge me in exchange for drawings.

If I had had the money to settle my bill at Pont-Aven, I should have gone already. In any case write to Pont-Aven until further notice. I send you a photograph taken here by an amateur. I hope you will show it to the children so that they do not completely forget what their father looks like.

The Copenhagen Exhibition ought to be keeping people in town this season and I hope the dead season will be of short duration.

Laval has returned from Martinique and is here for the present. He sends you his regards.

I embrace everybody.

PAUL.

71.

TO EMILE SCHUFFENECKER.   Quimperlé, 8 October, 1888.

My dear Schuff,

You are back in Paris ready to slip into harness again. I should like very much to see your pictures—return from the sea—I am sure they must be interesting.

I received your last letter and the next day one from Paris. Since then I have been confined to bed, with a return of that dreadful dysentery. Worry causes the bile to accumulate in the stomach and tortures me, then comes the moment of evacuation. But I am up and about again.

I have painted a picture[1] for a church; of course it was refused, so I am sending it to Van Gogh. Unnecessary to describe it, you will see it.

This year I have sacrificed all, execution and colouring, for style, intending to compel myself to do something different from what I usually do. It is a transformation which has not borne fruit so far, but will, I think, bear it.

I have done a self-portrait for Vincent who asked me for it. I believe it is one of my best efforts: absolutely incomprehensible (upon my word) so abstract is it. First the head of a brigand, a Jean Valjean (*les Misérables*), likewise personifying a disreputable impressionist painter burdened for ever with a chain for the world. The drawing is altogether peculiar, being complete abstraction. The eyes, the mouth, the nose, are like the flowers of a Persian carpet, thus personifying the symbolical side. The colour is a colour remote from nature; imagine a confused collection of pottery all twisted by the furnace! All the reds and violets streaked by flames, like a furnace burning fiercely, the seat of the painter's mental struggles. The whole on a chrome background sprinkled with childish nosegays. Chamber of pure young girl. The impressionist is such an one, not yet sullied by the filthy kiss of the Fine-Arts (School).

I send you a letter from Vincent, to let you see where I am with him and what is on foot at the moment. Show it to Miss Pouzin, so that she sees you are not alone in holding me in esteem. It will also serve to impress upon her that artists are beings apart who cannot be bothered with the practical business ideas mooted by her.

Van Gogh has just bought from me 300 francs work of pottery. So I leave at the end of the month for Arles, where I expect to stay

---

[1] The reference is to *Vision after the Sermon,* or *Jacob Wrestling with the Angel,* a first attempt at simplification which Gauguin, assisted by Laval and Bernard, carried to Nizon, near Pont-Aven, in order to offer it to the church of the little village. But the curé, startled and guessing that his flock would not understand this work, refused the gift.

a long time. The object of this sojourn is to free me from money.
worries, so that I can concentrate on my work until I can be
launched.

Henceforth he will send me a small monthly sum for my
living expenses. Do not forget me during my absence. I will write
to you and think of you.

Kind regards to everybody.

Yours ever,

PAUL GAUGUIN.

72.

LETTER FROM VAN GOGH attached to GAUGUIN'S letter to
SCHUFFENECKER.

My dear Gauguin,

This morning I received your excellent letter, which, however,
I have sent to my brother: your general idea of the impressionist,
of which your portrait is the symbol, is striking. I am more than
anxious to see it, but I feel pretty sure that this work is too important for me to have it by way of exchange. If you care to keep
it for us, my brother will take it from you, which I lost no time
in asking him to do at the first opportunity, which, let us hope,
will be soon.

For we want to urge you once more to see whether you cannot
come.

I must tell you that even whilst at work I do not cease thinking
of this enterprise of starting a studio with you and me for permanent residents, but both of us desiring to make it a shelter and
a refuge for the comrades when they are knocked out in the
struggle. After you left Paris my brother and I spent some time
together which will ever remain memorable. The discussions took
an ever wider sweep—with Guillaimin, with Pissarro father and
son, with Seurat ,whom I did not know (I only visited his studio
a few hours before my departure).

In these discussions what frequently cropped up was what my
brother and I have so much at heart, namely what steps can be
taken to safeguard the material existence of painters and to safeguard their means of production (colours, canvases) and secure to

them a direct share in the price their pictures may fetch at any time after they have parted with them.

When you come here we shall be able to go over all this ground again.

However that may be, when I left Paris, very dejected and pretty ill, and almost drunk owing to the necessity of stimulating my waning strength, then I crept back into my shell, and hardly dared to hope. But hope is once more dawning on the horizon, this delusive hope which has so often consoled me in my solitary life. And now I want you to take a full share in this confident belief that we are on the way to a lasting success.

When you arrive we can indulge in day-long discussions in the poor studios and the cafés of the little boulevard, and you will realize what my brother and I are driving at, which is not by any means the formation of a company.

Nevertheless, you will see that what is done in the future to remedy the desperate state of these last years, will be very much what we have advised. As soon as we have the whole idea worked out on and based on unshakeable foundations you shall have all details. And you will have to admit that we shall then be going beyond the plan which we have already outlined to you. If we have gone further it is only our duty as picture dealers. As you perhaps know, I, too, spent years in the business and do not despise a trade by which I earned my daily bread.

It is enough to say that I do not believe that in physically cutting yourself off from Paris, you will cease to feel in direct contact with it.

I have an extraordinary fever for work these days, actually I am struggling with a landscape, showing a blue sky above an immense vineyard, green, purple, and yellow, with black and orange vine branches.

Little figures of ladies with red parasols, little figures of vineyard workers with their carts enliven the piece. Canvas of 30 square millimetres for house decoration.

I have a self-portrait all ash-coloured. The ash colour comes from mixing veronese with orange mineral on a pale veronese background, and dun-coloured clothes. But in exaggerating my personality I sought rather the character of a simple adorer of the eternal Buddha. It has given me a lot of trouble, but I shall have to do it all over again if I want to succeed in expressing the idea. I must get myself still further cured of the conventional brutishness of our so-called civilization, in order to have a better model for a better picture.

One thing which has immensely pleased me. I received a letter yesterday from Boch (his sister is in the Belgian *Vingtistes*) who writes that he is staying in the Borinage to paint charcoal burners and miners. He proposes however to return to the South to vary his impressions, and in this case will certainly come to Arles.

I find my artistic ideas extremely vulgar compared with yours.

I have always the gross appetite of a beast.

I forget everything for the external beauty of things which I am unable to reproduce, for I reproduce it badly in my picture and coarsely, whereas nature seems to me perfect.

Now, however, the impulse of my bony carcase is such that it is going straight to the goal, whence results a sincerity that is something original perhaps in what I feel if, however, the *motif* lends itself to my coarse and unskilful execution.

I believe, that if, from now on, you begin to feel you are the head of this studio—which we will seek to make a shelter for several —gradually and in the degree that our intense *furious* work give us the means of carrying the idea to fruition, I believe that then you will derive some consolation for your present troubles and illness, in reflecting that we are probably giving our lives for a generation of painters yet to come.

These countries have already seen the cult of Venus—essentially artistic in Greece—then the poets and artists of the Renaissance. Where these things could flourish impressionism cannot wither.

I have taken special care to decorate your room with a *poet's garden*. In the Banal Gardens, a public park, flourish plants and bushes which make one dream of the landscapes associated with Botticelli, Giotto, Petrarch, Dante and Boccassio. In the decoration I have sought to bring out all that is essential in the unchangeable character of the country.

And I wanted to paint this garden in such a way as to remind one both of the old poet of these parts (or rather of Avignon) Petrarch, and of the new poet of these parts, Paul Gauguin.

However maladroit this attempt may be, it will show you that in preparing your studio I have thought of you with considerable emotion.

Let us screw up our courage for the success of our enterprise and go on thinking that you are in the right place here, for I verily believe that all this will last a long time.

Yours cordially,

VINCENT.

P.S.—I fear only that you will find Brittany more beautiful; here you see nothing more beautiful than Daumier shapes. The faces here are often absolutely Daumieresque. But you would soon discover Antiquity and the Renaissance dormant beneath all this modernity. And as for all that, you are free to resurrect them.

Bernard suggested that he, Moret, Laval and another should make an exchange with me. On principle I am really very keen on the system of exchange between artists, and I see that Japanese painters attach a considerable importance to this.

Accordingly, I will send you what studies in dry state I have available just now and you shall have the first choice. But I will not exchange anything with you if it should cost you anything as important as your portrait which would be too handsome. That I dare not, for my brother will gladly take it from you on return for a whole month.

73.

TO EMILE SCHUFFENECKER.   Quimperle, 16 October, 1888.

My dear Schuff,

What do you want me to say about your troubles concerning your name? You know my opinion of this, and it is that of all reasonable people. We have quite enough filthy vexations without creating them out of sheer folly. Don't bother yourself about it, sign " Schuffen " and leave it at that. If people like your pictures, they will not bother about the name, and won't concern themselves with precedents. They will always know who painted them and what his name is. Laval and Bernard, who want to be remembered, are of my opinion.

Send me back Vincent's letter.

Another thing, you know my itch for paying whenever I have money. Well, I have paid the doctor and something to Marie-

Jeanne without thinking, and now I have no funds for my journey.

Be good enough to go and see Van Gogh at once, and arrange for him to send me 50 francs. Telegraph me at once.

After I resolved to go South I managed to go down with fever. Now I am out of danger, and I believe I shall do good work.

I think that in a year's time I shall be out of the wood and able to settle my debts with you. In any case I shall none the less remain your obliged and devoted friend.

If you should see Guillaumin again, ask him why he has not written me. I sent him a portrait this summer and had no word from him. Is he annoyed because Van Gogh is running after me? In any event the good of one does not injure another.

So you talk about my *terrible* mysticism. Be impressionist to the very end and be afraid of nothing. Obviously this sympathetic way is full of rocks, and I have as yet only put the tip of my foot in it, but it is fundamental in my nature, and a man must always follow his temperament. I realize that I shall be understood less and less. What matters if I alienate others; for the multitude I shall be an enigma, for a few I shall be a poet, and sooner or later, merit will have its way.

However that may be, I tell you that I shall eventually do first class things, I know it and we shall see. You know well enough that in art I am always right at bottom. Mark this well, a wind is blowing at this moment *among artists* which is all in my favour; I know it from one or two indiscretions and rest assured, however much Van Gogh may be in love with me, he would not bring himself to feed me in the South for my beautiful eyes. He has surveyed the terrain like a cautious Dutchman and intends to push the matter to the utmost of his powers, and to the exclusion of everything else. I asked him to lower prices to tempt buyers, but he replied that he intended, on the contrary, to raise them. Optimist as I am, this time I really have my foot on the solid earth.

Cordially yours,

PAUL GO.

Telegraph me a reply.

Let me have the pleasure of sending you a fur overcoat. I shan't see the winter again for a long while and can go about in rags. I don't care for elegance any longer and should be delighted if you would accept something from me,

74.

TO EMILE SCHUFFENECKER.   Arles, 13 November, 1888.

My dear Schuff,

Thanks for your kindness. I received the parcel, for which I waited before replying to your last letter, which crossed mine.

I was keenly disappointed to see you were refused by the Salon Independante, and Dubois-Pillet accepted. Never mind, you must grow resigned to these trifling pinpricks, which happen more often to the deserving than to others. For years the " Vingtistes " have been inviting Signac, Dubois, and they have never even heard of me. I have managed to survive this.

To console me, I have received a very flattering letter inviting me to and I am this year organising an important exhibition at Brussels in opposition to the dotters.

I have just sent Van Gogh two canvases which you must contrive to see—on entirely different lines, painted simply on coarse canvas in thick impasto, so that the colour divisions are hardly noticeable, hoping thereby to get a broader view.

When you have time let me have your criticisms on all this. At the moment, it seems to me to be running along at full speed like a train and, like the engine driver, I can see the terminus ahead, but what chances there are of going off the rails! Yes, I am optimistic, but you are wrong if you think this optimism springs from the thought of money to come, which I should not spend in enjoyment and rest, but in preparing for the great struggle; what I am waging now is only a little artistic skirmish. I do not want to attack until I have all the necessary weapons in my hands. I know no other force than this and I say proudly: we shall see.

You can ask Pissarro if I am not talented. No constipation and regular coitus, with independent work, and a man can pull through.

I see you opening your eyes very wide, my virtuous Schuff, at these daring sentiments. Calm yourself, eat well, make love to the best of your ability, work the same, and you will die happy.

Warm regards to all the little family from the big fool who loves you.

P. GO.

75.

TO EMILE BERNARD.   Undated, Arles, November, 1888.

My dear Bernard,

I have forgotten your father's letter and there is nothing in it you ought to know. But this time you will be advised. I hope you are not being bothered too much by the mugs which I left in such an overheated state; in any case, you are working and experimenting. I fear cardboard is not strong enough for the glue; wood has too hard a surface and might peel. But if you use a simple material like thick paper on cloth, which grips and absorbs the colour, you will obtain good results. Theatre scenery is made like this and is very durable.

You discuss shadows with Laval and ask me if I am in accord. So far as regards the analysis of light, yes. Look at the Japanese who are certainly excellent draughtsmen, and you will see life depicted in the open air and in the sunshine without shadows, colour being used only as a combination of tones, diverse harmonies, giving the impression of warmth, etc. . . . Besides, I regard impressionism as an altogether new research, absolutely removed from everything mechanical, such as photography, etc. That is why I would avoid as much as possible that which gives the illusion of a thing, and as shadow is the *trompe l'œil* of the sun, I am constrained to suppress it. If shadows come into your composition as a necessary formula, it is quite another matter. Thus instead of a shape you would get only the shadow of a person; it is an original point of departure, the strangeness of which you will have to take into account. Like the raven on the head of Pallas who sits there rather than a parrot owing to the choice of the artist—a deliberate choice. So then, my dear Bernard, put in shadows if you consider them useful; or keep them out: it comes to the same thing, provided you decline to be enslaved by shadows. I explain my ideas on the subject by and large, and leave you to read between the lines.

I send you money to pay Gloannec 280 francs, Frédéric 35, 5 francs for despatching pictures, 5 francs for both to drink my health.

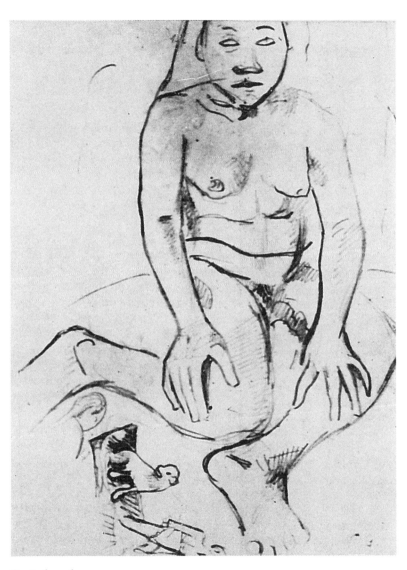

Seated nude
Pencil drawing (*Private collection*)

Now that the way is prepared by Van Gogh, I believe it is possible for all talented artists of our group to get on their feet, so you have only to walk straight on. I discussed you with the Zouave and believe that in Africa you would lead a life very useful to your art and fairly comfortable. I have looked into the money question and find we can get along cheaply, provided we eat at home.

It's odd that Vincent feels the influence of Daumier here: I, on the contrary, see the Puvis (de Chavannes) subjects in their Japanese colourings. Women here with their elegant coiffure have a Greek beauty. Their shawls, falling in folds like the primitives, are, I say, like Greek friezes. The girl passing along the street is as much a lady as any born and of as virginal an appearance as Juno. Anyhow, it must be seen. In all events, there is here a fountain of beauty, *modern style*. Greetings to both of you, and be friends with Laval, who has a fine and noble nature, despite his transcendent faults, when the Cossack re-appears. We are all the same you know, you as terrible as the rest of us. We must make up our minds to put up with each other and arrive holding each other's hands.

PAUL GAUGUIN.

76.

TO HIS WIFE.   Undated, Arles, November, 1888.

My dear Mette,

Enclosed is 200 francs.

I would ask you to *acknowledge safe receipt*, so that I may know that they have not gone astray. If, in addition, it would not tire you too much, you could at the same time give me news of the children. I have heard nothing about them for a very long time.

I am on the way to recovery, though not without relapses. And my affairs are assuming a better shape, although very slowly.

In any case, my reputation is being firmly established both at Paris and at Brussels.

I send you a letter from Schuffenecker, which will tell you better than I what is thought about my painting.

I am working to breaking point but I can see compensation in the future.

Your husband,
PAUL GAUGUIN.

2, Place Lamartine, Arles.

It is probable that I will send you something more this winter, if the Brussels exhibition, to which I have been invited, goes well, as it promises to do.

77.

TO EMILE SCHUFFENECKER.

Undated, Arles, December, 1888.

My dear Schuff,

Bravo! You have brought it off. See Van Gogh, arrange things to the end of my stay.

Only remember it is not an exhibition[1] for the others. So let us arrange it for a little group of comrades, and from this point of view I should want to be represented there as fully as possible.

Do your best in my interests to secure good positions for my pictures.

(1) Mangoes, Martinique.
(2) The tall Breton with the little boy.
(3) Breton woman, 1 standing, 1 on the ground.
(4) Winter (little Breton boy fitting his wooden shoe with village in the background.
(5) The Vicarage (landscape of 1886).
(6) Circle of little girls.
(7) Arles landscape.
(8) The mas of Arles at Van Gogh's.
(9) Pastel.
(10) Two children fighting.

---

[1] Referring to the exhibition of paintings of the impressionist and synthetist group, held in the premises of Volpini, Café des Arts, at the Universal Exhibition in 1889, where were shown numerous canvases of Paul Gauguin, Charles Laval, Léon Fauché, Emile Schuffenecker, Louis Anquetin, Daniel de Monfreid, Emile Bernard, Louis Roy and Nemo (Bernard). Guillaumin and Vincent Van Gogh did not exhibit.

Remember, it is we who are sending out the invitations, consequently :—

Schuff	...	...	10 canvases
Guillaumin		...	10 „
Gauguin		...	10 „
Bernard ...		...	10 „

40 canvases.

Roy	...	...	2 canvases
Man of Nancy	...		2 „
Vincent		...	6 „

making 10

This will do. For my part, I decline to exhibit with *the others*, Pissarro,[1] Seurat, etc.

It is our group.

I wanted to exhibit very little, but Laval told me it was my turn, and that I should do wrong in working for others.

Kindest regards to your wife and kisses for the children.

Yours, etc.,

P. GO.

78.

TO EMILE BERNARD.   Undated, Arles, December, 1888.

My dear Bernard,

Thanks for your letter and for carrying out the commission about the colours. You do not tell me if Tanguy considers himself repaid with the picture you have delivered to him. In any case the supplies sent must be paid for cash down and the money for this is with Van Gogh.

I am glad you have been to see our excellent Schuffenecker; you do not say anything about him; is he getting along; at the moment he is distressed because the Salon Independante does not want to exhibit him when it accepts Dubois-Pillet, Luce, etc.

I am at Arles quite out of my element, so petty and shabby do I find the scenery and the people. Vincent and I do not find our-

---

[1] From 1875 onwards, Gauguin had profited from Pissarro's advice. He even stayed with Pissarro at Osny in 1883, where he painted several canvases. Many works of his impressionist period reveal the strong influence which Pissarro exerted on his friend.

selves in general agreement[1], especially in painting. He admires Daumier, Daubigny, Ziem and the great Rousseau, all people I cannot endure. On the other hand, he detests Ingres, Raphael, Degas, all people whom I admire; I answer: "Corporal, you're right," for the sake of peace. He likes my paintings very much, but while I am doing them he always finds that I am doing this or that wrong. He is romantic while I am rather inclined towards a primitive state. When it comes to colour he is interested in the accidents of the pigment, as with Monticelli[2], whereas I detest this messing about in the medium, etc.

I do not know what to reply about the two drawings which your mother has kept. They are not mine but belong to Van Gogh, who sent me 50 francs this summer for a drawing. They are therefor to be handed to him. I do not understand how your mother has come to regard as a present what she took upon herself as a commission. I don't want to appear a miser, and this is what I propose: There is at Goupil's a little squat unpolished pot decorated with a bird on a blue green background. Accept this from me. Van Gogh will give it you if you show him this letter. I bequeath it to Madeleine.

Silence is the order of the day, but I hope she will sometimes think of her elder brother when she is putting flowers in it. It is a pretty rough thing, but bears far more the impression of myself than the sketch of little girls. She will therefore lose nothing in exchange. The pot is well cooled and it has withstood a temperature of 1600 degrees. Best respects to your mother.

Affectionate handclasp. Vincent sends you his regards and asks me to thank you for the study you sent him in exchange.

PAUL GAUGUIN.

[1] Gauguin's visit to Arles was to end dramatically. On the 24th December, about nine o'clock in the evening, Van Gogh, in a fit of madness, rushed at his friend with an open razor in his hand. Returning home he cut off his right ear, which he washed and slipped into an envelope, in order to deliver it to a prostitute whom he frequented. Gauguin, who had escaped with a bad fright, left the next day for Paris without seeing Vincent again.

[2] Born and died in Marseilles, fond of vivid colours, but discouraged by public indifference.

79.

TO HIS WIFE. Undated, Paris, February, 1889.

My dear Mette,

The day before yesterday a young man brought a parcel of vests from you. I thank you for this attention. Henceforth I shall be rich in waistcoats; the three other summer ones are still in good condition.

Business in Paris goes from bad to worse and I really don't know how it will end up. A slump on the Stock Exchange every day.

How are you getting on without Miss Engelman? I thought she was a friend you couldn't do without!

You tell me nothing of your family and complain of being alone; so they don't come to see you? I confess I cannot make out your solitude; you have your French lessons and admirers, who all flatter you—you told me yourself the last time that I saw you, that you were very much spoilt. Nobody to order you about, a thing you do not like, and charming children around you. True, your apartments may not be all you desire, but compared with me you are in Paradise.

Which reminds me. I read in the paper that at a Nice festival everybody noticed the attractive Miss de Falbe, wife of the Danish diplomat. Has the "imbecile of the yellow thread" perchance become a wealthy personage? After all, there would be nothing surprising in this, as there are no limits to human stupidity.

The Schuffeneckers send you their best wishes. Schuffenecker holds you in high esteem when he compares you with the millstone around his neck.

Another one who has marriage "over his head."

Let me have news of Copenhagen and of everybody. Will your friends come to the Exhibition this year?

Your husband,

PAUL.

80.

TO EMILE BERNARD. Undated, Paris, February, 1889.

My dear Bernard,

I do not know what to make of it; I sought you in vain at the

Exhibition. I have been to the Buffalo. At all costs, you must come and see that! It is great. Come on Wednesday and have breakfast with Schuff and we will go in the afternoon.

Tell me if you can't come.

P. GAUGUIN.

81.

TO EMILE BERNARD.   Undated, Paris, March, 1889.

My dear Bernard,

You missed something in not coming the other day. In the Java village there are Hindoo dances. All the art of India can be seen there, and it is exactly like the photos I have. I go there again on Thursday as I have an appointment with a mulatto girl.

Come on Thursday, but I don't want to be there too late; come either for breakfast at noon, or at 1 o'clock (at Schuff's). As to Buffalo we will go on Saturday.

I intend to leave on Tuesday next[1] and I must see about packing my traps.

P. GAUGUIN.

82.

TO HIS WIFE.   Undated, Le Pouldu, end of June, 1889.

My dear Mette,

Yes, you have not heard from me for over six months; but it is more than six months since I received news of the children. It seems there must be a serious accident[2] before I do hear, which scarcely disposes me to cheerfulness, although you say all danger is now over.

Does one ever know; one might become lame or imbecile as a result of a thing like that and the signs would not show until long after. Anyhow, I am hardened to adversity.

Do you realise the number of times I have written and my letter crossed yours, and because you seem to be the last to write, you play at silence? Whether I write or do not write, does not your conscience tell you that I ought to have news of the children

---

[1] Return to Pont-Aven.
[2] His son Pola had a fall.

whom I have not seen for five years? Yet you impress upon me, whenever opportunity offers, that I am their father!

When there was a possibility of my going to see them some six months ago (which arose quite suddenly) your Copenhagen people discovered that it was not worth while to incur such an expense. Money reasons always—those of the heart are not worth considering. Poor woman, to allow yourself to be advised so badly, and by people in short, who do not pay, either in money or in broken hearts. What money is lost when the partners are not in agreement, is something you will never understand.

What is it you want of me? Above all, what have you ever wanted of me? Whether in the Indies or elsewhere, I am, it appears, to be a beast of burden for wife and children whom I must not see. By way of return for my homeless existence, I am to be loved if I love, I am to be written to if I write. You know me. Either I weigh matters (and weigh them well) or I do not. Heart in hand, eyes front and I fight with uncovered breast. Your powerful sister has not abdicated her authority over you, but, in return, where is the protection she promised you?

Very well then, I accept the rôle that has been assigned to me, and then I must calculate—not to lose the substance for the shadow —(the shadow being the rôle of an employee). If I should get a job at 2,000 or 4,000 francs—your brothers' figures—there would be no complaint to make against me, and yet we should both be practically in the same position. As to the future, no one ever gives a thought to it.

I determined, despite the certitude which my conscience gave me, to consult others (men who also count) to ascertain if I was doing my duty. All are of my opinion, that art is my business, my capital, the future of my children, the honour of the name I have given them—all things which will be useful to them one day. When they have to make their way in the world, a famous father may prove a valuable asset.

You will retort that this will be a long time ahead, but what do you want me to do about it? Is it my fault? I am the first to suffer from it. I can assure you that if those who know about such things had said that I have no talent and that I am wasting my time, I would have abandoned the attempt long ago. Can it be said that Millet failed in his duty and bequeathed a wretched future to his children?

You want my news?

I am in a fishermans' inn[1] at the seaside, near a village of 150 inhabitants. I live here like a peasant, and work every day in canvas trousers (all those of five years ago are worn out). I spend a franc a day on my food and two pence on tobacco. So no one can say I am extravagant. I speak to nobody, and I have no news of the children. Only—only this—I am exhibiting my works at Goupil's in Paris, and they are creating a great sensation; but it is difficult to sell them. When this is going to happen, I cannot tell you, but what I can tell you is that to-day I am one of the artists who arouse the greatest astonishment. You have exhibited some old things of mine at Copenhagen. My opinion might have been sought first of all.

The 7th June, '89, passed without one of the children thinking of it. Anyhow, all's well that ends well. I am making inquiries through influential friends about a situation in Tonkin, where I hope I should be able to live for some time and await better times. As such posts are paid, you could have part of the pictures sold at Goupil's. As for the present I have nothing. I rather anticipate the sale of a wood carving. As soon as I have the proceeds I will send you 300 francs—you can rely upon getting them; it is only a question of time. I am writing to Paris to try to push the sale.

At the Universal Exhibition this year I have exhibited in a *Café Chantant;* perhaps some Danes will have seen it and told you about it. In any case, nearly all Norwegians see at Goupil's what I do and Philipsen, whom I met in Paris, has also seen them.

Once for all do not end your letters with that dry phrase ' Your wife, Mette '; I should prefer you to say plainly what you think. I have spoken to you about it before, but you have not wanted to understand.

PAUL GAUGUIN.

Pouldu, near Quimperlé (Finistère).

---

[1] Exasperated by the painters and bathers who flocked in growing numbers to Pont-Aven and prevented him from working, Gauguin moved to Pouldu, into a little inn kept by Marie Henry, nicknamed Marie Poupée. A few faithful friends accompanied him, a Dutchman, Meyer de Haan, Charles Filiger, Armand Séguin. Paul Sérusier looked them up several times, and Paul-Emile Colin, the engraver, spent several weeks with them in August and September, 1889.

83.

TO EMILE SCHUFFENECKER. Le Pouldu, July, 1889.

My dear Schuff,

I received a mournful letter from Copenhagen, the first for eight months.

Baby is in hospital; he fell from the third floor and it is a marvel that he escaped at all. As it is, he is in bad state with convulsions. Judge then, my poor Schuff, if life has any savour for me. If I had a few sous I would send a little money to them: to crown all, my paintings and carvings this year appal everybody!

I have been inquiring about a possible situation in Tonkin, which I am anxious to secure, to give me breathing space for a year or two, when the financial outlook will be better for impressionism.

I wrote recently to Bernard, from whom I have heard nothing. His father must have intercepted the letter. Tell him this.

No news from Laval.

Have you received a hare I had sent to you more than a month ago?

Regards to Madame and the children.

P. GO.

84.

TO EMILE BERNARD. Undated, Le Pouldu, August, 1889.

My dear Bernard,

I have read your letter to Laval, who showed it to me. I thought you were in Paris and you are at St. Briac—by your father's orders, which also forbid you to come to Pont-Aven. You are not losing much anyhow, as Pont-Aven is full of objectionable trippers. Fortunately, I have a studio[1] at Avains, where I can retire for shelter. Moreover, I have been more than a month at Pouldu with de Haan because I am floundering in a slough of despond and struggling with work which requires a certain time for completion.

---

[1] Gauguin had transformed into a studio the first floor of a little farm situated at Avains, near Pont-Aven. This studio was tenanted for several years by the painter Emile Compard.

I find pleasure, not in going farther along the lines I prepared formerly, but in trying something fresh. I feel it if I cannot explain it. I am certain to get there eventually, but slowly in spite of my impatience. In these conditions, my tentative studies yield only a maladroit and amateur result. Anyhow, I hope that this winter you will find in me an almost new Gauguin—I say almost, because I disclaim the pretension of inventing something new. What I am trying to get at is a corner of myself which I do not yet understand. Many things have happened therefore to explain my gloom.

I have received from Aurier[1] the *Moderniste*, with a part of your article. Good. Every little counts!

I am preparing an article on the purchase of pictures for the Louvre and attacking the contemporary art critic.

I return in three days to Pont-Aven, because I can live on credit there and my money is gone. I expect to stay there till the winter, and if I can then get any kind of post in Tonkin[2] I will slip off to study the Annamites.

P. GAUGUIN.

Vincent has written me and asks to be remembered to you. He is still in hospital.

85.

TO ALBERT AURIER.   Undated, Pont-Aven, end August, 1889.

Dear Sir,

I send you the short article hoping you will give it the same welcome as the first. I think it would be useful at the moment.

Make any alterations you like.

Kindly send me a copy of the number, if you insert it.

PAUL GAUGUIN.

---

[1] Albert Aurier (1865-1892), writer and art critic, one of the founders of the *Mercure de France*. Drawn into the symbolist movement, he contributed to the *Plume*, the *Décadent* and the *Moderniste*. It was he who hailed Gauguin as the leader of pictorial symbolism in a famous article on the *Vision after the Sermon*. He died early at 27 of typhoid fever caught at Marseilles.

[2] He hoped to obtain a minor post in the Tonkin civil service.

86.

TO EMILE SCHUFFENECKER.   1 September, 1889.

My dear Schuff,
        What a long time since I heard from you.
        On the other hand, I have received the pot you sent and which is very successful. I saw mother Reynier[1] who gave me word of you. You have made some sales, it seems. Fine, and you ought to be satisfied. I know of old what a pessimist you are, but everything comes to him who waits.
        As for the exhibition, Guillaumin writes me that people are ignoring it. There is an acid note in his letter—the intelligence has decidedly departed. But these days, I don't bat an eyelid.
        Write me at length all that is being said and done.
        Nothing much new here. Except that I am working. The Pont-Aven fight is over; everybody is humbled, and the Julian studio is beginning to tack about to humbug the school. Manet's triumph has crushed them.
        Greetings to all the comrades.

                                        P. GO.

        I do not remember Lambert's address. You would be doing me a good turn by asking him to make a wooden panel, which I want for a carving I hope to do here in the intervals. I should like it as soon as possible. Forgive me for always giving you commissions.

87.

TO EMILE BERNARD.

                        Undated, Pont-Aven, early September, 1889
My dear Bernard,
        Reading your letter I perceive that we are both pretty much in the same boat. Moments of doubt, results always below expectations; and the little encouragement we get, all this helps to drag us through the thistles and thorns.
        Well then, what can we do but fume and grapple with all the

---

[1] During Clovis Gauguin's illness in January, 1886, a neighbour, Mrs. Reynier, nursed him with devotion, while his father pasted up bills.

difficulties; when beaten, to get up and go on again. For ever and ever. At bottom, painting is like man, mortal but living always in conflict with flesh. If I thought of the absolute, I should cease to make any effort even to live. Let us be satisfied with what we are—whether incomplete or perfect. Although I have no patience, nor enough strength, and suffer the maximum agonies hoping for ultimate perfection, I labour and live always in hope. I am chary of giving advice (which is always a delicate matter) and yet I think that you would do well for some time to study according to your inclinations, since you believe at the moment that art is absolutely bound up with technical processes. If later you become, like me, sceptical in this respect, you will do something else. I confess that I feel in this language something quite different from the words, however harmonious. Corot, Giotto—seduced me by some quality quite apart from the solidity of their painting. You know how I esteem the work of Degas and yet I feel that there is something he lacks—a heart that beats. The tears of a child are something, but they can't be said to show wisdom. In short, I much admire masterpieces of every kind, those of emotion and those of technique; hence there is work to be done in both spheres. It is obvious that you are highly gifted and also that you know a great deal. Why bother about the opinions of idiots or jealous people? I do not think that this can disturb you for long.

As for myself, I have not been spoilt much by others, and I even expect to become more and more incomprehensible. What do I care. You are young and I think you lack something, a void which age will soon fill. It is a great deal that you yourself feel that, in spite of all you have seen, felt and suffered, you have not found yourself. But all this will right itself. There have been old men who affirmed their youthful beliefs, but they, unlike us, had nothing to disturb them such as the turmoil of existence and the pictures of others. You have seen too much in too short a time. Take a rest from seeing—for a very long time. Take whatever pleases you from what I tell you. In any case be assured that on my part there is nothing but the best intentions.

I have returned to Pont-Aven until the end of September, and I have just finished two good canvases, for myself, in the sense that they nearly express what I wanted to say at the moment—I say nearly and I am so far satisfied, hoping that the more of them I do, the better they will become.

I have also designed a large panel of 30 in carving[1] to be carried out later in wood when I have money to buy it. Not a penny in my pocket. I have also carved something better and even more remarkable. Gauguin (as a monster) seizing the hand of a protesting woman, saying to her: Be amorous and you will be happy. The Indian fox symbol of perversity, then little figures in the interstices. The wood will be coloured.

This winter we may have a large house which Haan wants to rent. It has a studio 12 by 15 metres overlooking the sea. In this case Laval and Moret would join us, and we could live very cheaply. You might be able to complete this group.

Now to bed.

Cordially yours,

P. GO.

88.

TO ALBERT AURIER.   No date, Le Pouldu, October, 1889.

Dear Sir,

Some time ago I sent you an article. Have you received it? I should be grateful for a word from you that it has arrived.

Yours very sincerely,

PAUL GAUGUIN.

Pouldu, near Quimperlé, Finistère.

89.

TO EMILE BERNARD.   No date, Le Pouldu, October, 1889.

My dear Bernard,

Your letter was a little delayed.   Pouldu is not Morbihan, but Finistère, near Quimperlé. Your letter, written in haste, is a trifle obscure. I gather that we have to exhibit in Lisbon. That you are going to Lisbon and your cousin is bringing the canvases. You mention a picture sold, but I have no knowledge of it. Van Gogh

---

[1] Gauguin was in the sequel very pleased with this wood carving, which gave concrete form to his ideas about love. This magnificent work belongs to Mrs. Jeanne Schuffenecker. A sketch is shown on this letter.

has sold for me the little dancers in the kiln. Is it this? I have decorated our enormous studio with lithographic subjects, P.G. O and Bernard, Japanese, etc. It is splendid and we are working at this moment with storms raging in front of us—for we are immediately above the sea.

You promise that you will write me a long letter explaining your enforced sojourn far from us.

Are you working much? I am working on a great wood carving (panel of 30 with nude figures). I have made a conquest here of a new Countess; she is enchanted with impressionism, and intends, on her return to Paris, to win over to our side many of her acquaintances—(Rouvier, Finance Minister, among others) whom she will persuade to buy my carving. In the absence of something concrete, we must live on hope. Laval has left for Paris and now wants to go to another district—perhaps he will work there? In any event he did not touch a brush during his six months in Brittany. Chamaillard[1], on the other hand, has done an excellent portrait of his wife. Moret nothing much. De Haan gets along splendidly here. He sends you his regards.

Sincerely,

P. GO.

90.

TO EMILE SCHUFFENECKER.

No date, Moelan, October, 1889.

My dear Schuff,

What has become of you? It seems that you are cross with me. Because I rebuffed Champsor[2]. First. the picture he wanted was sold for 500 to Montaudon, and I cannot sell it over again. Moreover, he is a vulgar scribbler not worth the rope for hanging. Second his articles mean nothing. You may find worth in them, I cannot. Yet again, his attitude in this matter was menacing, and I do not like this. Besides—that is all.

I have this year made disciples more important than Champsor. Another Countess who is well know in Parisian society, is

---

[1] Ernest de Chamaillard deserted the Quimper Bar for painting and joined Gauguin, whom he admired. His works, which are mainly owned by Breton collectors, are little known.

[2] The writer Champsaur.

smitten with me and the Impressionists. She is now in Paris beating the drum for our pictures. Her daughter paints and has now begun to do so on our lines, and so on.

I haven't done much painting recently—working on a carving in wood which I am sending to Paris next month and with which I am pretty satisfied. However, you will see it. The Countess has promised me she will make Rouvier the Minister buy it. If this happens, it will be seen to the best advantage.

Another thing. I am on the coast in a large house immediately overlooking the sea. When storms rage it is magnificent. I am working here with a Dutchman who is my pupil and a very good fellow. I do not think of going to Paris until the winter, and then for a month only, provided I sell something. I am reckoning on enough for a trip to Holland, to see the Rembrandts at close quarters. But these are all projects.

Anyhow, this planning is better than weeping.

You have submitted again to the teaching yoke[1], my poor Schuff. Have you done any work this year?

Guillaumin has been to Auvergne, which has yielded good results.

Write me a line. Greetings to children, wife, brother, mother, in short everybody.

Cordially yours,
P. GO.

91.

TO EMILE BERNARD.   No date, Le Pouldu, November, 1889.

My dear Bernard,

What can I say to you, at this moment when everything is crashing around me? I am tied to Pouldu by debts, which I have little hope of seeing paid. Van Gogh gives no sign because he can do nothing and according to what I divine and what Schuff tells me, our affairs are in a bad way, while Van Gogh has got married and is tied to the whims of the home, which is not healthy for us. Then what! the only person who up till now has bothered about me, is obliged to go off, and I am not on the spot to try to remedy matters.

---

1 Schuffenecker was professor of drawing at Vanves, later Michelet, College

I have made application to go to Tonkin, but the replies up to date are, for all intents and purposes, negative. The people they send to the Colonies are generally those who play pranks, steal the cash box, etc. . . . But me, an impressionist artist, that is to say, a rebel—it is out of the question. And on top of this, I am ill, suffering from accumulated spleen and gall, the physical result of the redoubled blows of misfortune which oppress and depress me, so that at the moment I have scarcely the energy or the will to work. And work used to make me forget. In the long run, this isolation, this concentration upon myself, while all the chief joys of life are cut off and intimate satisfaction is denied me, cries out for relief as an empty stomach for food. At the last, it proves a delusion so far as happiness is concerned, unless one is made of stone and is absolutely insensible. Despite all my efforts to become such an one, I fail. Mother Nature gets the upper hand all the time. Such is Gauguin in the toils, his hand burning in the furnace, and he is not able to suppress his cries. No doubt I shall get over this. What is man in this immense creation, and who am I to complain more than another. But unfortunately I see a different result in the case of others, and what might help a rascal to tolerate loneliness has the opposite effect on me.

Your phrase: " You know how fond we are of you," gives me pleasure, and, whether deliberate or otherwise, the plural " we " considerably adds to it. Did you send the critical periodical? What lunacy this article is! However, the nonsense fails to wound. Fénéon does well in saying that I imitated Anquetin[1] whom I don't even know. It seems that Eve did not speak negro, but good God! what language did she speak, she and the serpent? Thanks for photographs.

Your beautiful group of the Magdalen supported by two women is so well arranged in line and effect and expresses so well the essence of this scene that there is no room for the other personages to share in it as sorrowfully—personages necessary perhaps to the arrangement of line, but I would have them more stupid than suffering. This fine representation of the Magdalen who has done more by her love for belief in the resurrection is sufficient. And, I

[1] Louis Anquetin, born at Etrapagny in 1861, died in Paris in 1932. Admirable artist, friend of Emile Bernard, with whom in late 1887 he had made the first attempts at synthesis. He, too, repudiated these theories in order to indulge a passionate admiration for Rubens.

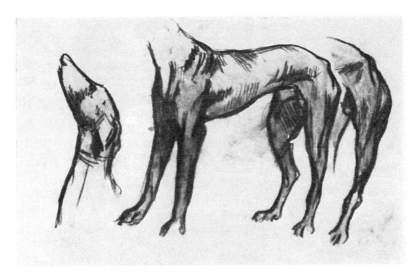

Gauguin Dog Studies
Water colour drawing

repeat, you have caught her admirably; I look at her now as at a different Magdalen than the one I knew. Don't take my criticism in bad part; it may be wrong, as I am just now so morose that everything bothers me.

Greetings to you both from my troubled heart.

P. GAUGUIN.

92.

TO EMILE BERNARD.   No date, Le Pouldu, November, 1889.

Your disconsolate letter reaches a countryside as sorrowful. I understand the bitterness which sweeps over you at the foolish reception of you and your works. They should be very beautiful this year—Schuff tells me that they were of fine mystic quality. What would you rather have? a mediocrity which pleases everybody or a talent which breaks new ground. We must choose if we have free will. Would you have the power of choice if choosing leads to suffering—a Nessus shirt which sticks to you and cannot be stripped off? Attacks on originality are to be expected from those who lack the power to create and shrug their shoulders. At your age you have a lifetime before you. As for me, of all my efforts this year, nothing remains but howls from Paris which penetrate here and discourage me to such a degree that I dare not paint any more, and can only drag my old body about on the sea shore of Le Pouldu in the bleak North wind. Mechanically I make a few studies (if you can call brush strokes in accord with the eye, studies). But the soul of me is absent and is mournfully regarding the pit which gapes in front of it—the pit in which I see the desolate family deprived of paternal support—and no heart on which to unload my suffering.

Since January my sales have totalled 925 francs. At the age of 42, to live on that, buy colours, etc., is enough to daunt the stoutest heart. It is not so much the privations now as that the future difficulties loom so high when we are low. In face of the impossibility of living, even meanly, I do not know what to do. I am making efforts to obtain some kind of a post in Tonkin, where I might be able to work peacefully as I wish.

As for painting for the market, even impressionist pictures, *NO*.

I have been groping within myself for a more elevated sensibility, and I seem almost to have grasped it this year. Then, good God! I mutter, I may be wrong and they may be right, and that's why I have written to Schuff to ascertain your views, to guide me a little in the midst of my trouble. I see that you have read between the lines, that you see I seem to have hit upon something: and I am strengthened in my opinions, and I shall not renounce them, but forge ahead steadily all the time.

And this in spite of Degas, who, next to Van Gogh, is the chief author of the whole collapse. He does not, in fact, find in my canvases what he says he sees there—the model's bad smell. He divines in us a movement contrary to his. Ah! had I, like Cézanne, the sinews of war, I would enter the fray with delight. We are not alone in giving battle; you see that Corot, etc., have been justified by time. But what poverty assails us to-day, what difficulties! As for me, I own myself beaten—by events, by men, by the family, but not by public opinion. I scorn it and I can do without admirers. I won't say that at your age I was like this, but by the exertion of sheer will power, that is what I am like to-day. Let them study carefully my last pictures and, if they have any feelings at all, they will see what resigned suffering is in them—a cry wrung from the heart. But thus it was written—that I have no heart, that I must be wicked, cross-grained and prickly. However, let that pass. But you, why do you suffer, too? You are young, and too early you begin to carry the cross. Do not rebel; one day, you will feel a joy in having resisted the temptation to hate, and there is truly intoxicating poetry in the goodness of him who has suffered. Moreover, if there is yet time, do not love. It takes it out of you. I seem to be saying two contradictory things, but on reflection, you will see that it is only apparently so. At your age, you have need now and then to burst out. I am in no mind to blame you since it is a need, but choose your twin soul with care. When you are forty, you will weigh the twin souls in the balance, and see what little remains.

I do not want to shatter your illusions, but what would you, friend. I am passing through such a phase of disillusionment that I cannot help a cry escaping me.

I have heard nothing of Laval for a month. I fear the poor fellow has been seduced into idleness.

If you see Aurier ask him about the second article that I sent him about the Millet sale.

Be good enough to send me my grandmother's book.

Courage, dear friend. Once more into the breach. The Templars may one day be expelled from the Temple.

Always,

P. GAUGUIN.

Greeting to your sister. Write sometimes.

93.

TO EMILE SCHUFFENECKER.   Moelan, November, 1889.

My dear Schuff,

Yes, I had your postcard and letter, and I intended to write you last night. In your letter you tell me to apply to Van Gogh, which I did at once, but have had no reply. In any event, I don't rely much on business of this sort —always offered below prices which are not high to begin with.

If you see Laval, tell him I am still awaiting the long letter that he promised me.

I have just sent my wood carving to Paris; it should reach Goupil in a fortnight. Let us hope it will sell better than the painting, but not at Champsor's price. I am in real straits.

I have no news of Bernard. Is he back in Paris?

Yours,

PAUL GAUGUIN.

Pouldu, Finistère, near Quimperlé.

94.

TO EMILE SCHUFFENECKER.

No date, Le Pouldu, 16 November, 1889.

My dear Schuff,

For the time being 30 francs is a consideration. The frame costs 8 francs, which makes the drawing 22 francs. Done! I am toiling up the steps of a rugged Calvary. From Paris I am deafened by the cries my latest pictures have provoked. I don't say they are good, but I am sure they will lead to something more perfect than my old pictures.

As to Degas I hardly bother about him, and I am not going to spend my life rubbing pumice stone over an inch of canvas during five sittings of a model. With butter the price it is, that is too much!

Despite this, I shall have to sail close to the wind.

If you see Bernard, ask him to enquire of Aurier of the *Modernistic* what has become of a long article of mine, and what he thinks of my last roughed paintings.

Look at the carving at Van Gogh's; it should be there now.

PAUL GO.

95.

TO EMILE BERNARD.

No date, Le Pouldu, 16 November ,1889

My dear Bernard,

Thanks for book and photos. Of these two I like the Christ better. True you can't see much from the photo, but colour apart, the Christ seems to me not only better, but really fine. From one end to the other the canvas reflects a meaning, an imaginative style which knocks me flat. The disproportionate length of the figure in prayer is very bold and adds to its movement. You did right to exaggerate it; one can forget the model and this damnable flesh. The soldiers are well arranged. I see a head of Judas which slightly resembles me in the photo. Don't be alarmed. I shall not take offence. Strangely enough, I have used the same *motif*, but in another way. I am keeping this canvas[1]; no use showing it to Van Gogh; it would be understood even less than the rest. I sent the sketch of it in a letter to Vincent, who wrote me a gloomy letter. I am tired, I have just written Van Gogh a letter of sixteen pages on the subject of all this furore of which I see the reason clearly enough. Our exhibition—you and I raised a few storms. I said as much to Van Gogh, when explaining to him what the two of us are after, why we are working etc., I have told him bluntly that he was wrong in listening to Degas and everybody, and that he ought to form his own opinions.

---

[1] *Christ in the Garden of Olives.*

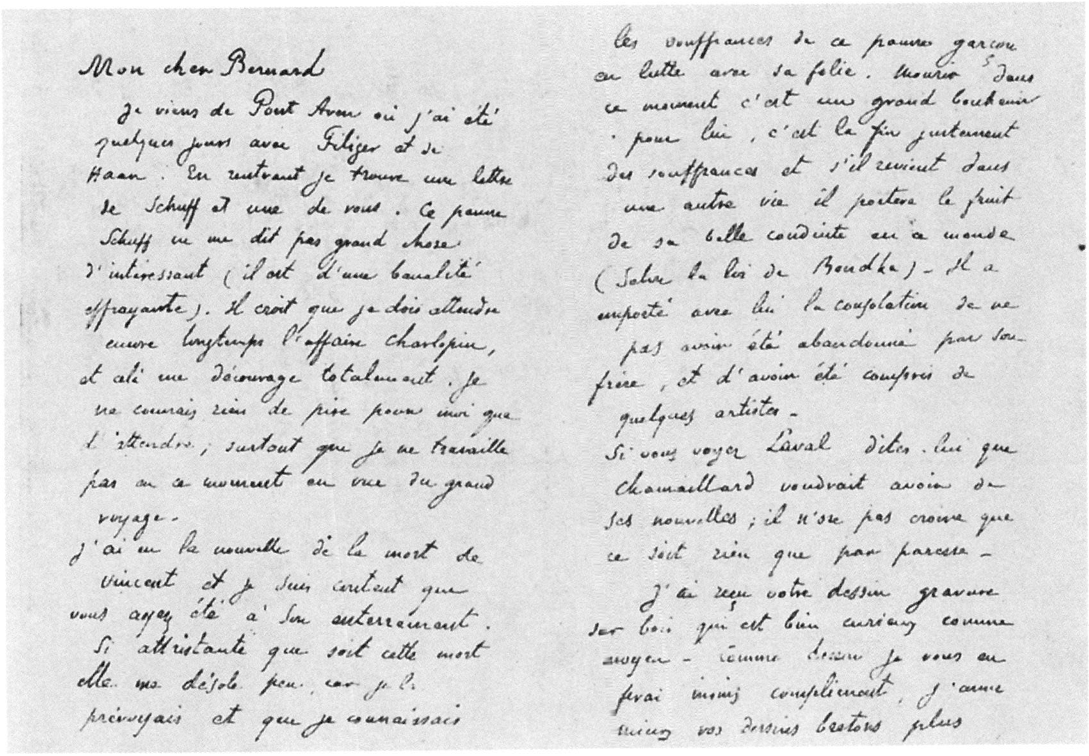

Mon cher Bernard

Je viens de Pont Aven où j'ai été quelques jours avec Filiger et de Haan. En rentrant je trouve une lettre de Schuff et une de vous. Ce pauvre Schuff ne me dit pas grand chose d'intéressant (il est d'une banalité effrayante). Il croit que je dois attendre encore longtemps l'affaire Charlopin, et ceci me décourage totalement. Je ne connais rien de pire pour moi que d'attendre; surtout que je ne travaille pas en ce moment en vue du grand voyage.

J'ai eu la nouvelle de la mort de Vincent et je suis content que vous ayez été à son enterrement. Si attristante que soit cette mort elle me désole peu, car je la prévoyais et que je connaissais les souffrances de ce pauvre garçon en lutte avec sa folie. Mourir dans ce moment c'est un grand bonheur pour lui, c'est la fin justement des souffrances et s'il revient dans une autre vie il portera le fruit de sa belle conduite en ce monde (selon la loi de Bouddha). Il a emporté avec lui la consolation de ne pas avoir été abandonné par son frère, et d'avoir été compris de quelques artistes.

Si vous voyez Laval dites-lui que Chamaillard voudrait avoir de ses nouvelles; il n'ose pas croire que ce soit rien que par paresse.

J'ai reçu votre dessin gravure sur bois qui est bien curieux comme moyen. Comme dessin je vous en ferai moins compliment. J'aime mieux vos dessins bretons plus

Letter to Emile Bernard August 1890
(*Private collection*)

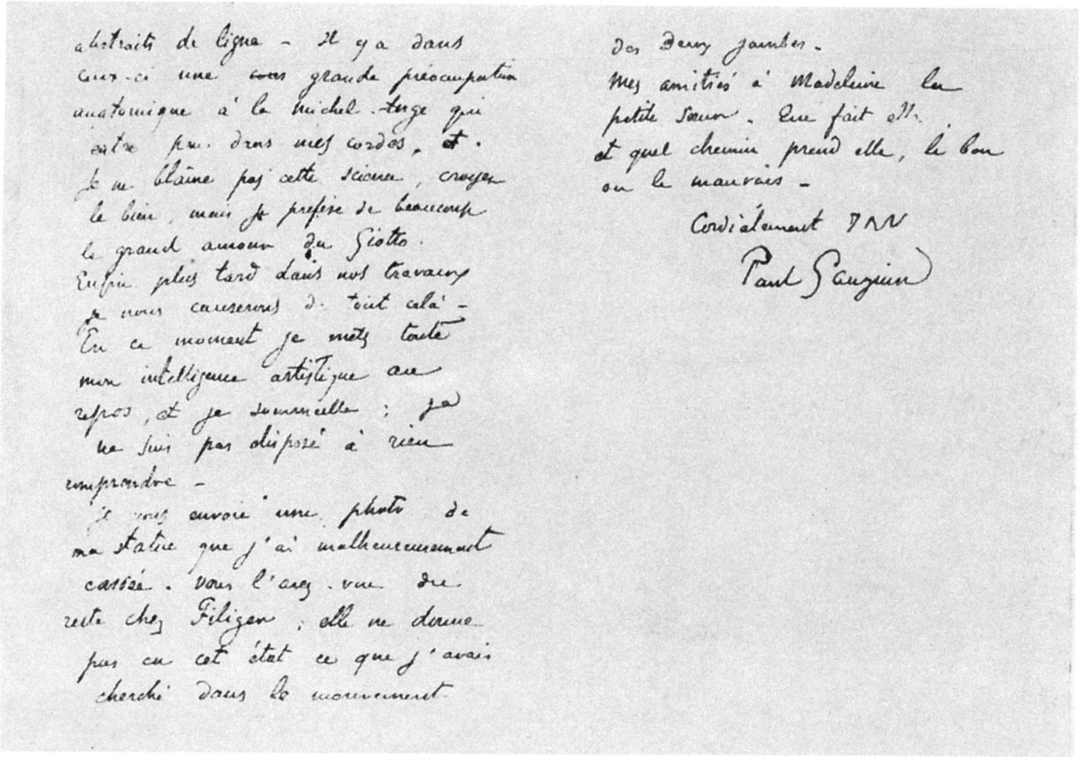
abstraits de lignes — Il y a dans
ceux-ci une grande préoccupation
anatomique à la Michel-Ange qui
entre peu dans mes cordes, et.
Je ne blâme pas cette science, croyez
le bien, mais je préfère de beaucoup
le grand amour du Giotto.
Enfin plus tard dans nos travaux
je vous causerons de tout cela —
En ce moment je mets toute
mon intelligence artistique au
repos, et je sommeille ; je
ne suis pas disposé à rien
comprendre —
Je vous envoie une photo de
ma statue que j'ai malheureusement
cassée. Vous l'avez vue du
reste chez Filiger ; elle ne donne
pas en cet état ce que j'avais
cherché dans le mouvement
des deux jambes —
Mes amitiés à Madeleine la
petite sœur. Que fait elle
et quel chemin prend elle, le bon
ou le mauvais —
Cordialement à vous
Paul Gauguin

Letter to Emile Bernard (*continued*)

I am glad you have seen the carving and that you understand it; nobody else appears to. But what does it matter? It is either a work of art or not. If you see the *Moderniste* with my second article, send it to me or get Schuffenecker to do so.

Sincerely,
P. GAUGUIN.

96.

TO MADELEINE BERNARD.

Le Pouldu, end of November, 1889.

Dear Sister,

I shall scold Emile for having shown you my letter revealing something of my state of mind, which I confided to none but him; but I don't like scolding, his intentions being so excellent, and having brought me a letter from you. A year has gone by since we both had a chat. The misfortunes of us painters must not make you miserable; there are sweet pleasures in store for you.

My advice to Emile to distrust his heart means this. That he is not made to play with friendship. The man who is deceived suffers and loses strength for the struggle, which strength he needs as artist. The torments of self esteem wear themselves out and sometimes stimulate talent more than flattery; but those of the heart—for him who possesses it—are terrible indeed; enough! Friends, good people, do exist but they have to be found. Far be it from me, whom suffering of every kind has aged, to beguile you young people of twenty into the general belief in deceptions. I am attached to both of you because you are both starting modern life, which is so difficult, egoistic and venal, with an equipment different from the majority; the love of beautiful things, hearts that ask nothing but to confide, and disinterestedness—three fine flowers which make me fond of you, but which also make me afraid. My horizon is black, and I see no rift in the clouds unless I can offer you my co-operation in life. At all events, rest assured that I will do all that I can do. In spite of all the social conventions which keep a young girl away from any friend, never fear to ask my advice on the day of misfortune or sorrow. At this moment I want to please you and sign our fraternal treaty. Ask Emile to obtain from Schuff a large pot that he saw me make; it is meant to represent the head of Gauguin the savage, and please accept it from me as a slight token of the pleasure your letter has given me in my Pouldu solitude.

Kindest regards.

P. GO.

Note.—This letter is written on the back of the preceding.

97.

TO ALBERT AURIER.   No date, Pont-Aven, December, 1889.

Dear Sir,

I requested Bernard to send me the *Pleiade*[1] which contains your " Salon and Modernism," which has interest for me. Herewith a few stamps.

Sincerely,

PAUL GAUGUIN.

98.

TO EMILE SCHUFFENECKER.

No date, Pont-Aven, January, 1890.

My dear Schuffenecker,

Best of thanks for your letter and its contents. It happens that I have written to Bernard that I want to leave for Paris, so your offer to send me the money for the journey comes at the right time and I accept it most gladly. Moreover, in Paris I can bestir myself to sell something, and I think I can pay you back in a short time. I will come by train on the 4th or 5th. And if I should not succeed in my Tonkin project, I will try to work at something outside painting, for I must hold my course for some time.

Or better still I will urge the Minister of Finance to give me something in France, no matter what. But I must be in Paris for this. I gathered from your letter that, in spite of all, you have grandiose ideas about the house you intend to build. Let us hope you will not repent them.

PAUL GAUGUIN.

[1] Forerunner of the *Mercure de France.*

99.

TO HIS WIFE. Paris, January, 1890.

My dear Mette,

I think everything is going well if not for the immediate present at least for the future. This year the Meissonnier group is organising a section for sculptural art and yesterday I received here an emissary from these gentlemen, Renan's son, who was instructed to invite me expressly to exhibit my ceramics and my carvings. Being almost alone in this class or at any rate the most conspicuous, I stand a chance of achieving some success, having from Mirbeau and his colleagues the promise of quite a new campaign in my favour. The two things combined might launch me.

Speaking of Mirbeau, I send you a letter of his which will explain his article, that you Northern people thought full of exaggeration.

It will show you in any case that it was the result of genuine enthusiasm, and not merely puffing. Keep this letter, which I may one day need for my defence. I assume that my affairs interest you, that they are our joint concern, despite the maledictions unjustly heaped on my head by your family.

I will not discuss all my interests with you, but only our common cause as man and wife, unless what you said during your visit is sheer hypocrisy, designed to appease and avoid conflict in anticipation of a better pecuniary state in the future.

Because I have loved you alone and love you still without return on your part (save upon terms), you may believe that my judgment and calculations are nothing but wishful thinking. Well, never mind. The result differs only in happiness and by this even you can judge whether I am able to remain cold before our intestine war.

I will certainly not fail you in duty whatever you may do, but—there is too much for me to explain—read between the lines. The past can never be wiped out, but the future may hold compensation.

Kisses for you. Your family need have no fear: these kisses

are not dangerous and will not increase your family. Farewell, dear Mette, be good to the children—kiss them for me. All the best for both of us.

P. GAUGUIN.

Before sending this letter which I wrote some days ago, I have been awaiting the photos you were to send me. What has become of them?

100.

TO HIS WIFE.   Undated, Paris, February, 1890.

My dear Mette,

Your letters are rare but are also short. I was despairing at having your address and news of the children when your young friend came to see me in my temporary lodging, lent by a friend. He gave me your address and the news. It was as far back as May since I had news of you and your family through Fritz, who appeared very happy in his new marital situation; I did not offer my congratulations.[1] In spite of all our quarrels with Ingeborg I must say as a matter of truth that this woman is the limit. She seemed to me as coarse and as dull as possible, with sharp and slavish appetites. Perhaps that is what is lacking in him. Happiness is reserved for the few.

In your brief letter you affect to believe that I am pretty miserable and you rightly say, why weep? But wrongly that our lives are broken. Obviously weeping won't help. The past can never be cancelled—we may sometimes forget it.

I have some satisfaction, if not in money at least in self-esteem: every day I see my reputation growing and an increasing promise for the future. But I am miserable enough when I reflect on my solitary life, without mother, without family, children. Cursed by my relations. Your two years silence, which started when I went to Martinique, tried me sorely, made me more

---

[1] The Norwegian painter, Fritz Thaulow, married to one of Mette Gauguin's sisters, had been divorced and married again shortly after. The famous picture, *The painter Thaulow and his family* (1895), represents the artist's new wife and with her children.

wretched than my financial reverses. But it had one advantage—
it hardened me and strengthened me to scorn everything.

May the day come—and perhaps soon—when I can flee to the
woods on a South Sea island, and live there in ecstacy, in peace
and for art. With a new family, far from this European struggle for
money. There, in Tahiti, in the silence of the lovely tropical night,
I can listen to the sweet murmuring music of my heart, beating
in amorous harmony with the mysterious beings of my environment. Free at last, with no money troubles, and able to love, to
sing and to die. Our two lives are broken, you say? You are wrong.
Yours is unshackled, and in the midst of your family and your
children, your days are gliding by if not without irksome labour,
at least free from marital constraint, adulated, respected and loved.
Your efforts are rewarded.

The children's photos are excellent, and the group very intelli-
gently arranged. Aline seems strangely beautiful, and Clovis, my
dear Clovis, both neat and refined. Thanks for sending them to me.

                            PAUL GAUGUIN.

It is advisable to write me care of Schuffenecker. I do not
know how long I shall be staying here.

                            101.

TO HIS WIFE.   Undated, Paris, early April, 1890.

My dear Mette,
    What am I to think of your changeable mind? Of your con-
tradictory letters and most of all, of the spirit that prompts them?
I should like to see you again, and embrace you once more! I
have so many things to say to you—before last letter—do not come
before the 15th April so that I can receive you, etc. . . . .

    And this last letter— I am afraid of your meeting my brothers
and I love my peace of mind *above all*. Think well before coming
and think of the separation. Come at the end of April and leave
at the end of April!

    I find all this difficult to reconcile. Gratuitous difficulties are
piled on this journey: you leave for the country so early and in

the winter the room is occupied. This is just what happened before I went to Panama. You write me in terms of admiration, then, when I get stuck—I am nobody, etc. . . . .

Anyhow, I prefer to know nothing except how to extricate myself for the future, when it will be better. In spite of all the difficulties, I do believe the future will be *better for me*.

Moreover there is the expense of the journey, and whilst I should have a holiday and save the cost of my food, I am likely to annoy your dear brothers and your dear mother and prevent you going into the country for the summer. I prefer to hold back and do without seeing the children. After all, I should be seeing them all too soon and all that goes with this.

I must be in Paris on the 20th to fire a statue which I believe I have sold, and could not therefore come to Copenhagen before the end of April. So don't refer to it any more—have a good time this summer, and may God come to your assistance.

Are the 60 crowns for Emil's first communion really necessary? Always the fripperies of vanity for the children before the things that matter. If they are necessary, although I have not a shirt to my back, I will do what I can to send them.

Salut.

Your husband,

PAUL.

102.

TO EMILE BERNARD.   Undated, Paris, April, 1890.

My dear Bernard,

I have read your letter to Schuffenecker. Why do you not write to me? So you find commercial designing disappointing! It is work that goes against the grain for an artist gifted as you are. An artist clever, really clever in the execution of such work, would never have the necessary bad taste. Well, well, go on so that you may learn to know all about it. After all, these disappointments are less harmful than others—a good shove of the shoulders gets you clear—and also of love and what follows. God keep you! (I refer to this because you touch on the subject in your letter.)

As you know my opinions thereon, I need not repeat them.

Artistic matters don't advance much. And I have already reached a mature age, nearing the end of the road, as they say, and I deem it futile to continue the struggle without trump cards in my hand. And as for doing commercial work in order to live, I would not, even if I could.

Just at this moment there is a rift in the clouds.

I am on the eve of selling, apart from Goupil, a parcel of canvases for 5,000 francs—very cheap of course. I am in direct touch with the buyer, who will not have the funds for a month; I shan't believe it until the money is actually in my pocket.

I have made up my mind to go to Madagascar. I intend to buy a little place in the country which I can enlarge myself, to plant and live simply. There are models and everything necessary for studying. I will then found the Studio of the Tropics. Whoever likes can come and see me. I have made inquiries in various quarters, and understand that 5,000 francs would keep one there for 30 years, if necessary.

It costs nothing to live for those prepared to live like the natives. One can easily obtain all one's food from hunting alone.

So, if things can be arranged, I will go there and do what I say—live in freedom and practise art. I shrink from giving you any advice, but all my heart goes out to the man who is suffering, to the artist who cannot work at his art here in Europe. If after your exertions you fail to find satisfaction, and you are released from military service, come and seek me out. Without needing money, you will find an assured existence in a better world. I believe that by taking a little trouble the journey out could be made free of charge.

As they say, the prettiest girl in the world cannot give more than she has.

This applies to me. And if you are unhappy, I cannot give you any other consolation than this.

The half of my cloak. It is still the best kind of Christianity.

Yours ever,

P. GAUGUIN.

P.S.—After Wednesday or Thursday next, I shall be at Pouldu, where I shall await the upshot of this business and get ready for the journey.

103.

TO EMILE BERNARD.   Undated, Paris, April, 1890.

My dear Bernard,

I really do not know how to answer you, as I thought I had said everything in my letter.

You are in a nervous condition and over-excited, like a wild boar surrounded by dogs. The life of an artist without means and lacking support is difficult, and especially affecting, and here in Europe you are only at the *commencement*. I may say that from every point of view I have had to bear ten times the burden, but this is not the question. There is nothing fresh to report. The prospective buyer told me last Sunday that he will clinch the matter when he has the money in a month, perhaps two. So keep cool and no nonsense before then—I shall require another month in which to pack my luggage and collect everything we shall require, so as not to be caught unawares. The voyage costs 700 francs.

It is now possible to get your passage paid by the Government, but I propose to pay my own fare. You have to write to the Ministry of Marine, stating that you want to be a colonist,[1] and are too poor to pay for the journey. I have an old college friend, who is captain of a packet steamer. I do not know whether he calls at Madagascar, but we should certainly be able to fix something up with him.

From another angle I have arranged for a friend to send a letter of recommendation to Bourgeois, the Minister of Fine Arts, to whom I will explain our position.

As you see, I am working on various lines, moving heaven and earth to achieve our aims. If you should happen to have 200 francs, more if possible, they will come in handy for your tropical outfit.

Have courage then, and refuse to be cast down, and all will go well. In your misfortunes it is a lucky thing for you to have

---

[1] Gauguin sought to draw Bernard into his new adventure, as he tried at the same time to persuade Schuffenecker to sell some land in order to accompany him and finance their journey. But the cautious Schuff had no illusions about the chances of success of this kind of expedition. On the other hand, de Haan, who was ill, could not think of going abroad, while Gauguin had had enough of Laval.

such support as mine, something that I never had when I was your age. What I did there I will never repeat having tried the experience with Laval. And I know what it cost me. Laval thinks he is uninjured into the bargain; a little more, and it would have been he who had made the sacrifice.

Anyhow, it is dead and buried. Now, if you look at the matter all round you will see that you will be trying a new life, which offers excellent chances at 22; whereas I am trying it at 42 with very little time before me to forget the past. And with family responsibilities!!!

Do not mention the above to Laval. I have no need of any gratitude, and dislike the wranglings caused by misunderstandings. To conclude, keep calm until you hear from me again.

(Unsigned)

104.

TO EMILE SCHUFFENECKER.

Undated, Pont-Aven, June, 1890.

My dear Schuff,

Many thanks for your colours, if I did not acknowledge them at once, it was because I was awaiting the 50 francs, and wanted to kill two birds with one stone.

I know, from Bernard's blabbing, that Van Gogh has written you. Tanguy told him that we are leaving for Madagascar immediately. Van Gogh wrote me a fairly encouraging letter, promising in effect to give me effective and regular help, while raising the price of my pictures at the same time.

If I go to Madagascar, it will facilitate matters, inasmuch as my needs will be practically nil. How I would like to see the Charlopin[1] transaction terminated, so that I could know how I stand! These 12 millions appear to me to smell bad, it is too much. I should have more confidence in 500.000 francs. Ask Roy then what he thinks, as more than a month has gone by since our interview, and the matter ought to be settled by now.

[1] Eventual buyer of a parcel of canvases for 5,000 Frs.

Your holidays are approaching and you will soon be able to invigorate yourself in outdoor work. And how is the garden?

Kind regards to everybody,

PAUL GAUGUIN.

Ask Bernard to get me a book about the language, there ought to be one in Paris.

105.

TO EMILE BERNARD.   Undated, Le Poûdu, June, 1890.

My dear Bernard,

I answer at once your somewhat anxious letter, which I quite understand. Perhaps I have explained myself badly, as you have not understood me.

1. I shall not leave until about the 15th August; you have therefore plenty of time to think about the matter beyond the 28th June. Besides I shall not leave unless this sale of pictures really comes off, but it is almost certain.

Thus I am not going out to look for a situation nor to offer you one.

What I want to do is to set up a studio in the *Tropics*. With the money I shall have I can buy a hut of the kind you saw at the Universal Exhibition. An affair of wood and clay, thatched, near the town but in the country. This would cost almost nothing. I should extend it by felling trees and make of it a dwelling to our liking, with cows, poultry and fruit, the chief articles of food, and eventually it ought to cost us nothing to live. Free . . .

As to the future, if I were single, I would just stay there and not bother myself any more. When I have worked for three or four years I shall see.

You must realize, my dear Bernard, that a hard life and an easy life are in inverse ratio to abundance of money and needs. So if the object is to make a fortune, one should not go where life is primitive and you can subsist upon the fruits of the earth gathered without toil—in Madagascar money is scarce; the people up country have none and live without it.

If you want to maintain a wife out there and earn money in business, I have nothing to say.

Do you think that I am incapable of love and that my 42 years are an obstacle to the impulses of youth?

I stick to what I say. I shall go and live there like a man retired from the so-called civilised world, who intends to mix only with so-called savages. And of my daily bread I will place half at your disposal.

A woman out there is, so to speak, obligatory, which will provide me with an everyday model. And I can assure you that a Madagascar woman has a heart just as much as a Frenchwoman, with far less calculation in it.

As for money, you will want very little, and nothing for the voyage. With very little effort you should be able to get a free passage—see the Minister of Marine. If not, once at Marseilles, there is a way of embarking without paying, viz. as a waiter (see the head waiter for this). I must admit it is a great trial to one's self esteem. But in this world we must make sacrifices to gain our ends.

Ponder on these things. I have now told you everything.

When you write to your sister, say farewell for me.

P. GAUGUIN.

106.

TO EMILE BERNARD.   Le Pouldu, June, 1890.

My dear Bernard,

I thank you for your nice, friendly letter. Yes, I am vexed, which is why I did not answer you. All the things that lie close to the affections touch me more nearly than I can say, in spite of all my efforts to harden my heart. As to the cliques that rage in front of my pictures, this bothers me not at all, the more so as I know myself that they are imperfect, and rather an approximation towards something similar.

Sacrifices must be made in art, in one age after another—ambiant attempts, a floating idea without direct and definite expression. But ah! the moment when one touches the sky although it eludes one immediately; in compensation this *glimpsed* dream is more potent than all material things. Yes, we are destined (we pioneer artists and thinkers) to succumb to the blows of the world, but to succumb so far as we are flesh. The stone will decay, the word will remain. We are in the dismal swamp, but we are not dead yet. As for me, they won't even have my skin. If I manage to get what I am now trying for, a snug berth in Tonkin, I can work at my painting and save money. The whole of the East— lofty thought written in letters of gold implicit in all their art— all this is well worth studying, and I feel that I shall be rejuvenated out there. The West is corrupt at the present time and whatever is herculean can, like Anteus, gain new strength in touching the soil of the East. And, one or two years later, we can return solvent.

At the moment I am gathering my strength, tired but not exhausted. There is very little light in the day time. I am relaxing by doing wood carving and still life studies. The ten days storm is still blowing, the sea is breaking on our beach, and in the absence of news from Paris, the outlook is melancholy at the moment.

I find the purchase of *Olympia*[1] very funny, now that the artist is dead. Will the Louvre take it? I hardly think so, but it is to be hoped they will.

Because the wind is howling and this would be an appeasement, it is better that the tide should come in at full flood. Then *Olympia* could be sold very dear like the Millets. At present the more follies there are, the clearer the signs of better times on the horizon, and you who are young will see this. As to writing an article on the subject I am hardly encouraged by the reception accorded to the one I wrote this year. Aurier has not replied to two letters, the dirty dog. The *Moderniste* has not come and I have not been able to read *le Maudit*.

I smiled at the thought of your sister in front of my pot. Between ourselves, in making it I had in mind the idea of testing the extent of her admiration for similar objects, I want later to give her one of my best things, although not very successful in the firing.

You have long known, and I have written it in the *Moderniste*, that I seek the character in every lump of matter. Now the

---

[1] Wishing to offer Manet's *Olympia* to the Louvre Museum, Claude Monet, in November, 1889, started a subscription. A lively discussion ensued. Finally, an official decree of acceptance by the State appeared in the *Journal Officiel* of 17th November, 1890.

character of grey pottery is the emotion of the furnace, and this figure calcined in this inferno, expresses, I think, the character pretty distinctly. Such an artist was glimpsed by Dante in his visit to the Inferno.

Poor devil driven in upon himself to endure suffering. However that may be, the prettiest girl in the world cannot give you more than she has.

Vincent has written me on very much the same lines as you. I have answered him accordingly.

Do me the favour of having a photograph taken of the pot, in a clear light, showing the reflections on the surface.

Yours, etc.,

P. GO.

Give all my regrets to Madeleine for the roughness of my pot.

107.

TO EMILE BERNARD.   Undated, Le Pouldu, June, 1890.

My dear Bernard,

I am astonished at your news. Schuff wrote me two days before and nothing in his letter gave me a hint. Besides, when I left, father Charlopin told me that it was a matter of a month, and now six weeks have gone! Anyhow, we must hope for the best. However, the suspense is trying, above all, the uncertainty. Now let us talk as if the voyage were certain. I picked up some information about Madagascar lately from a naval officer who stayed there a long time. It comes to this, the coast is unhealthy, although yellow fever is unknown there. But life is healthy in the hill country. According to official returns, there were 15 deaths in Mayotte from 1877 to 1889, of which 8 were due to dysentery and 7 to fevers. Population is 10,000, of which 3,000 are Europeans, but look how trifling the mortality is. As for the women, they are as in Tahiti, sweet, etc . . . besides, many come of a Polynesian race. In Madagascar meat costs almost nothing and game is most abundant. Life there is however dearer than one would think for a merchant who wants a certain degree of senseless luxury.

The same thing goes for Tahiti; there are also English and French. Loti saw things as a writer, and he had his own boat and plenty of money. Bread trees, wild bananas, etc. But all this is to be found in the tropical zone, coco-trees, etc. You need a certain time to get used to this sort of food. Ask Laval.

Despite this I recognize that Tahiti is certainly favoured and that you can live there in fact (almost without money) as we have dreamed. What a pity it is so far away, farther than China.

By warship via the Cape of Good Hope—the voyage would take three months—like the packets 40 to 45 days. Find out how much the voyage costs.

Whether Schuff has sold his land and wants to do me another good turn, we shall see. For myself I should like Tahiti, especially for de Haan,[1] whose health is not too good. And I should have more security out there.

Goodbye for the present, and don't be afraid to write.

P. GAUGUIN.

108.

TO EMILE BERNARD. Undated, Pont Aven, early July, 1890.

My dear Bernard,

Don't get upset; whatever doubts there are prompted by interest or jealousy, are not directed against you. And in my recriminations I meant to speak to Schuff, to whom I wrote a letter about it. I ought to have guessed that your letter crossed that. So do not get alarmed. As my habit is to do things quickly I wrote to you by way of reply and to confirm my intention. You must realize that with all the annoyances I have suffered at each exhibition, I feel I have the right and duty to take precautions. And my anticipations were partly founded on G's behaviour. You see for yourself how he vacillates (surely owing to my decision to be well to the fore). So exhibit all you feel inclined to send, and I am positive you will have acted for the best.

In all these matters I may seem to be running amuck because

---

[1] Gauguin tried to entice Meyer de Haan, who possessed a small income.

I do things in telegraphic style, taking the shortest cut, but in my own mind I know what I am doing. I should be the first to recognize anybody's talent, even if superior to mine; but wickedly to trip me up is quite another thing. I have all the old impressionists against me, and all this year I have been watching G. I am content with my own view.

So the incident is closed and no bones broken. Let us get on with our painting and fight on nobly.

You know that I take the keenest interest in your artistic progress and aspirations, and you have my best wishes for your success. I shout from the housetops " Watch little Bernard. He is going to be somebody."

Here at Pont Aven we have seen some changes. We no longer see Chamaillard, who is tied to his women's apron-strings and has been taught to distrust me.

Sérusier[1] has just arrived and talks of nothing but the progress he is making.

(End of letter missing.)

109.

TO EMILE BERNARD.   Le Pouldu, end July, 1890.

My dear Bernard,

Your letter reached me at the same time as I heard from Filiger[2] that you had organized a lottery. You ought to have sent us twenty tickets; Sérusier could have disposed of them among the Julian circle at Pont Aven. Unfortunately he is leaving to-morrow for Auverge, and I do not know enough people to offer them to. Filiger also tells me that you have someone who intends to launch

---

[1] Paul Sérusier (1863-1927), painter and theorist, whose meeting with Gauguin at Pont Aven in 1883 had a considerable influence on his artistic development. Started the Nabi movement, which attracted Bonnard, Vuillard, X.-K. Roussel, Ibels, Ranson, Piot and Maurice Denis, he taught at the Julian Academy and wrote for his pupils " The A.B.C. of Painting." In 1903 he settled at Chateauneuf-du-Faou, in Brittany.

[2] Charles Filiger, painter of Swiss origin, born at Colmar, died at Plougastel in 1930. He met Gauguin at the Colarossi Academy and followed him to Pouldu, where he became one of his most faithful disciples. He is best known for his water-colours of a mystical inspiration. He lived wretchedly all the time he was in Brittany.

you. Splendid!! In that event you may change your mind about Madagascar.

It is true that Tahiti is a paradise for Europeans. But the journey costs much more, as it is situated in Oceania.

Madagascar, however, offers more attractions by way of types, mysticism and symbolism. There you have Indians from Calcutta, tribes of black Arabs and the Hovas, a Polynesian type. Notwithstanding, make inquiries about the journey via Panama, etc. I am very much afraid that our business, which tarries so long, will fall through. Schuff and Roy have gone off on holiday for two months, and when I am not on the spot, our business is at a standstill.

Thank Aurier for his good will. And has Schuffenecker sold his land?

I am no longer working. The suspense about Madagascar is telling on me. That is where the future of painting lies.

Yours,

P. GAUGUIN.

110.

TO EMILE BERNARD.   Le Pouldu, August, 1890.

My dear Bernard,

I am glad that you saw Charlopin and are seeing him again. These matters must be followed up until the deal is clinched. God grant it may be next month, as I am consumed with the sickness of hope deferred. If Charlopin would even like to buy a little from you it would be so much profit for the Company P. Go. & Co., but we must wait for one deal to be concluded before seeking another. Now another thing. You must make the most meticulous inquiries. Transports leave for the Antipodes every six months, but they take three to four months. I believe the Emigration Society employs the packets for the journey. In any case, it is essential for my calculations to know the dates of departure, the fare and length of the voyage.

De Haan, who is Dutch, can only leave by steam packet. Find out all these things while you are in Paris, and write me as soon as possible, so that I may know how long I have to stay in Brittany.

I don't know who has told you that I am in the habit of strolling on the beach with my disciples. The only disciples I know of are de Haan, who is working outdoors, and Filiger who is working in the house. I myself walk about like a savage, with long hair, and do nothing. I have not even brought colours or palette. I have cut some arrows and amuse myself on the sands by shooting them just like Buffalo Bill. Behold your self-styled Jesus Christ. On the very day you have sure news about Charlopin write me immediately just two words.

Yours, etc.,

P. GAUGUIN.

What has happened to Van Gogh, I hear nothing of him.

111.

TO EMILE BERNARD.   Undated, Le Pouldu, August, 1890.

My dear Bernard,

I am just back from Pont Aven, where I have been for a few days with Filiger and de Haan. On reaching here I find a letter from Schuff and one from you. Poor Schuff has nothing very interesting to say (he is frightfully banal). He thinks I shall have to wait a long time for the Charlopin deal to be completed, and this utterly discourages me. I know nothing worse than to be kept in suspense; especially as I cannot work at the present time in view of the long voyage in front of me.

I have had the news of Vincent's death,[1] and am glad that you were present at his funeral.

Distressing as this death is, I cannot grieve overmuch, as I foresaw it, and knew how the poor fellow suffered in struggling with his madness. To die at this moment is a piece of good fortune for him, it marks the end of his sufferings; if he awakens in another life, he will reap the reward of his good conduct in this world

---

[1] On the 27th July, 1890, Vincent Van Gogh, who felt a fresh attack of madness coming on, aimed a pistol at his heart, but the bullet lodged in his groin. He died a few hours later, in spite of medical attention. A commemorative plaque has been affixed to the hotel at Auvers-sur-Oise where the painter died.

(according to the teaching of Buddha). He died in the knowledge of not having been abandoned by his brother and of having been understood by a few artists . . .

I have received your drawing, engraved in wood, which is very curious as a medium. As a drawing I cannot give it much praise, I like better your Breton drawings with less conspicuous lines. This drawing shows a great anatomical preoccupation *à la Michelangelo*,[1] which hardly enters into my calculations. I am not condemning that discipline, believe me, but I much prefer Giotto's great love. However, we will discuss all this when we get to work later. At present I am letting my artistic intelligence slumber and do not feel inclined to apprehend anything.

I send you a photo of my statue which I have unfortunately broken. You saw it at Filiger's, in this state it does not convey what I sought in the movement of legs.

Regards to little sister Madeleine. What is she doing, and what path is she taking, the good or the bad.

Yours, etc.

PAUL GAUGUIN.

112.

TO EMILE BERNARD.   Le Pouldu, September, 1890.

My dear Bernard,

I do not find in your letter the information I asked for.[2] It is not at the Ministry that you should make inquiries. There is a concern in Paris called the French Emigration Society, and it is there you must inquire whether there is any way of getting a free passage or a reduction in the steamboat fare. The transports take too long, and we have to wait four months for them. Moreover, I asked you what it costs via San Francisco. I must know that. As de Haan can only leave by steamer I will go with him paying my

---

[1] After 1905, Emile Bernard, repudiating the experiments of his youth and in reaction against Gauguin, moved towards the classicism of the Venetian painters of the Renaissance.

[2] Abandoning the Madagascar project, Gauguin was making preparations to go to Tahiti.

own fare, and you shall come and join us. It is possible and even probable that, without interfering with our intention of "going native," de Haan would do some business there in pearls with first class Dutch merchants. In any case, we shall leave together, de Haan and I, because he would not venture to go there alone without us. Inquire, therefore, if you could leave, like us, by steamer, otherwise you could leave by a transport and come out there after us; I would leave you a little money for incidental expenses and the accidents of the voyage. As to Etienne, I cannot forward the letters of recommendation, which are already dog-eared by so much use, not to mention that he was of no use to me about Tonkin and was also disagreeable. Moreover, the Emigration Society will look after that—have no fear, *we will go*. I am more determined than ever, and if Charlopin does not come up to the scratch, I will go to Paris and move heaven and earth to find someone else who will. Unfortunately, I am still kept here in debt, by the end of the month I shall owe nearly 300 francs, and I see nothing coming from Van Gogh.

Hang Pissarro, but when we are in Tahiti I shall defy Pissarro and his associates. I have been in labour lately, and am delivered of a wood craving, a counterpart of the first " Be mysterious," with which I am pleased, in fact I do not think I have done anything approaching it.

Enclosed is a letter for Charlopin, which please deliver at once, as I do not know his address. And if you go quickly to work, you might influence the reply.

Write me often and neglect nothing connected with our departure, our liberty, in fact. For you know, I am not going out with the intention of remaining there for good, to practise art out there without any thought of returning to Europe. And remember, we shall have to work hard for six months. I want to build a comfortable and solid house, to sow and plant what we need for our support. Later on, if we have no money, we shall have something to live on without worry. All for the *Company*.

Yours sincerely,

PAUL GAUGUIN.

And Aurier's article.

113.

TO EMILE BERNARD.   Pont Aven, October, 1890.

My dear Bernard,

I was very surprised yesterday to receive a letter which I wrote you a month ago and which was wrongly addressed. Your silence is explained, if not excused!

For a month past things have been going wrong; and nothing right; I have decidedly more than my share of ill-luck. Van Gogh's[1] stroke is a hard knock for me, and if Charlopin does not give me the means of going to Tahiti, I am done. When shall I be able to live, free at last, in the woods? God, but it is taking a long time.

And to think that subscriptions are pouring in every day for flood victims, but as for painters! Not a soul to help them. They can starve if they like. De Haan is at present in Paris trying to fix up things with his family, who have been cutting off his supplies for some time. People of good will are in a jam.

I have arrived at the stage of not believing in anyone. The worse the calamity, the quicker everybody runs away.

Look at Laval, I have heard nothing from him for a long time.

I want to go to Paris to fix things up and I cannot slip the painter here except for a day's journey, and I owe the hotel over 300 francs. So you see how I am stuck in this place.

I write in haste and scrappily.

Yours,

PAUL GAUGUIN.

I open my letter because I have received one from Sérusier telling me that you are organizing an exhibition of Vincent's works. What stupidity. You know I like Vincent's art. But given the folly of the public, it is quite the wrong time to remind them of Vincent and his madness just when his brother is in the same boat. Many people say that our painting is all mad. It will do us harm without doing Vincent any good. However, go on, but it is *idiotic*.

---

[1] Stricken with paralysis shortly after Vincent's suicide and having returned to Holland, Theo had died there in January, 1891.

114.

TO HIS WIFE. Paris, December, 1890.

My dear Mette,

My uncle should still be living at 7, rue Endelle, as he is not a man likely to change his habits. Knowing his melancholy disposition, I preferred not to write him until I had better news to report, but I should like you to send him these photos which ought to please him.

This time the photograph does you a little justice, but the others are made to look uglier than they are in reality. Aline's hair, neither long nor short, does not improve her. It is better to cut it quite short up to 15, but Clovis has a thick crop, which rather hides his ears.

Little Paul is greatly changed. Emil looks more and more like a stiff Danish officer, which I don't like at all. Otherwise, they seem to me to be very well dressed. In my present clothes I would not dare to go out with them, and this confirms my doubts about a trip to Denmark.

I intended, if I could scrape together a little money, to go to Brussels to see my show, and then go on to spend a month in Copenhagen to embrace the children, in default of talking to them, as not one of them would be able to say to me " Bonjour." Well, we shall see.

Schuffenecker flatters me (you say) far too much, and yet he is only repeating what many others are saying, not to mention Degas. I am a corsair, he says, but sacred—the very incarnation of art.

It may be that these people divine in me something different from the impression you Danes seem to get. However, we won't discuss this. I have only sent you this to keep you in touch with what is going on.

In your letter you make use of an extraordinary word: affectionate. I confess that I do not understand, having learned from long experience that this is a fiction. I believe that affection has some connection with gold. The more gold one has, the more affection. What a lot of people have brain and hearts of flint!

I kissed the Schuffeneckers on your behalf. They wish to be remembered to you.

> Your husband,
>
> PAUL.

When you write to my uncle mind you address the envelope legibly. Have you heard from my sister?

115.

TO HIS WIFE.   Paris, January, 1891.

My dear Mette,

It is curious to notice how all your letters fall short of replying to mine. Is it because you don't read them or skip them? Or are you adopting an attitude of diplomatic finesse? I won't waste my time looking for the reason.

Have you sent the portrait to my Uncle?

Have you any news of my sister?

Emil has written me a letter in worse French than he spoke when he talked to me in Denmark. At his age I could write a letter in Latin less childish than this. Although he is not a genius, he ought to occupy a somewhat better position than number ten in his class, as he has a good memory. He is not industrious enough. By way of compensation, his hair is nicely parted and he seems very well turned out. If anybody had behaved towards you like Master Otto behaved towards me, I would not send my son to spend his holidays with him.

You have now told me several times in your letters that you are the mother of my children. Inquiry into paternity is forbidden, but not into maternity, which is never doubtful. In my letter I told you that I toyed with the idea of going to see the children, but would not dare to go out with them in my soiled and shabby garments. And you know full well that no scandal is permitted in Denmark, Hence, in spite of my wishes, it is very doubtful indeed whether I shall go, especially as I should not be able to leave before the end of the winter. The Brussels exhibition opens sooner than I thought, in the next few days. I cannot go, not having the money.

And yet this journey would have been a most useful one for me to make.

> PAUL.

116.

TO JEAN DOLENT.[1]

Dear Mr. Dolent,
I return Madame Vallette's letter to you.
Of course I accept with pleasure your choice of draughtsman.
I will read the book[2] in question otherwise it would be difficult to
suggest an idea that is not hackneyed.
Hoping to see you soon, my regrets to Mr. Dolent, Senr.

PAUL GAUGUIN.

10, Rue de la Grande Chaumière.

117.

TO RACHILDE.[3]   Paris, 2 February, 1891.

I hope for a letter on Thursday.
Madam,
Although long wanting to express my feelings for you, I have
not ventured to write you, but not being able to repress them, I
implore you to be kind enough to grant me an interview, the time
and place to be as you like, preferably the evening. Allow me to
conceal my identity until we meet, which I hope will be soon, you
will readily understand why.
Hoping you will condescend to answer a sincere appeal from
the heart, I beg to remain,

P. G.

I am unable to say what I mean by letter, but rest assured I
am none the less sincere.

[1] Jean Dolent (1835-1909), whose real name was Charles Antoine Fournier,
was employed for fifty-three years by the firm of Caplain as a gold refiner.
An amateur in art matters, he held Sunday receptions, and had some slight
influence on artists.
[2] Referring to the *Théâtre* of Rachilde, published by Savine in 1891.
Gauguin made a sketch: Madam Death, for the frontispiece. The original
drawing preserved by Rachilde was given to the Louvre Museum in
March, 1946, thanks to the intervention of Mr. Paul Hartmann, publisher
and manager of the *Mercure de France*.
[3] Rachilde, author of *Monsieur Venus*, had married Alfred Valette, the
moving spirit of the *Mercure de France*, and for forty years was closely
connected with the development of this great French review.

118.

TO RACHILDE.   Paris, 5 February, 1891.

Madam,

In reading your drama *Madam Death* I find myself truly perplexed. How can I express your idea with a mere pencil, when to
put it across the footlights you require powerful aids—the actress
herself, words, gesture.

I would therefore ask you to excuse me for falling short of
your ideas in the feeble sketch which I send you—and if I send
you two instead of one, it is because by putting them together
(which is possible, is it not?) the one will supplement the other.

Be kind enough to regard my two bad sketches as a well-
meaning effort.

PAUL GAUGUIN.

119.

TO HIS WIFE.   February, 1891.

My dear Mette,

I waited some time to reply to you, your last letter being better
than the others.

The reason being this: I am engaged in making a bid for
fortune, and I did not want to answer your letter before having
some certainty of the result.

The Figaro[1] article strongly impressed the Manager, who had
not been enthusiastic. It is finally settled for Tuesday. Others will
follow in the *Gaulois, Justice,* the *Voltaire,* the *Rappel,* and perhaps
the Débats. As soon as they appear, I will send you the lot. If
you could translate the *Figaro* article for a newspaper, it would be
useful, as it would have some influence on the Danish movement.
Your friend Ballin[2] owes me 250 francs. I have transferred this
debt to your account, and he will probably pay you next month.

[1] In the days preceding the auction, such journals as *Le Figaro* published
articles on Gauguin. That of Octave Mirbeau, appearing in the *Echo de
Paris* of 16th February, 1891, paid high tribute to his work.
[2] Moggens Ballin, Danish Jew, friend of Jean Verkade, Sérusier and Maurice
Denis, was converted to Catholicism. By his marriage with a Frenchwoman Ballin had several children, all of whom entered the priesthood.

After the articles there will probably be an auction at the Hôtel Drouot. If this goes well, I shall go to Brussels about the 20th February for a show I am having there (solicited). Thence I could go as far as Copenhagen to kiss the children without being taunted by you and your family as a light-minded man. Don't be afraid I shall put you out. I will stay at a hotel for the few days I shall be in Copenhagen incognito. I realize that the burdens you are bearing are heavy, but there is always the future to look forward to, and I think that one day I shall be able to lift them all off your shoulders. The day will certainly come when the children will be able to appear anywhere and before anybody with their father's name for protection and honour. Do you imagine that the influential friends I have gained will refuse to start them in life. I doubt whether business life would have yielded as much.

Kiss the children for me and tell me what you think about the visit to Copenhagen.

Cordially,

PAUL GAUGUIN.

120.

TO HIS WIFE. Paris, 19 February, 1891.

My dear Mette,

I write these few lines in haste as I am very nervous, the day of my sale being at hand, Monday next.[1] Everything has been well prepared and I am waiting for all the articles to be published in order to send them to you. The matter has made a great stir in Paris, and in the world of art there is a great agitation, which extends as far as England, where a newspaper speaks of this as an event.

If my sale produces enough money I will then go to Copen-

---

[1] Determined to leave France, Gauguin had finally chosen Tahiti on Madame Redon's advice. A sale of thirty pictures realised 9,860 francs. A performance of the *Théâtre d'Art* by Paul Fort, took place later at the Vaudeville for his benefit and that of Verlaine, but showed a loss.

hagen, where I shall arrive about the 2nd or 3rd. I will advise you by telegraph 24 hours beforehand.

I will bring your corsets.

Love and kisses,

PAUL GAUGUIN.

121.

TO HIS WIFE.   Paris, 24th February, 1891.

My dear Mette,

I send you the best of the articles. The sale took place yesterday and was successful. It is not colossal and hardly up to the expectations aroused by the pre-view, but the moral success is enormous, and I fancy it will bear fruit before very long. I shall be in Copenhagen on Thursday. Try to be at the station if you can.

Goodbye for the present.

PAUL GAUGUIN.

Mad. Bendix bought a picture. I believe she is the wife of a musician of the Theatre Royal.

122.

To an unknown correspondent.   Paris, March, 1891.

Dear Sir,

On the occasion of my departure, mutual friends are good enough to be giving me a dinner on the 23rd at the Voltaire,[1] at 7. Your presence would give me great pleasure. The cost is 5 francs.

---

[1] On the 23rd March, a banquet in honour of Gauguin attracted some thirty guests, including: Rachilde, Odilon Redon, Jean Dolent, Charles Morice, Jean Moréas, Alfred Valette, Albert Aurier, Saint Paul Roux, Eugène Carrière; Adolphe Rette recited verses. Stéphane Mallarmé, fearing no repetition of the disorder of the Moreas banquet of a short time before, agreed to preside and was the first speaker.

123.

TO HIS WIFE. Paris, 24 March, 1891.

My adored Mette,

To be sure, an adoration pretty often tinged with bitterness. As you will see, our letters have crossed and if this last is late, it is because I have been awaiting the photographs—but, apart from this, do not let us render letter for letter (I implore you), let us write what we have to write, and when it can be written. I know how difficult the present is for you, but now the future is assured and I shall be happy—very happy—if you want to share it with me.

In the absence of passion, we can—our hair whitening—enter an epoch of peace and spiritual happiness surrounded by our children, flesh of our flesh. As I have said over and over again, your family were wrong to set you against me, but, in spite of this, I am not going to worry about them.

Yesterday a banquet was given for me at which forty-five persons were present, painters and writers; Mallarmé being in the chair. Verses, toasts and heart praise. I tell you that in three years' time I shall have won a battle which will enable us—you and me—to live at our ease. You will rest and I shall work.

Perhaps you will understand one day what kind of a man you chose as the father of your children. I am proud of my name; and I hope—I am even certain—you will not sully it, even if you should meet a smart captain. If you come to Paris, I urge you to visit respectable and simple people, and not charlatans.

If you come here, let Morice[1] know by letter in advance, for he is a bachelor. He will immediately assist you to meet suitable people. I have received from the Government an official mission, which will enable me to have the services of the naval personnel and hospital staff when I land. I have, also, an order for a picture—for three thousand francs—when I return. All these things will facilitate our coming together.

Goodbye, dear Mette, dear children, love me well. And when I return, we will be re-married. It is therefore a betrothal kiss that I send you to-day.

Your

PAUL.

[1] Charles Morice, symbolist journalist and writer, author of *Current Literature* and of a work on Gauguin, published in 1920.

124.

TO HIS WIFE.   Oceania, 250 miles from Sydney, 4 May, 1891.

My dear Mette,

In two days I shall be at Nouméa, where I shall be picked up by the boat for Tahiti. I had an excellent voyage with superb weather created specially for me. But what extraordinary passengers on these ships. I am the only paying one.[1] All of them are employés of the Government, this benevolent Government which foots the bill for all these little outings, with removal expenses for the women and children thrown in. They are worthy people at heart, and have only one drawback, which is fairly common, however, that of being utter mediocrities.

Many calls on the way. The last two were truly astonishing, Melbourne and Sydney. Imagine two towns hardly 50 years old, of 500,000 inhabitants, with houses of 12 storeys, steam trams and cabs as in London. The same smart clothes and abounding luxury. Fancy coming 12,000 miles to see that! At Sydney a dock labourer earns 20 to 25 francs a day and meat costs 4 sous a pound. It is very easy to earn money in Australia, but even on 25,000 francs a year, you can only live very modestly. In spite of all these caustic remarks, I am obliged to admit that the English people have truly extraordinary gifts for colonising and running up great ports. A burlesque of the grandiose!

On the bridge of our ship, in the midst of all these civil servants in their stiff collars with their children, etc., I alone am really a little peculiar with my long hair. I, too, it appears, have a family and (it hardly appears). Are they thinking of me? I hope so. Shall I have news occasionally out here in Tahiti? Without counting letter for letter? I hope, however, I shall not always be a pariah. I long to get to work.

Thirty and more days have slipped past during which I have been eating and drinking, and, for the rest of the time, staring vacantly at the horizon. The porpoises sometimes jump out of the water to bid us good morning and that is all. Happily I can think sometimes of you and the children and take out the photos to

---

[1] Gauguin regretted taking a 2nd class ticket, the 3rd class accommodation being almost as good, and 500 francs cheaper.

Pahoura.   One of Gauguin's Tahitian
Models   *Photographed in* 1938

reassure myself. I dare not believe that all this will, perhaps, recoil on me one day. A question of money? After all, the English in Australia might be right.

I have been here at Nouméa two days, and on the 21st I leave for Tahiti in a warship. The Government has received me very well and given me a passage on the vessel with the officers: my official letter is opening doors. What a funny colony Nouméa is! Very pretty and amusing. Officials and their wives; households with their 5,000 francs salary manage to keep their carriages and their women in wonderful toilettes. Solve the problem! Impossible! The released convicts are the richest, and one day they will be top sawyers.

This makes me truly envious of the pleasant results of committing crimes; if we are condemned, within a short time we lead a happy life. However, everybody finds his happiness in his own way.

When this letter reaches you, you will perhaps be in France, in the midst of those funny Frenchmen you used to dislike so much. Well, you know there is some good in these people. Comparing them with the English (in the Colonies), they are insignificant and very serious; but what roughness, what egoism do you find among the former. And with all their frivolity, the French nation always remains great and good. It has a genius of a quite special character.

I hope Paris will please you a little and that you will not dislike my friends.

Think a little of me and of our first days in that city.

For the moment much love and kisses *to you first* and to the children.

                                             PAUL GAUGUIN.

                                125.

TO HIS WIFE.   Tahiti, 4 June, 1891.

My dear Mette,

A few lines in haste. The post happens to be leaving to-day, three days after our arrival. A prosperous voyage, in good health in a wonderful country. Thanks to the *Figaro* article and to some letters of recommendation, I am known already. Very well received by the Governor and by the Secretary for the Interior, a worthy family man, with his wife and two daughters. I lunched with them and they cannot do too much for me.

Tell your cousin Gad that I travelled with two officers who were once his shipmates, unless there is another Captain Gad.

There is a Danish Consul here, who happens to be a Dane. Ask your cousin whether he knows him, and if there is any way of sending him a letter of recommendation. I want to have as many acquaintances as possible. I think I shall soon have some well-paid commissions for portraits: I am bombarded with requests to do them. I am making the utmost difficulties about it at present (the surest way of getting good prices). In any event, I think I can earn money here, a thing on which I did not count. To-morrow I am going to see all the Royal Family. All of which is advertisement, however tiresome.

What I have been writing is very disconnected, but I am very busy visiting, looking for lodgings as well as a little tired.

I will write at greater length next time.

Heaps of kisses for the children and the best for you from your faithful lover and husband,

PAUL GAUGUIN.

126.

TO HIS WIFE.   Tahiti, July, 1891.

My dear Mette,

I begin my letter before the post goes so as not to be caught napping; and I am too lazy to write, especially at stated periods.

I have been here now 20 days; I have already seen so many new things that I am quite unsettled. I shall need some further time before I can paint a good picture. I am gradually getting into things, studying a little every day. The King[1] died a few days after my arrival; his funeral had to wait until everybody in the island and the neighbouring islands had been informed; each village grouped itself on the grass in the evening and sang in turn their choral chants in several parts, and this lasted all night long. This was a real treat for music lovers, as this people is extraordinarily gifted for music. Two chants heard simultaneously in the piercing voices of men and

---

[1] Pomare V., last king of Tahiti.

women, then some parts of accompaniment forming strange harmonies. A group of bass voices imitating the sound of the drum accompanied merely to render the cadence. It is impossible to conceive anything more harmonious. Not a false note was sounded.

The hearse all covered with flowers was drawn by mules dressed in fillets of black wool. At the grave side the pastors and chiefs made speeches in Tahitian. It would take a long time to tell.

I am writing this in the evening. The night silence in Tahiti is even stranger than anything else. It can be felt; it is unbroken by even the cry of a bird. Now and then a large dry leaf falls but without even the faintest noise, rather the rustling of the wind. The natives often move about at night, barefooted and silent. Nothing but this silence. I understand why these people can remain hours and days sitting immobile and gazing sadly at the sky. I apprehend all the things that are going to invade my being and feel most amazingly at peace at this moment.

It seems to me as if the turmoil of life in Europe exists no longer, and to-morrow it will be the same, and so on until the end. Don't conclude from this that I am an egotist and intend to abandon you. But leave me a little time to live thus. Those who reproach me entirely fail to realize what an artist's nature is, and why should they seek to impose on us duties similar to theirs. We do not thrust ours on them.

Such a beautiful night it is. Thousands of persons are doing the same as I do this night; abandon themselves to sheer living, leaving their children to grow up quite alone. All these people roam about everywhere, no matter into what village, no matter by what road, sleeping in any house, eating etc., without even returning thanks, being equally ready to reciprocate. And these people are called savages! . . . They sing; they never steal; my door is never closed; they do not kill. Two Tahitian words describe them: Iorama (good morning), good-bye, thanks, etc. . . . and Onatu (I don't care, what does it matter, etc.) and they are called savages! I heard of the death of King Pomare with keen regret. The Tahitian soil is becoming quite French, and the old order is gradually disappearing.

Our missionaries have already introduced a good deal of Protestant hypocrisy and are destroying a part of the country—not to mention the pox which has attacked the whole race (without spoiling it too much, to be sure). The handsome men you are so fond of are numerous here, much taller than I am and with limbs like Hercules.

I should like to have your memory to learn the language quickly, for very few here speak French. I often say if Mette were here, she would not take long to speak Tahitian, which, besides, is very easy.

I put out my lamp in kissing you and bidding you good-night.

The post has just come a little before time. I expected news, two words to show I am not forgotten. But nothing! Perhaps a letter will come via Auckland. Letters should be posted before the 6th of the month marked via San Francisco, otherwise they go all over the place. I try to think this is the reason of your silence. I am still thinking of you tenderly, and kiss you.

                                        PAUL GAUGUIN.

                        127.

TO HIS WIFE.   Tahiti, March, 1892.

Dear Mette,

I did not write last month in reply to your letter, as the American mail, delayed by bad weather, arrived very late and left again two days after. Then your letter was very short, quite insignificant. Now comes the first letter that tells me anything, the one you have written from Paris.

In this connection you are in too much of a hurry to write and do not re-read your letters, as a result of which you forget many things important for business. This is awkward, especially when I am so far away. Thus you tell me that Morice advised you to see Calzado; how did he know that Calzado knew Castelar and so on. It is not very clear. You were going to see Marie Calzado, and then what? What did they say to you, and can we hope for anything? I had written to Morice because he has access to Clemenceau, who is more influential than Castelar. In short, I have taken great trouble to learn a little about men and things. When I am not there, my affairs are at a standstill.

Of Morice you speak in a very enthusiastic way, which suggests a woman enamoured of a cause, and your letter, moreover, is much more affectionate than usual, as if you had to forgive yourself something. I hope you have only sinned in thought with the *Danish Captain*. I am capable of jealousy, but I have no right to talk, being away from you for so long. I realize that a woman who spends her years of youth away from her husband may have moments of desire both of the flesh and of the heart. What would you? It is not my fault that I was born at a time so little propitious to artists.

For I am an artist and you are right, you are not mad, I am a great artist and I know it. It is because I am such that I have endured such sufferings. To do what I have done in any other circumstances would make me out as a ruffian. Which I am no doubt for many people. Anyhow, what does it matter? What distresses me most is not so much the poverty as the perpetual obstacles to my art, which I cannot practise as I feel it ought to be done and as I could do it if relieved of the poverty which ties my hands. You tell me that I am wrong to remain far away from the artistic centre. No, I am right, I have known for a long time what I am doing, and why I do it. My artistic centre is in my brain and not elsewhere and I am strong because I am never sidetracked by others, and do what is in me.

Beethoven was blind and deaf, he was isolated from everything, so his works are redolent of the artist living in a world of his own. You see what has happened to Pissarro, owing to his always wanting to be in the vanguard, abreast of everything; he has lost every atom of personality, and his whole work lacks unity. He has always followed the movement from Courbet and Millet up to these petty chemical persons who pile up little dots.

No, I have an aim and I am always pursuing it, building up material. There are transformations every year, it is true, but they always follow each other in the same direction. I alone am logical. Consequently, I find very few who follow me for long.

Poor Schuffenecker, who reproaches me for being wholehearted in my volitions! But if I did not behave in this manner, could I have endured the endless struggle I am waging for one year? My actions, my painting, etc., are criticised and repudiated every time, but in the end I am acknowledged to be right. I am always starting all over again. I believe I am doing my duty, and strong in this, I accept no advice and take no blame. The conditions in which I am working are unfavourable, and one must be a colossus to do what I am doing in these circumstances.

I drop this subject, on which I have dwelt so long only because I know that at bottom you are interested in these questions. You have taken a dislike to art because it has brought you worry and toil, whereas the world has gilded for you the pill of other occupations. If these occupations have their proportion of lucky ones, there are also many who can hardly keep their heads above water in business and other employments, and they have no remedy. Whereas a fine day will dawn at last for art. Not much comfort, it is true. But confess that in your heart of hearts you are flattered to be the wife of a somebody. Would you prefer to be called Madame Uribe ?

Let us now talk about our own concerns. I have had plenty of annoyances, and were it not *essential for my art* (I am pretty sure of this), I would leave at once. Ever since I left Paris it has been nothing but difficulties and setbacks and unforeseen expenses arising out of the voyage and settling down. The transport of the luggage turned out very expensive. On my arrival I expected much from the King, but his death 15 days later was something like a calamity for Tahiti and for me in particular. However, you know I am not easily discouraged; well, I started spitting blood by the cupful. They treated me at the hospital for 12 francs a day. I resolved not to stay there on such onerous terms. The warden peremptorily forbade me to leave, expecting me to perish if I did. It seems that great injury has been done to the heart, which is not in the least surprising. I left the hospital, however, and have not had a relapse. I take digitalis from time to time.

Every month I have been expecting money from Morice, with whom I left it, plus the proceeds of pending picture deals, but I have had neither money nor news from him.

In spite of all these vexations I am working hard and believe that on my return I shall have collected enough material to paint for a long time.

You tell me that you cannot see very clearly into the future. I am in exactly the same position. But with me it is different. I am used to looking no farther ahead than the next day. Is not life always the opposite of what we expect and hope ? What is the use of thinking passively about the future, it only makes us forget the present? Every day, I say to myself, here is another day gained. Have I done my duty? Good, then let us retire to rest, for to-morrow I may be dead.

I am glad to know that *Suzanne*[1] goes to Philipsen, an artist. This proves that I had a little talent at that time and a little money in my pocket. You made enough outcry at the time I bought these pictures; what do husbands do and specially stockbrokers; on Sundays they go to the races or to the café or with whores, for men must have a little amusement, otherwise they cannot work, and besides it's only human nature. For my part I worked, and that was my dissipation. Add all this up over a period of years and ask yourself if I have not saved money which you have found useful. In short, I am glad you have sold the picture.

The more you sell, the greater the proceeds, the brighter the future. For one buyer brings along another. Painting is now our lifeline (and you know that I can see no other and want no other). On your part, you must work to break down sales resistance. Danish customers are not to be despised, although I am French. It needs only the caprice of a rich and influential man to launch a painter. Such a caprice may often be aroused by working away gradually day after day. You know what I mean.

Do you know what Claude Monet earns to-day? In the neighbourhood of 100,000 francs per annum. Do you think this is an accident? You may tell me that his painting is easier to understand and all that. Fifteen years ago he found it difficult to sell a picture for 100 francs and his painting was easier to understand, and yet Fritz did not understand. No, the truth is that Claude Monet had Hoschedé[2] in his pocket, and then the customers brought by his brother from Rouen. In short, his relatives, instead of casting him off, supported him and praised him to the skies. In the end, people believed in him.

Enough of business, I am tired. You will be satisfied when I succeed. I am in process of regaining my beautiful figure of yore, without becoming too lean. I eat very little and then scarcely anything except roots and fish like the natives. On the other hand, I

---

1 *Suzanne*, a canvas in his impressionist manner, painted while he was with the exchange broker Bertin.

2 Ernest Hoschedé, business man and amateur in the arts, who took a great interest in the Impressionists, and especially in Claude Monet. The sale of his collection on the 5th and 6th June, 1878, was a very important event. Monet's *Saint-German-l'Auxerrois*, fetched 305 francs.

have gone very grey, but have not had a headache for 4 months. Write me at length (take your time) with my letter in front of you. Reply to my letters.

Love to the children who are to kiss you for me.

Your Paul who loves you.

PAUL GAUGUIN.

128.

TO HIS WIFE.   Tahiti, May, 1892.

My dear Mette,

Here is a beginning of the harvest at last. You see that all hope is not lost; you know what I told you (one customer leads to another); from every point of view I am satisfied with the result you have obtained with my canvases; in the first place this had relieved you a little and assured you a peaceful summer and it gives you a little confidence. This beastly painting ! How often you have insulted it, not as talent, but as a breadwinner.

I quite understand how hard it is to be patient. Your hurried letter does not explain much, I have to guess your meaning. The exhibition in Denmark of next spring is probably next year. I will send you some good canvases from here at the end of the year if I am not condemned to bring them myself.

For I am now on tenterhooks all the time. I am making every effort to get hold of a 1.000 franc note. If I succeed I shall go to the Marquisas, to la Dominique, a tiny island which has only three European inhabitants, and where Oceania is not yet swamped by European civilization. Living is very expensive here and I am ruining my health through not eating. In the Marquisas I can eat; an ox costs 3 francs or the trouble of hunting it. And I could work. When shall I return, you ask ?

I very much want to see you all again and take a little rest, but we must be reasonable. A voyage like that cannot be undertaken lightly, like going out for a walk. I must do everything that I can here, so that I do not have to come back. And this will be the end of my wanderings. Just a little more confidence, dear Mette, for the sake of us all.

I have 11 months of effective work and I have 44 fairly important canvases, which should amount to 15.000 francs a year, provided the customers buy them.

You want to send Aline to a boarding school, good, you know what she needs. When I come back I hope to find all the children as nice and healthy as I left them. If funds permit, would you like to spend two months with me next summer in the country in Denmark, with the children as well?

Kisses to all.

PAUL GAUGUIN.

P.S.—You mention a good article by Aurier on the symbolists. In what review? And who does it mention? For I receive nothing from Paris. Morice is supposed to send me from time to time news of anything published about me. But I have heard nothing from him, although I wrote him 5 months ago.

I know Aurier and doubtless he has not overlooked me in this article. I created this new movement in painting and many of the young people who have profited are not devoid of talent, but once more, it is I who have shaped them. And nothing in them comes from themselves, but through me.

However, your Danish friend, whose name I forget, he who is enamoured of Aline, knows these youngsters and what it all amounts to. And I have a few letters from them which elucidate the matter. Ask Pasteur if I did not know him at Orleans? The Zevor boys and Pasteur played with me at St. Mesmin. That was a long time ago. And which does not make me feel younger. Here I am, old already, and I have done so little in this world, the time being so short. I am always afraid of becoming senile before I have finished what I have undertaken. Not that I am conscious of any weakening, on the contrary, I feel my brain is as strong as ever at this moment, but who can answer for to-morrow. There is certainly something the matter with my heart, which grows worse every day. The least surprise, the slightest emotion upsets me completely. When I am riding the least swerve terrifies me and for four or five minutes I do not know what I am doing. And the poor beast pays the penalty. Here riding is an amusement which costs nothing.

When I get back, if I have a little peace, I will undergo some treatment. You say nothing about Emil's studies. How is he getting on at school, will he be an engineer some day?

Looking forward to the next letter.

PAUL.

129.

TO HIS WIFE.   Tahiti, June, 1892.

My dear Mette,

You are irregular in your correspondence. There is nothing for me by this mail—no letter to distract me and relieve my anxiety about my family.

You can continue to write me until further orders, I have got here 400 francs for a canvas. The portrait is postponed. In any case I reckon to stay here four months.

Perhaps Morice will be prompted to send me the money in his care, which would keep me for some months.

I learn from Paris that you expect to sell some canvases in Denmark. If you succeed in doing so, try and send me a small part of the proceeds. I am in a fair way to ruining my health with the little food I take. I should prefer even that than to abandon the struggle I have embarked upon. Anyhow, see what you can do.

When I return I shall have something to show customers, and when I am on the spot, things will move a little. When I am not there, nothing happens.

I am fairly pleased with my last works and feel there is dawning in me an Oceanic character, and I can assert that what I am doing here has not been done by anyone else and nothing like it is known in France. I hope that this novelty will turn the scale in my favour. Tahiti is not devoid of charm and its women, in default of regular beauty, have an indescribable quality that is penetrating and utterly mysterious. Anyhow, you will see. Three months ago I sent to Paris a specimen of my work, which I think was well done. We shall see what Paris has to say about it.

I am going to ask you something that may seem strange, but is perhaps not altogether unreasonable. I regard piano lessons as utterly useless for Aline. For proficiency long years of application, as well as a gift that way, are necessary. If then, instead of the piano, there are facilities for her to learn the guitar, which would give pleasing results within a short time, I should be more than satisfied. She could accompany me in my old age, and I confess that my old mandoline is a dreary companion when I am alone.

Music is my great distraction. Look then to it. Philipsen's brother is a musician, who should know musicians able and willing to teach Aline.

Kisses for all,

Your

PAUL.

130.

TO HIS WIFE.   Tahiti, July, 1892.

Dear Mette,

I have at last received from you an explanatory letter in answer to mine. The last mail brought me nothing and I am always a little downcast when I have no news from France. At this moment I am almost at the end of my strength, and in any case at the end of my tether, thanks to Morice, who says he is very fond of me but does not prove it. He has money of mine and, owing to my not receiving it, my calculations have all gone awry. The result being that I have 50 francs in my pocket at the present time, and do not know what to do in order to return home.

It will be necessary to make application to the authorities to repatriate me as a pauper. And it is very hard for me to make this application. On the other hand, I don't want to do so before another two or three weeks as I shall then be expecting the captain[1] of a schooner who promised to let me do his wife's portrait for 2,000 francs. But here is the snag. The captain is a bit of a rip. Will he keep his promise. I am wracked with anxiety. I rely no more on Morice and on my return I shall have a bone to pick with him. I do not relish my path being blocked in this treacherous fashion. The two residents at Marquisas and Raiotea have just left on leave and their reliefs have arrived. Here was an opportunity to appoint me in their place without any dismissal. But Morice lost my letter and forgot what I asked him, spoke neither of Geffroy[2] nor to

[1] Gauguin had met him on his way to the Governor soliciting repatriation.

[2] Gustave Geffroy, novelist and art critic, author of *l'Enferme*, *l'Apprenti*, member of Goncourt Academy, Director of Gobelins, very intimate with Georges Clemenceau and Claude Monet, to whom he dedicated an important biography. He met Gauguin only once at Pouldu. Cézanne painted his famous portrait of him about 1895.

Renan,[1] both of whom I should have thought were as influential as Castelar. But enough of this, let us think of the present.

If I do this portrait I shall stay another year. If not, I will return soon, unless the authorities decline to grant me a passage.

Every day I have been expecting this money from France, otherwise I would have written the Minister of Fine Arts to get me home. Now it is too late. If I stay another year, I will then take the necessary steps for my return.

Do not be offended at my determination to stay another year. I am in the midst of work, now that I know the soil, its odour and the Tahitians whom I draw in a very enigmatical manner, are closer to the Maories, and not like the Orientals of the Battignoles. It has taken me nearly a year to understand this, and now I have my foot in the stirrup, the thought of having to leave all this is maddening.

I have by now 32 canvases, one of 3 m. by 1 m. 30; 3 of 1 m. 20 by 90 and the remainder by 70. A fair number of drawings and sketches, a few carved knick-knacks.

I thank you for the photograph. How the children are changing every day. Now Clovis looks like me at his age. As to Aline she is the spit of Emma Gad. Paul's eyes make him look very funny. For my part you will find I have grey hair. On the other hand, my figure is like what it was in my younger days, and I have lost the tendency I once had to grow round-shouldered. The habit of walking about nude, or almost so, together with physical exercise, has made my gait seem youthful. I have not coughed since I was ill, and it is extraordinary that I have not caught the influenza that is raging in Tahiti. Every day children and old people die and everybody around me is coughing.

Kisses for all.

PAUL GAUGUIN.

Do not write after receiving this letter until I tell you in case I have to be leaving.

---

[1] In February, 1891, Ary Renan, son of Ernest Renan, secured from the Ministry of Education a promise to entrust the painter with an art mission, to be rewarded by the purchase of some canvases. In 1896, the Director of Fine Arts, M. Roujon, declined to keep this promise, but sent 200 francs to Gauguin, who returned them.

131.

TO HIS WIFE. Tahiti, August, 1892.

My dear Mette,

Several mails have come with no letter from you; your silence is the reverse of affectionate. However busy you are, you can always find half an hour a month to write me, if you want to. But this you don't want to do.

I hope the children are well and that there is no illness in the house. It being now summer you are probably with them in the country on holiday. Emil must be very busy if he can't write a few lines to his father. At his age I would write to my mother when I was away and could always find a few affectionate words for her. But then I was brought up on different lines, with less calculation and a little more heart.

I am still here working and struggling, for I have no more money and they send me nothing from Paris. When I am not on the spot, things are at a standstill. I do not know when I shall return as I can't walk to Paris and they won't let you come on the boat without money. I don't know what saint to pray to for money. I have, however, merchandise and good stuff in hand, but it is not saleable here in Tahiti. Nobody has any money, and besides the only potential buyers are tallow merchants and pen pushers. Never a word from Morice, and I don't know his address to write to him. You who are in correspondence with him should be more up-to-date than I am.

Reach for your pen and give me some news.

PAUL GAUGIN.

132.

TO DANIEL DE MONFREID.[1] Tahiti, August, 1892.

My dear Daniel,

You rejoice in your letter at alleged good news on which you congratulate me, viz., on my remaining in Tahiti. But do you realize that it is nearly 5 months since I wrote you to this effect and

---

[1] Daniel de Monfreid, born in 1856, was the faithful correspondent and trustworthy agent, who looked after all Gauguin's business while he was in the South Seas. A good painter, he was rarely influenced by his friend. He was also called the "Captain," because he loved the sea and owned a sailing boat.

that the 400 francs have almost vanished and I am in the same position as formerly, i.e., in a state of indecision. Every time the mail brings your letter I hope for money, which is important. More than a year has passed since I left. My reputation is growing, but nothing has been sold whereas when I was on the spot I nearly always managed to raise the wind to the tune of about 2,000 francs. Neither Tanguy, nor Portier, nor Goupil. I can hardly believe it. As to Morice, I am resigned to the loss of the money he has of mine, and am astonished at his silence and his behaviour.

However, let us chat and banish this dark cloud.

Happily, I have made supreme efforts here to stave off the evil day. I have recently made two wood carvings, which I managed to sell for 300 francs, and I can stay here another three months. But what will happen then ? I dare not ask myself.

I have had no canvas for a month and dare not buy any, as I have so little money, so I cannot do anything. But I am studying with the brain and eyes, then I rest a little, which won't do me any harm. Lying fallow from time to time is necessary for active people like me. I see that you have a livelihood in the artistic sphere, on which I congratulate you, and this can do you nothing but good in forcing you to decorate. But beware of modelling. The simple window attracts the eye by its division of colours and shapes. Here is something that is still better. Music in some way. Which means that I was born to practice *an art trade* and that I could not succeed. Windows, furniture, faience, etc. . . . my real aptitudes are for these things rather than for painting in the strict sense of the word.

As to your reference to feminine attachments, I very much fear you will one day give way to the sentiment of gratitude and habit, especially with the maternity of your wood warbler. But it is your business and I only mention it because you were the first to speak of it and, besides, I take an interest in your welfare.

My regards to Maitral and thanks for his excellent souvenir. When you receive this letter it is probable that everybody will be in Paris, so my regards to everybody.

I have recently done a fine nude, two women by the side of a stream, I think it is my best thing to date.

That is all.

Cordially yours,
PAUL GAUGUIN.

133.

TO HIS WIFE.   Tahiti, 5 November, 1892.

Dear Mette,

I have heard from you by this mail, although your letter was very nearly lost. The mailboat capsized and a little schooner brought us the letters ten days later. This leaves me little time to reply, which I am doing to-day. I see that everybody is pretty well. Emil will not get his degree until next year when he will be 19. If the degree corresponds to ours it seems to be quite late, and I do not see how he can enter a crammers at 20. Our maximum age for the Navy is 17 and the examination is more severe than that for a bachelor of arts, that of St. Cyr and the Polytechnic 20 years. I hope therefore that things are not the same in your country. However that may be, we must not be angry with the boy if he is backward, it is we who have made him so. Moreover, the future will look after all this. Why are you so worried about the children's future ? When people have reared boys up to the age of 18, they have done their duty, and even more; not everybody has money to settle on their children, who have to make their way in the world in their turn just as their parents did themselves. We have not bequeathed infirmities to ours or fettered them with a bad name. They are intelligent and fit, which is more than is necessary for their future. Half a loaf is better than no bread; without money, one cannot live like a nobleman, and so on. As to the girl, it is another matter, but you say she promises to be pretty, and her face will be her fortune. She has four brothers into the bargain; this is more than needful for her settlement in life.

I feel myself growing old, and that quickly. Owing to lack of food, my stomach is being atrociously ruined, and I get thinner every day. But I must go on with the fight, always, always. And the responsibility rests with society. You are without confidence in the future, but I have that confidence, *because I want to have it.* Without that, I should long since have thrown up the sponge. To hope is almost to live. I must live to do my duty until the end, and I can only do so by forcing my illusions, by creating hopes out of dreams. When day after day I eat my dry bread with a glass of water, I make myself believe it is a beef-steak. I implore you then, dear Mette, not to speak of false hopes, what is the use of it ?

I cannot send you any studies from here, the cost of transport being too dear, and I have no money to pay for it.

If by chance someone I can trust should be going to France, and would take my case with his luggage, I will profit by such an opportunity, but there is not much likelihood of that, and we had better leave it out of account.

I have received 5 lines from Morice, who professes to be astonished at my silence, and alleges he has written me many letters and sent me money. Lies ! I have received letters every month. I am replying to him and sending the letter to J. Dolent, who will hand it to him, and ask for explanations. I have also instructed Joyant to deal directly with me. But this poor fellow is not much of a business man. Since Van Gogh's death he has not been able to sell anything. Had you known Van Gogh, you would have known a responsible man devoted to the good cause. If he had not died like his brother, I should be out of danger at the present time. And it is thanks to him that the firm of Goupil is doing anything for us.

I receive every month a letter from Daniel or from Séruzier, two pupils who are very devoted to me. Séruzier tells me this month that Ballin and Clement are progressing in painting and that they will do something. You tell me that Juan Uribe is better; I thought he had left for America.

Goodbye for the present and kisses for all.

PAUL GAUGUIN.

134.

TO HIS WIFE.   Tahiti, 8 December, 1892.

Dear Mette,

No letter from France this month, which is not cheering. It must be confessed that you do not much like writing. I expected to leave by the January mailboat, but now I am chained here for 6 months. The Minister wrote to the Governor, requesting him to repatriate me if possible. The Colonial Budget being very poor, the Minister was told that it was impossible. I hope the Minister will reply in 5 months on favourable lines, that is, to charge up the cost to the home authorities. If not, I do not know when I shall return and how I shall do so. I am here without money.

Gauguin pencil drawings from Tahiti

I found an opportunity to send 8 canvases to France. They will be in charge of Daniel, 55, Rue du Chateau. Write him for information regarding the Danish exhibition. If by good fortune you should manage to sell some of my canvases the money *must be put aside for my return to France.*

Once back in France I shall have need of it to set me on my feet. Below is the translation of the titles I have put on the canvases. This translation is for you only so that you may give it to those who ask for it. But I want the titles in the catalogue to be the same as those on the pictures. This language is fantastic and has several meanings.

1.	Parau Parau.	(Word, Word).
2.	Eaha oe feci.	What, you are jealous, cnvious.
3.	Manao tupapau.	The Spirit of the Dead Watches.
4.	Parahi te Marae.	Temple place reserved for worship of the gods and human sacrifices.
5.	Te faaturuma.	Silence or Mournful Spirit.
6.	Te Raau Rahi.	The Great Tree.
7.	I Raro te Oviri.	Under the Pandanus.
8.	Te fare Maorie.	The Maorie Dwelling.
9.	Te vahine note tiare.	Woman with a blossom.

I send you a landscape medley.

I am indeed afraid that the canvases will be ruined on such a long journey. Now listen to me. Except for three canvases I leave it to you to fix the price, but I want the prices to be higher than my French canvases.

No. 2 not less than 800 francs.

„   3 „   „   „ 1500   „

I would even keep back the latter for much later.

No. 4 not less than 700 francs.

Many of the pictures, of course, will be incomprehensible and you will have something to amuse you. To enable you to understand, I proceed to explain the most questionable and the ones I would keep or sell dear. *Le Manao tupapau.* I have painted a young girl in the nude. In this position, a trifle more, and she becomes indecent. However, I want it in this way as the lines and movement interest me. So I make her look a little frightened. This fright must be excused if not explained in the character of the person, a Maorie. This people have by tradition a great fear of the spirit of the dead.

One of our own young girls would be startled if surprised in such a posture. Not so a woman here. I have to explain this startled look with an economy of literary effort as was done formerly. So I did this. General harmony, sombre, mournful, startled look in the eye like a funeral knell. Violet, dark blue and orange yellow. I make the linen greenish yellow (1) because the native's linen is different from ours (flattened bark of a tree), (2) because it suggests artificial light (the Kanaka woman never goes to bed in the dark) and yet I do not want the effect of lamplight, (3) this yellow binding the orange yellow and the blue completes the musical accord. There are some flowers in the background, but they are not real, only imaginary, and I make them resemble sparks. The Kanaka believes the phosphorescences of the night are the spirits of the dead and they are afraid of them. To finish I make the ghost merely a good little woman because the young girl, unacquainted with the sprites on the French stage, could not visualise death itself except as a person like herself. Here endeth the little sermon, which will arm you against the critics when they bombard you with their malicious questions. To end up, the painting has to be done quite simply, the *motif* being savage, childlike.

All this must be very boring, but I am sure it is necessary for you over there.

Kisses for you and the children.

PAUL GAUGUIN.

135.

TO HIS WIFE.   Tahiti, early April, 1893.

My dear Mette,

At last I have a letter from you. I am always afraid there has been an accident when I go so long without news of you and the children. Your letter is affectionate but melancholy. I realize your complaints, which are justified, but what is the use? What shall I say about myself? For nine years I have been living without seeing my family, without home, and often without eating. For two months I have had to stop spending any money on food. I have every day some maioré, an insipid fruit which is like bread, and a glass of water. I cannot even indulge in the luxury of a cup of tea, sugar being so dear. I endure this situation stoically but it has affected my health and my eyes,[1] which I cannot do without, are very much dimmed at the present time. If you had sent me the money for the last picture, it would have saved my life. Why . . . Can you explain it? The Minister wrote to the Governor to ascertain if he could expatriate me. The Colony replied that it had no money and must have definite instructions, which has postponed any reply until the month of April. If the reply is unfavourable, how can I leave? With the money you could have sent me, it would have been possible, as a warship sometimes leaves for Nouméa on the 1st May. I could have joined it and at Nouméa I could have taken a 4th class ticket on the steamer, whereas the journey via America costs 1,500 francs. You preferred to keep the money, I do not reproach you, but it was of prime urgency. Now it is too late.

Let us hope for something from the Ministry, in which case I shall be in Paris about the 4th July. Joyant has sent me a statement of my account with Goupil, he has remitted 250 francs to Morice for him to send me, and this in the month of May, '91, which makes 1,350 francs which Morice has stolen, but I have received neither money nor letters from him. Joyant also writes me that sentiment has considerably changed in our favour and that my corner, that is to say those who have followed me, is very much to the fore.

A good idea has just occurred to me, and I am writing to Paris about it. Paris maintains a number of drawing inspectors for the schools. These inspectors are not very busy but are very well paid, 10,000 francs a year. Reganey who once had a mission is an inspector. I am therefore asking friends in Paris to bestir themselves to get this position for me. Puvis de Chavannes[2] who belongs to the Institute (it is the Institute which appoints the inspectors) is favourably disposed towards me. If possible, Pasteur's son, who stands very well with Bonnet, should be seen. With these two members of the Institute on our side, something should be doing. I do not want to raise false hopes, but we must bestir ourselves, and I hope you will do what you can in this matter. It means for us, dear Mette, the

---

[1] Privations, abuse of tobacco and sexual excesses had such severe effects on the painter's sight that at this time the colouring of his pictures, which was very vivid, seemed to him dull.

[2] Puvis de Chavannes, born in Lyons in 1824, died in Paris in 1898, author of numerous and important wall paintings, the most famous of which are those of the Pantheon, the Paris Town Hall, and Lyons and Boston museums. Gauguin liked his canvas *The Poor Fisherman*, which he regarded as a first attempt at synthesis.

chance of being happy and united with our children in our old age. No more uncertainty.

What you tell me about an exhibition in England is excellent provided a trustworthy Englishman is prepared to look after matters on the spot. You have enough canvases available. Moreover, it is a little distraction. In the evenings I study the language a little, I have such a bad memory. To bed at 9 and up at 5. A bathe in the river and then to work. I make tea in the morning and go on till noon. If de Haan had come, life would have been very pleasant, I could have talked about art. He made a mistake in not coming, as life is no dearer for two, and this poor fellow needs a moral force besides him, such as the primitive and the new, to excite his imagination. However, it's his affair. Nevertheless, I am very much alone.

I have your photographs nicely arranged on a hanging shelf in the hut, which provoke many questions from the kanakas who come to see and admire my painting, if astonishment can be regarded as admiration. So these are your children, they say, what do they do? And the vahine is pretty, why is her hair like that of a tane (man)? Why isn't she with you, etc. . . So to dismiss the subject I tell them that she is dead and that trouble killed her. Well then, they say, why don't you stay in Tahiti for good, very good soil here, have children by kanaka woman. You see I am on the way to going native.

Poor Aline, I do not think that Denmark is the country she would choose. I know she is a little like me, which is why you treat her a little like a foreigner. She realizes that you do not love her much and she is not happy. You are wrong when you say she has no affection for you; the opposite is the case.

We shall see all that later. It now being late I will retire and end my letter.

Kisses for the children and you.

PAUL GAUGUIN.

136.

TO HIS WIFE.   Tahiti, April/May, 1893.
My dear Mette,

I have your letter advising the sending of 700 francs but your letter is torn and the money missing. On the other hand, Daniel sends me the same sum which he had from Schuff, who told him that it came from you. I therefore assume that you opened your letter to take out the money. If so, it is difficult to believe that neither Denmark, nor San Francisco, nor Tahiti noticed the torn envelope or drew attention to it. I must as a matter of logic cling to the former supposition and not lose courage, as otherwise it would be altogether too bad. You ought either to have written your letter again or sent a post office order or (in the latter case) written a word of advice in the letter. Careless!! But recriminations are useless, and everyone is liable to be careless. I am all the time in a fever of impatience to be off. If the Ministry sends a favourable reply next month, I will leave in May.

You can write me until further notice but do not send any money. Your letter is encouraging for the future, it will not be too soon to leave harbour, for we have both suffered, and it seems to me that we have done more than our duty. I hope you received in good time the canvases I sent for the Danish Exhibition. You are right, I must return, I should have done very well working in the Marquisas, which would have been immensely useful to me, but I am tired and it is urgently necessary for me to look after things in France. Unfortunately, I shall get back in the summer, which is a bad time for business. On the other hand, this exhibition in Denmark may have prepared the ground. However, we shall see.

Have you made a mistake in giving Emil's height as 1 m. 96 c. which gives a growth of 18 cm. in 6 months? And Aline's nose! When I saw it it promised to be enormous. But if it doesn't make her ill, I see no particular drawback.

You say that Morice has written me. In spite of my letters to France I have received no explanation of his conduct. On my return I will go into the matter at close quarters. If I get hold of the money I left there (and I will do so) I shall have 1,300 francs from this source, which will be very useful for my arrival. Soon I shall not have a coat to put on my back.[1] If you can make me a present of half a dozen shirts, they would be most useful on my arrival. I don't attach much importance to dress, but I must be neat and not have a slovenly appearance in order to do any business.

I end my letter with kisses for you and the children.

Good-bye for the present. It may be that I shall arrive a month and a half after the receipt of this letter.

PAUL GAUGUIN.

[1] About 1902 he found himself in the same sartorial state, and, being silent about his poverty, Europeans and policemen reproached him for dressing like a native.

137.

TO HIS WIFE.   Undated, Marseilles, 3 August, 1893.

My dear Mette,

Here I am at last at Marseilles[1] safe and sound, and I have wired Daniel to send me, if possible, some money to pay my train fare and hotel bill. The money I had was used up in the course of the voyage. As soon as you receive this letter write me in detail how everything is going on in the house (this will make 5 months since I had your news). Tell me also what is the state of our finances, so that I can make my calculations accordingly. Of course, the work I am bringing back with me cannot yield immediate results and there are certain preliminary expenses to be incurred on arrival. I have heard nothing of the canvases which I sent (except that they arrived in good condition). But what effect did they produce at the Exhibition in Denmark? To enable me to organise my show in Paris you must give me the fullest information up to date. The return voyage has been terribly tiring, the Red Sea in particular was extremely hot, and we were obliged to cast into the sea the corpses of three passengers stifled by the heat.

I am thankful to arrive as well as I am; in the last six months I have been regaining my strength and developing a corporation. You will find a husband to embrace you not too much like a skinned rabbit and by no means impotent.

I write you this on board ship to lose no time and post my letter as soon as I land.

I am in a state of great apprehension as I near port. Is Daniel at present in Paris and can he send me some money. I have only enough in my pocket to send a telegram and pay for a carriage to convey my luggage to a hotel where I shall wait for money. I have some heavy luggage in the shape of paintings and carvings which will involve me in some expense.

Good-bye for the present.

News quickly. Best love.
                                                              PAUL.

[1] Gauguin returned to France via Nouméa and Sydney on a troop transport. " For the third class," he wrote Monfreid, " there is just about two feet to move in the fore. I had to pay extra to go 2nd class. What a filthy voyage." At Marseilles which he reached on Wednesday, the 4th August, with four francs in his pocket, he found lodged at the Post Office 250 francs lent by Paul Sérusier, and sent by the forethoughtful Monfreid, before he left for Algiers. On the 6th August, Gauguin was in Paris.

138.

TO HIS WIFE.   Undated, Paris, August, 1893.

My dear Mette,

I shrink from writing you, not knowing what to say or what to think of your silence. I had hoped that you would have answered at length immediately on receipt of my letter. As soon as I arrived I saw Durand-Ruel, who was very cordial and promised me his premises for an exhibition. This is a great point gained and I think that, with a few notices in the newspapers, this exhibition will be a success. And if this goes well, I believe that Durand-Ruel will push me. I therefore attach great importance to this and would like you to tell me exactly what pictures you have still unsold (only of those done in Tahiti) and then I will advise you which of them must be forwarded on to me.

I am in Paris at this moment without a penny and cannot undertake anything unless I know what I can rely on.

I am eager for a letter from you.

Love and kisses.

PAUL GAUGUIN.
8, Rue de la Grande Chaumière.

139.

TO HIS WIFE.   Undated, Paris, end August, 1893.

My dear Mette,

Decidedly I understand things less and less. You have my address since you sent a telegram to my new abode and you have not yet found an opportunity to write me a line. Everybody I see in Paris, however, asks me how you are, and I do not know what to reply. Were it not for the little restaurant that lets me eat on credit,[1] I do not know how I should subsist.

Séruzier is in the country and is sending me 100 francs to-morrow, as a loan to enable me to go to Orleans to-morrow.[2] How-

---

[1] It was the restaurant Caron, Rue de la Grande Chaumiére. Madame Caron, who welcomed artists, retired to Noyon with a collection of pictures, including several by Gauguin.

[2] The painter was obliged to go to Orleans, where his uncle Isidore had just died.

ever, it cannot be helped, everybody is away, I know not where, (Schuff also is on holiday), and without Séruzier I should still be in the Marseilles hotel. Good God, how difficult it is to act when those on whom you rely leave you completely in the lurch—and especially your wife.

Frankly, what is the matter? I want to know where I am. Why has not Emil or you come to Paris to greet me? This would not have killed you. But enough of discussion; I await long letters for my information, and replies to all my questions.

PAUL GAUGUIN.

140.

TO HIS WIFE.   Undated, Paris, 4 September, 1893.

Dear Mette,

I am back from Orleans. Everything is finished except the settlement, which will take place in about 2 months, as there are shares to be transferred. After setting aside a sum of 4,000 francs for his housekeeper and the expenses, there remains barely 9,000 francs each.[1]

I am up to my ears in work here, and must see about the exhibition.[2] Everything depends on that. Will you send me the Tahiti pictures you have? I must have them for the show.

Of course, send them without frames, well packed and carriage paid.

Why does not Emil come to study in France since he has to study abroad, and why is he going abroad? I do not understand it.

I will write soon a letter in reply to yours.

PAUL GAUGUIN.

[1] Gauguin had to share the inheritance with his sister Madame Uribe.

[2] The exhibition was held at Durand-Ruel's from 4th November to beginning of December, 1893. Gauguin exhibited thirty-eight canvases from Tahiti and six from Brittany, as well as two carvings. The catalogue contained a preface by Charles Morice. The eleven canvases which were sold hardly covered expenses, but the interest aroused exceeded all expectations. Many visitors came to the exhibition for the amusement of it. Paul Durand-Ruel had agreed to organise this exhibition on his premises solely to please Degas, for he had no faith in Gauguin's art.

141.

TO HIS WIFE. Undated, Paris, 10 September, 1893.

My dear Mette,

I received your letter at last which reached me from the Pyrennees, Schuff having forward it to Daniel, who in turn sent it on to me; I was at Schuff's place all right on my arrival, but he was at Dieppe, whither your letter was forwarded. What you tell me is not cheerful and, really had not my uncle died, I do not see how I should have been able to organize without any money at all and the fruits of my toil having been unproductive.

However, a truce to this topic. My uncle's death makes it possible to arrange everything. I hope to get my share in two months' time, unless my sister makes difficulties. She has left her brother-in-law a power of attorney with instructions not to let me act alone in anything. And if my uncle had not been the man of integrity whom you know (according to the tales of the housekeeper) he would have left everything to Marie. In short, my share ought to be 10,000 francs net.

I intend in November to risk a bold stroke upon which our entire future will depend, and according to what I have already divined on my visits, I think everything will turn out all right. Consequently, I must not lose a minute and you will realize that I cannot be away before this exhibition; that is to say the end of November.

Since you have a little free time why don't you come with little Paul to Paris, which would give you a little rest, and I should be happy to embrace you. Moreover, we could discuss matters, for which there is much need (letters are very unsatisfactory). I have a studio nearly ready, so there would be no embarrassment or expense, and from every point of view it would be very useful. And if you can find the money for the journey,[1] it would be repaid in two months at the most. There are in the house two Danish ladies whom you know and it would be very easy to accommodate one of the children.

We could make some useful calls and later on would reap the fruits of this little expense. Don't raise a whole crop of objections and calculations, shake them off, and come here as soon as possible.

Write me at once the day of your arrival. Quick, I am closing it is late for the post.   PAUL GAUGUIN.

[1] This suggestion provoked protests from his wife.

142.

TO HIS WIFE.   Undated, Paris, September, 1893.

My Dear Mette,

I am up to my neck in work, having errands to run, and many canvases to repair and retouch ready for my exhibition.

I await eagerly the Tahiti canvases for which I asked. Let me hear as to this soon. I wonder why you reproach me for not sending you any of uncle's money. I have told you, however, that I shall not get it until 2 months' time, and we must consider ourselves lucky if we don't have to wait for papers from Colombia, in view of the fact that my sister is married to a foreigner subject to American law. It may be that her share will have to be transferred to her children. Pablo is busy about the matter at the Embassy and perhaps things will get a move on. In any event, we have to wait, which is annoying in every way, as my uncle's Italian bonds have fallen considerably in recent years and are falling every day, which appreciably diminishes the estate.

Don't forget to send my canvases, I must have them for my show.

Kisses for the children.

PAUL GAUGUIN.

143.

TO HIS WIFE.   Undated, Paris, October, 1893.

Dear Mette,

Not until the day before yesterday did I receive the case of pictures in good condition sent by passenger train. Two of the best pictures are missing. I should be glad if you would tell me what has become of them. I shall henceforth need to keep an account of all this and when you have time write down a list of the pictures you have and a list of those you have sold since my departure for Tahiti, with the prices.

At present the dealers are on the look out for any of my old pictures, even including a snowscape done at the Trocadero which I gave to Helene Uribe, and which sold for 500 francs.

No news yet from the Orleans lawyer, and I am overwhelmed

with the preliminary expenses of my installation and exhibition, which will open on the 4th November, at Durand-Ruel's.

I am also preparing a book on Tahiti, which will facilitate the understanding of my painting. What work!

I shall soon know whether it was an act of lunacy to go to Tahiti.

Kisses for the children.

PAUL GAUGUIN.

144.

TO STEPHANE MALLARME.[1]

Paris, 3 November, 1893.

Dear Sir,

I learn that you are back in Paris, but do not know if you have yet resumed your Tuesdays. I was anxious, however, to come and see you. Taking my chance I will come Tuesday next to tell you a little about my journey.

Believe me, yours sincerely,

PAUL GAUGUIN.

145.

TO HIS WIFE.

Paris, December, 1893.

My dear Mette,

For some time I have had a little rheumatism from the right shoulder down to the hand, and I confess that my courage in facing affairs is not great.

My show has not in fact given the results that might have been expected, but we must look facts in the face. I fixed very high prices: 2 to 3,000 francs on an average. At Durand-Ruel's I could hardly do otherwise, having regard to Pissarro, Manet, etc. But many bidders went as far as 1,500 francs. What can I say but that

[1] Stéphane Mallarmé, the great poet, whose life has been described by Henri Mondor, in a magisterial biography, published in 1841, liked Gauguin's painting, about which, on the occasion of his visit to the Durand-Ruel exhibition, he stated " It is extraordinary that so much mystery can be put into so much splendour." Gauguin made a drawing of Mallarmé, which he reproduced as an etching.

we must wait, and, in short, I have proved to be right, for now a price of 1,000 francs for my work does not seem enormous in the market.

Let us forget it. The most important thing is that my exhibition has had a very great artistic success, has even provoked passion and jealousy. The Press has treated me as it has never yet treated anybody, that is to say, rationally, with words of praise. For the moment I am considered by many people to be the greatest modern painter.

Thanks for your suggestion to come to Denmark, but I shall be kept here all the winter by a huge volume of work. Many receptions, visitors who want to see my pictures. And buyers, I hope. A book[1] about my voyage, which is causing me much labour.

What is killing me is that damnable struggle for money. The lawyer makes no progress, and I have to keep postponing repayment of the small sums which I borrowed under promise to repay in October. This ties my hands and I cannot buy for myself many things that are necessary. But enough!

Hear what I propose, and I think that of all suggestions, this is the most reasonable. Would it not be possible to hire a fisherman's cottage on the coast of Norway, where I could work and where you could come with the children in the holidays?

(End of letter missing.)

146.

TO HIS WIFE.   Paris, near end December, 1893.

Dear Mette,

How can you suppose that I have money and do not send you any. Unfortunately, the winding up of the estate threatens to last another 6 months; another power of attorney is supposed to be necessary, and it takes a long time to get it from America. The result being that since I have returned to France I have been worried on all sides by shortage of money; I dare not do anything; as a general principle you have no need to call me to order to do what I ought to do; as soon as possible I will help you.

At the moment I have influenza, which stupefies me very con-

---

[1] *Noa, Noa.*

siderably, head, heart . . . nothing moves. Here is the children's
first letter at last. It is not often that I have such Christmas greetings. Better late than never.

And I will reply.

PAUL GAUGUIN.

Very dear Aline. Here you are grown up already, sixteen years
old . . . I even thought it was 17, weren't you born on 25/12/1876?
You don't remember for obvious reasons but I myself saw you
quite small and very quiet, you opened bright blue eyes such as
you will have, I think, always. Mademoiselle is off to the ball. Can
you dance well? I hope the answer is a graceful YES, and the
young gentlemen talk to you a lot about your father. It is a way
of indirect courtship. Do you remember 3 years ago when you
said you would be my wife? I sometimes smile at the recollection
of your simplicity.

You ask me if I have sold many pictures; unfortunately, no,
otherwise I should take great delight in sending you some pretty
things for your Christmas tree.

You see, my poor children, you must not be too cross with
your father if money is not plentiful in the house, a day will come
when perhaps you will find that he is the best father in the world.

Kiss all the children and your mother, dear Aline, for your
papa who signs

PAUL GAUGUIN.

147.

TO HIS WIFE. Paris, December, 1893.

My dear Mette,

' Let me beg you to remember that you have children. It would
be fair for you to give them half of the amount, 4,500 francs[1].' So
you say, and for the second time in a month. As I am 45 years
of age and have strong reasons for believing that I know what is
fair and unfair, I find advice a little too much and a trifle ridiculous.

As you have lately told me, I must get out of my difficulties

---

[1] This legacy intensified Mette Gauguin's resentment towards her husband,
for she had hoped to get half. Thus she wrote: "This time I am angry.
One can expect nothing from him. He never thinks of anyone but himself
and his welfare.

alone (don't I know it only too well) and *with what*? with my goods? (You have them all with you). I shall take precautions to prevent a recurrence of what happened to me on my arrival at Marseilles.

Since I have been back in France I have had to borrow:

½ term in advance (lodgings)	75	francs
Journey and stay in Marseilles ...	250	„
1 term in advance „	150	„ [1]
Pictures from Denmark	40	„
Frames and stands for the exhibition ...	750	„
Linen	100	„
Bedding	100	„
Dental and ocular treatment	75	„
Orleans expenses	50	„
Living expenses	200	„
Exhibition catalogue	125	„
Tobacco and petty expenses	50	„
1 coat and shoes	125	„
	2,090	
Remittances to Tahiti	400	

money lent for voyage home.

It is strange that I have to make out an account for you, and convince you that I must live elsewhere than in the street, and that, coming home ill after living in a warm climate, I cannot walk about quite naked, and have to keep myself warm. Convince you still that I must, for our children's future, incur some expense to enable me eventually to win a livelihood for us. Moreover, half of barely 7,500 francs does not come to 4,500 : " put the two children in a large expensive school "; in this case why not send them to France, where I might be able to obtain scholarships.

When the time comes, I will send you 1,000 francs to cover immediate necessities. After my exhibition when I can see what I

[1] When he received the 9,000 francs of his uncle's legacy, Gauguin moved with a mulatto, called Annah the Javanese, into a large studio at 6, Rue Vercingétorix. He painted the walls' himself in yellow chromium. He decorated them with his Tahitian canvases, as well as Maori and negro warlike trophies. In this strange studio, with Annah, his monkey Taoa, and a parrot, he gave numerous receptions,

am able to earn (without being told either), I will help you according, but once again a budget must be made out. Consequently, I must have exact information, and be advised as to precisely what pictures you are selling[1]. On the basis of such accounts made up every two months, I will do what I ought to do. Of this duty I alone am judge.

You must understand, and everybody would agree with me in this, that I must be kept informed without any *trickery*.

Let us be good friends always, and there is everything to gain by being open.

PAUL GAUGUIN.

148.

TO HIS WIFE.   Undated, Paris, 5 February, 1894.

My dear Mette,

The accident I suffered at Tahiti has almost finished me; my heart has been affected badly by the privations and worry I endured and I began to spit blood which was difficult to stop. The doctor says a relapse would be fatal, and I must take great care of myself in the future.

If therefore the only letters you can write me in the future should be like those you have written me since my return, I implore you to desist. My work is not finished and I must live. Remember that—and cease your perpetual complaints which do no good and much harm. I might ask you, on my side—if, apart from the children, you had any heart to understand—if you think that I am on a bed of roses.

Please see whether it is possible to exchange the Cézanne[2] with the red roofs for one of my canvases. You told me some time ago that Brandès bought them from you with the option of your taking them back at the purchase price. In this case I should much prefer redeeming them with interest on the money. *I am tremendously*

---

[1] Mette Gauguin never told her husband the titles of the pictures she sold.

[2] Canvas belonging to Gauguin's impressionist collection which Mette brought to Denmark in 1884, and which also included a Manet, several Monets and Renoirs; some by Sisley, Guillaumin, Jongkind, etc.

anxious to have this picture. In this case, will you send it to me together with the pair of swords which I may need one day or another.

I await a reply to all these questions.

PAUL GAUGUIN.

149.

TO HIS WIFE.   Undated, Paris, April, 1894.

My dear Mette,

Here is Brandès reply. I send it so that you need no longer suffer from the unjust imputation that my pictures are bought at a *loss* and for reasons of *charity*.

I have obtained information about military service. He (Emil) must be registered before the end of December of this year in order to serve in the years 95-96-97. I thought he registered as a Dane. So the end of all his careful education is that he becomes a mere soldier. In any case, he must be registered at the French Embassy or become a naturalised Dane.

Your husband,

PAUL GAUGUIN.

P.S.—Can you give me a list of the pictures sold apart from those to Brandès; I really need this to ascertain the actual ownership of my works.

" Sir,

I have during the last two years bought from Mette pictures for a sum of 10,000 francs. This now forms quite a little collection which I like; I have not the least intention of parting with any of them.

I quite understand your caprice as an artist, but you will understand that you are really asking too much.

BRANDES."

My reply to Brandès:

" Sir,

Kindly excuse the importunity of my request. I was under the wrong impression, which your letter rectifies, that out of sheer benevolence and in order to render Mette a service, you bought

"Where Do We Come From? What Are We? Where Are We Going?" (detail)   Oil   1897–98   (Museum of Fine Arts, Boston)

some very queer and at the same time very questionable canvases, all mad works, which would be restored to Mette when better times came.

I would repeat that my intention was good—I wanted to relieve you. Nothing more than that. But you like your collection: you appreciate all its . . . intellectual value.

As artist I can do no less than congratulate you, and remain . . . "

150.

TO WILLIAM MOLARD[1].   Pont-Aven, May, 1894.

My dear Molard,

I have received a letter from the landlord accusing you of having put into my studio a young man on the day I left. Moreover, a letter I wrote to Leclercq[2] has been returned, " unknown." I hope that with my letter you have been able to settle things. Tell Leclercq that I have written to Fassy.

I feel too seedy to write much. My leg is broken close to the ankle. They started throwing stones at Concarneau, when I was walking with Annah. I knocked down with two punches a pilot who attacked me. He then rallied the crew of his boat and fifteen men fell on me. I took them all on, and kept the upper hand, until my foot caught in a hole and in falling I broke my leg. Whilst on the ground I was kicked mercilessly but at last I was extricated. I had to be carried to Pont-Aven[3], and am nursing my wounds.

Cannot more——

P. GO.

[1] William Molard, son of a Mentes organist, talented composer, but extravagent, tried to compose revolutionary music, which, according to his friends, it was impossible to play. He also had his studio at 6, rue Vercingétorix, and made Gauguin's acquaintance when the latter moved into the house. He died in Paris in 1936.

[2] Julien Leclercq, journalist and writer on art, born at Armentières, great friend of Rictus and admirer of Gauguin, who sometimes used his services as secretary. Died in Paris 2nd November, 1901.

[3] Tired by the life he was leading in Paris, Gauguin had gone to Pont-Aven in the Spring of 1894, but no longer found in Brittany the old atmosphere. Marie-Jeanne Gloanec had sold the little tavern and had opened the hotel *des Ajoncs d'Or*, sharing the clientèle of painters with the hotel *Julia* kept by Madame Julia, the good hostess. Bathers and tourists were soon flocking to the scene. During a stroll at Concarneau, Gauguin's fantastic attire, the sight of Annah and her monkey, provoked a fracas with sailors, in the course of which Gauguin was wounded.

151.

TO WILLIAM MOLARD. Undated, Pont-Aven, early June, 1894.

My dear Molard,

I have been allowed up for two hours the last few days but it will be a good month yet before I can think of any kind of work.

It is a great pity that the Grieg translation is stopped; it means I shall not have the pleasure of seeing you this summer. If you thought of sending Judith[1] to Brittany, I would look after her like a father, but perhaps from the standpoint of the proprieties it would not altogether do.

I asked Leclercq for the newspapers which reported my accident. It is absolutely necessary to show them to the legal officer before sentence is passed, which it will be in three weeks' time. You will appreciate that I am trying to get my considerably increased expenses refunded—it is sheer bankruptcy.

If you see the old man, tell him that I cannot write without fatigue, that everybody writes to me and that I cannot reply to any without undue exertion. Tell him that my pictures cannot be sold easily.

Kindest regards to Madame and to Judith. To friends also.

Yours, etc.,

PAUL GAUGUIN.

152.

TO WILLIAM MOLARD.

Undated, Pont-Aven, September, 1894.

My dear Molard,

Your letter surprised me in utter idleness : in front of me a heap of unanswered letters growing higher each day.

I have had to take morphine every night for two months and

---

[1] Judith Arlberg, daughter of the Swedish baron Arlberg, first husband of Madame Molard. Aged 13 years in 1894, much liked by Gauguin, she was present at all the receptions in the rue Vercingétorix, attending to the guests like the young daughter of the house. Painter and pastellist, known under the name of Judith Gérard, she exhibited for many years at the Salon d'Automne. In 1906 she painted a portrait of Annah in a pearl grey dress and a nude in pastel. Judith Gérard retired some years ago to Ballancourt (Seine-et-Oise).

I am now very weak; to ward off insomnia I must take alcohol every day, which gives me four hours sleep a night. But this weakens and disgusts me. Yes, I can manage to limp with a stick, but it is most disappointing not to be able to get far enough to paint a landscape; However, during the last eight days I have begun to handle the brushes again. All these misfortunes, piling up one after the other, the difficulty of earning a *regular* income in spite of my reputation, reinforced by my taste for the exotic, have led me to make an irrevocable decision, which is as follows.

In December I will return to Paris and will exert myself to sell everything I have, either " en bloc " or piecemeal. The proceeds thereof once in my pocket, I will set out again for the South Seas, this time taking two comrades with me, Séguin[1] and an Irishman. Concerning this project but me no buts. Nothing will stop me from going and it will be for good. What a foolish existence European life is!

Best wishes to Leclercq. I have not the courage to answer him; I wish him success in his diplomatic career since he desires it. It has its seamy side, however—one must listen a lot, speak very little and every day grant something different from what is expected of you.

Annah goes in a fortnight to Paris to look for a place, if possible; not always easy to deal with the good little woman.[2]

Taoa is dead and more's the pity; she ran about in perfect freedom and followed me like a dog even into the water. But her curiosity prompted her to eat the white flower of the Youcka, and when we found her in the morning we could not save her from the effects of the poison which had been working all night.

Would you do me a service by sending me three treble-strings for guitars and two fifth cords. If it were a large outlay I would send you the money, but please give me credit for such a bagatelle.

[1] Armand Séguin, died at Chateauneuf-du-Faou on 30th December, 1903. Friend and disciple of Gauguin, he was with him on the occasion of the Concarneau affray. Gauguin wrote the preface to the catalogue of his exhibition at the Barc de Boutteville in 1895. He illustrated *Gaspard de la Nuit* for Vollard. His rather unimportant work is wholly influenced by that of Gauguin, whom he admired passionately.

[2] Annah, whom Gauguin represented in a famous picture entitled *Annah the Javanese: Aita Parari*, profited by Gauguin's immobilisation to return to Paris and pillage his studio. She then disappeared entirely out of his life.

Can you also get for me a French-Samoan dictionary at the missionary bookshop kept by the Picpus Brothers, for which I will send you the cost.

Thursday last I was at the Police Court. In spite of all the pleading of my Counsel, in spite of all the brutal assaults proved, there was only a nominal sentence, which proves that in these country places justice is administered in accordance with political edicts. I am to have 600 francs compensation. And I have already spent 475 francs on the doctor, 100 francs on the advocate and all the expenses which an invalid incurs at a hotel—which amounts to this—that I am completely ruined.

And in spite of this, the defeated party is appealing to the Court at Rennes against the sentence—which should be much better for me.

Leclercq should see Dolent so as to get into touch with Geoffrey, who would insert in the *Journal* or *l'Echo de Paris*, a stinging article attacking Quimper justice, and giving full details of my case. It seems that the Rennes judges are very susceptible to these articles.

Apparently people have the right to assassinate or lame for life an innocent man because he is a stranger in the Concarneau country, and his illness, his suffering and his lost time count for nothing—because the Concarneau brigands are *voters* and my attacker is a friend of the Republican authorities.

I ask therefore *en grace* for an article in the Parisian journals. It must appear.

Kind regards to Ida,[1] Judith.

Yours ever,

PAUL GAUGUIN.

153.

TO HIS WIFE.   Undated, Paris, January, 1895.

My dear Mette,

I begin to wonder whether my family knows of my existence, as my birthday, Christmas and New Year's Day all go by without a word from them. Well, it doesn't matter. But I have been

[1] Ida Ericson, born in Sweden, died in Paris in 1927. Very eccentric, often dressed like a man and smoked cigars, she married William Molard in 1891. A sculptress of some talent, she made a medaillion of Gauguin in bronze.

expecting some papers to sign regarding Emil's naturalisation and fear that by negligence the child may be exposed some time in the future, to vexation. In this matter, should you condescend to attend to it, perhaps you would tell me what has happened, to relieve my anxiety.

Devil take it! there are sometimes other letters to write in life than those asking for money.

Yours,

PAUL GAUGUIN.

6, rue Vercingétorix.

154.

TO AUGUST STRINDBERG.

Undated, Paris, 5 February, 1895.

Dear Strindberg,[1]

I received your letter yesterday; your letter which is a preface for my catalogue. The idea of asking you to write this preface occurred to me when I saw you the other day in my studio playing the guitar and singing; your Northern blue eyes studying the pictures hung on the walls. I felt your revulsion: a clash between your civilisation and my barbarism . . . A civilisation from which you are suffering: a barbarism which spells rejuvenation for me.

Studying the Eve of my choice, whom I have painted in forms and harmonies of a different world, she whom you elect to enthrone, evokes perhaps melancholy reflections. The Eve of your civilised imagination makes nearly all of us misogynists: the Eve of primitive times who, in my studio, startles you now, may one day smile on you less bitterly. This world I am discovering, which may perhaps never find a Cuvier nor a naturalist, is a Paradise the outlines of which I shall have merely sketched out. And between the sketch and the realization of the vision there is a long way to go. What

---

[1] August Strindberg (1849-1912), Swedish dramatist and novelist, frequented Gauguin's receptions in the rue Vercingétorix. The painter had asked the writer to preface the catalogue of the exhibition he was organizing before his departure to the South Seas. Strindberg replied in a long letter explaining his refusal: " Behold! I cannot consecrate your art and I cannot love it—(I can get no grip on your art, this time exclusively Tahitian): but I know that this confession will neither astonish nor wound you for you seem to be particularly fortified by the hatred of others." Gauguin inserted this letter and his own reply in the place of the usual preface.

matters! If we have a glimpse of happiness, what is it but a fore taste of *Nirvana*?

The Eve I have painted—and she alone—can remain naturally naked before us. Yours, in this simple state, could not move without a feeling of shame, and too beautiful, perhaps, would provoke misfortune and suffering.

To make clearer my ideas to you, I will not compare the two women themselves, but rather the languages they speak—the Maorie or Touranian language spoken by my Eve and the language spoken by your chosen woman, language with inflexions, European language.

Everything is bare and primordial in the languages of Oceania, which contain the essential elements, preserved in their rugged forms, whether isolated or united, without regard for politeness.

Whereas in the inflected languages, the roots, from which—as in all languages—they spring, disappear in daily ·use which wears away their angles and their contours. They are like a perfected mosaic where one forgets the more or less skilful joining of the stones in admiration for the fine lapidary painting. Only an expert eye can detect the process of construction.

Excuse this long philological digression, which I deem necessary to explain the barbarian drawing which I had to employ to represent a Touranian country and people.

It remains for me, dear Strindberg, to thank you.

When shall we see each other again?

To-day, as yesterday, with all my heart,

PAUL GAUGUIN.

155.

TO ARSENE ALEXANDRE.[1]

Undated, Paris 10 February, 1895.

My dear Arsène,

First I must thank you for having replied to my appeal for the Séguin exhibition and for having understood it, lover of art as you are! Of course I am at your entire disposal as regards my neighbour's secrets (Polichinelle's secret as well).

---

[1] Arsène Alexandre, journalist and art critic, author of a biography *Paul Gauguin, sa vie et le sens de son oeuvre*, published by Bernheim Jeune & Co. in 1930.

1. Varnish of extra quality is nothing but a layer of resin. However white it is, it always reverts to its original colour which is yellow; moreover, by its very nature it has the fault of suppressing the air on the painting without having the merit of preventing the acids from decomposing the tones. Resin is an excellent conductor of everything. You know as I do that the varnish on the Rembrandts remains as fresh and grey as on the first day. What is it due to if not the varnish? White wax has none of these drawbacks, as we know from ancient pictures done in wax. My neighbour has experimented by applying wax thereon and has obtained the same result. Wax on a picture as on wood stops every kind of crack and deterioration.

For restoring pictures I describe a delicate operation which must be made by deft hands. First I want to explain the defects of restoring oil paintings. The colours are laid on the canvas with an agglomerative substance, either glue or oil. When they are old, and therefore their oil has evaporated, the perfectly dry colour is a hard but porous material like a plump body. It is beyond question that all the fresh oil will gradually be absorbed by the dry colour surrounding the defective part. Hence these yellow patches which grow larger every day. Make a test on a porous block of dry colour, Spanish White, for example. You will then see for yourself that oil is the enemy. I now describe a different process.

The holes must be filled with colour agglomerated by caseine glue, the only glue exempt from the influence of humidity, and only soluble by prolonged immersion in ammonia. To discover by this means the exact tone is not easy, I know, but it is easy to finish the process by a layer of oil colour very much scoured by a volatile essence such as mineral essence or benzine. The fleshy body disappears almost entirely and a hard substance remains.

Yours very sincerely,
PAUL GAUGUIN.

P.S.—Enclosed are two letters to be printed in the *Revue Blanche* of the 15th February and in the catalogue of my sale to be held on the 18th instant. I am sure they will interest you. This sale will herald my departure in case of success.

I am sure you will do all you can for the 18th without being asked.

Thanks in anticipation.

156.

TO STEPHANE MALLARMÉ.

Paris, 23 February, '95, Saturday.

Dear Mr. Mallarmé,

The sale has put nothing in my pocket.

In this moment of disappointment, the royal hand of Stéphane Mallarmé cordially extended gives delight and strength.

I do not by any means abandon hope of my intended departure. As the auction did not succeed, I hope to sell the pictures piecemeal.

I will come and see you one of these days, if you still hold your Tuesdays.

Yours very sincerely,
PAUL GAUGUIN.

157.

TO MAURICE DENIS.[1]

Undated, Paris, early March, 1895.

Dear Sir,

You have just written an admirable article on Séguin in the *Plume*. I might quarrel with you about certain details but this I refrain from doing as I am chiefly interested in artistic manifestations.

In conclusion, my sincere congratulations.

What prompts me to write you is the pleasure it gives me to see painters looking after their own business. I believe you wrote something in the *Revue Indépendante* a few years ago, but this was all, and it was not very much.

For some time, and especially since my design to bury myself in the South Sea Islands, I have been conscious of the obligation which rests on you young painters to write rationally on artistic subjects. This Séguin preface in short fills a long-felt want.

Soon I shall disappear, but I have good hope that the work

---

[1] Maurice Denis, born at Granville on 25th November, 1870, died in Paris on 13th November, 1943. Painter and writer on art, friend of Paul Sérusier, one of the founders of the Nabi group, he started with Georges Desvallières the Studios of Sacred Art, which had a considerable influence in the revival of modern religious painting.

begun will be completed. I can therefore sincerely congratulate you on your good intention. Go on all of you fighting with the brush as well as with the pen, and in my retreat I shall cherish this fervent hope.

Yours, etc.,

PAUL GAUGUIN.

158.

TO HIS WIFE.   Undated, Paris, March, 1895.

Dear Mette,

I have been expecting your letter for some time. I know what the newspapers have said about me. Even five years ago you believed in the accuracy of *figures* in spite of what I told you. This time it is a different matter.

I have been fighting a battle to raise the prices of my canvases and caused a rumour of my departure to circulate in order to give a rarity value to my pictures. Here is the true statement of account :

The sale[1] realised		23.640 francs
except for 1.370 francs of genuine sale, *everything was bought in* by me under borrowed names		
7% on 23.640 francs makes		1.654.80
hire of premises		150.—
transport		30.—
		1.834.80
	less	1.370.—
making a net loss of		464.80

Now let us have a little talk. It must be confessed that since my return any man in my place would have made melancholy reflections on life, the family, and everything else.

---

[1] The auction held at the Hôtel Drouot comprised 49 canvases, the greater part of which Gauguin re-sold shortly after. Before leaving his studio in the Rue Vercingétorix, he distributed the knick-knacks on the walls amongst his friends and bestowed all his wood engravings upon Madame Molard.

1. Your own words: "You must get out of your troubles yourself."

2. Written by the children: nothing.

3. I broke my ankle, which laid me up: not a word from my family.

4. A terribly long winter. I was all alone in lodgings nursing a chronic bronchitis to no avail; literally I cannot live without the sun.

In these circumstances and with the enemies my painting has raised up, I must take all sorts of precautions to keep going at all. At 47 years of age I do not want to fall into abject poverty and yet I am not far from it; if I am down nobody in the world would give me a hand; your own words, "you must get out of your troubles yourself" embody deep wisdom; I will cling to it.

By the way, as I am very well known at the Ministry of War, they communicated with me because they were disturbed by Emil's failure to present himself for enlistment. I told them that I knew preparations were being made in Denmark for that and that I expected any day to have papers to sign, etc.

You see how your negligence leads to trouble.

Meanwhile I am your husband,

PAUL GAUGUIN.
6, Rue Vercingétorix.

159.

TO WILLIAM MOLARD.   Albert Hotel,
Queen Street, Auckland,
end June, 1895.

My dear William, my dear Ida, my dear Judith,

I embrace you all and am writing you from here, Auckland, New Zealand, where I have been for 8 days, and for 8 days the Tahiti steamer has been expected but has not arrived. It is cold and I am bored, and am spending money to no purpose.

And how dirty I am; impossible to change my things owing to the uncertainty of the time of leaving, and to the luggage being in the Customs House. With the little English at my command I manage, but how hard and long it is.

And what food! However, I shall arrive one of these days.

By the way, inform my friends who have to come to Tahiti to go via America; it will be both cheaper and quicker. By this route it is always uncertain.

When my letter reaches you, you will probably be in Brittany, at the end of the holidays; I hope the three of you will be enjoying yourselves.

I do not propose to write four pages, I am on a voyage, which means in a lethargic state.

My dear William, my dear Ida, my dear Judith, I embrace you all.

Write me by next mail.

P. GAUGUIN.

160.

TO WILLIAM MOLARD.   Undated, Tahiti, July, 1895.

My dear friends,

Here I am at last and the mail leaves tomorrow : I hasten to write you to give you reassuring news of me. Arrived in good health. What a change here since I left ! Papeete, the capital of this Eden, Tahiti, is now lighted by electricity. The big lawn in front of the old garden of the King is spoilt by a roundabout, 25 centimes for a ride, a phonograph, etc.

My ears are deafened by all the gossip about politics, which are very embroiled. Chené, the General Commissioner, is here on a Government mission to settle the affairs of the revolting islands, and, diplomatically speaking, after a lot of nonsense, everything is at a standstill. So we must have troops and shooting or give way to the natives, who are encouraged by the English. However, all this hardly interests me. What is, for instance, a disaster for the trade of the Colony is a windfall for me, that is, the rate of exchange. Just think, they formerly gave me 125 Chilean francs for 100 French francs, whereas to-day they give me 200, which considerably increases my litle capital. Kindly tell Lévy[1] whenever he is sending

---

[1] Lévy, the picture dealer, who had told Gauguin: "You can leave for Oceania with an easy mind, we will not let you down. It is perhaps a matter of time, for your painting is not easy to swallow, but I will do what is required." In fact, he never sent him any money.

me money to send either English gold or any draft of the Crédit
Lyonnaise or the Comptoir d'Escompte.

Next month I shall be at La Dominique,[1] a little island of the
Marquisas, a delightful place where one can live almost for nothing
and where I shall meet no Europeans.

I shall live there like a lord with my little capital and my studio
properly arranged.

By next mail I will write at greater length.

Good health to all.

                                        P. GAUGUIN.

Let Morice know that I have received his letter, which gives
me great pleasure. It seems that *Noa-Noa* is going to be published.

Until further orders keep writing to me at Tahiti.

                            161.

TO WILLIAM MOLARD.   Undated, Tahiti, December, 1895.

My dear Molard,

At last I have word from you, the first since my departure, each
mail day I hurry to the post office, at first perplexed, and then despairing, I go away. For some time I have been on tenter-hooks and
in this state, of course, I cannot work.

I am at the end of my tether and really do not know what to do.

Of the 4.000 francs that is owing to me and which would keep
me for two years I have received nothing and at the rate things are
going, I am afraid I shall be penniless. So what can I do. Even
Baudonne, who is supposed to pay on the 20th July, gives no sign
of life. The more I advance in age and renown, the more I retreat in
a pecuniary sense. Do not forget the 800 francs from Talboum and
mention the matter to Morice, who is his friend, some time before
the due date so as not to be caught napping. Speaking of Morice I
see that *Noa-Noa* has tumbled down the sixth flight of stairs.

I see that Strindberg is back in France. She is still the country
where a foreigner finds most sympathy and where ideas are

---

[1] In reality he settled in the district of Pounoaouia, not far from Papeete,
and did not leave for La Dominique until September, 1901.

broadest I read an article on Strindberg in the *Mercure*, which is very good.

Enjoy yourselves on my Wednesdays with a thought for our old Thursdays.

Kisses for your women folk.

P. GAUGUIN, Tahiti.

I should have thought that Paco[1] would have written me and sent the guitar strings.

162.

TO CHARLES MORICE.   Undated, Tahiti, May, 1896.

My dear Morice,

I have a letter from Séguin, which reminds me that I ought to have written you long ago in reply to the only letter from you since our arrival in Tahiti. But I am laid up with a broken ankle which hurts excruciatingly; big sores have appeared and I cannot get rid of them. This robs me of all energy, of which I have more need than ever to cope with the other vexations. The vexations of a man of 50 who is to-day left without resources, thanks to his friends. I departed with a light heart, as I thought, but on every side my debtors have let me down and I have been unable to regain my liberty for lack of the little money required to set me up here. In your letter you say that I did not want you at the station, which is true. But this decision did not concern you alone, it applied to everybody. I wanted to avoid farewells at the station which would have unmanned and tired me. At the moment of leaving in the omnibus, which I had ordered, the Molards insisted on coming with me, as also did Pacot who had come specially to say good-bye to me at the house. They came then and that is all. Do not think that I slighted you on this occasion. You must know that this is not my habit so far as you are concerned. You say that I have not enough faith in your friendship for me, and that you hope to prove it one day. If I believed in it—but I believe also in your impossibility, I know your life and that you have not a moment to spare for anyone else,

---

[1] Francisco Durrieu de Madron, known as Paco Durrio (1876-1940), Spanish sculptor and ceramist, disciple of Gauguin, for whom he had a passionate admiration all his life.

in spite of all your good will. Séguin tells me that he heard *from you* that the book *Noa-Noa* was *sold in Brussels,* and it did not occur to you that this news coming from other than you would come as a severe disappointment, for you know the poverty in which I am living. Left in the lurch by Lévy and everybody. And if the book is sold, who has the proceeds? You know, moreover, that I left with Molard a power of attorney to represent me in any publishing negotiations. And if this is true (I can hardly believe it) in spite of appearances, how can this action be described? Is it an act of friendship on your part, you who owe me already? Believe me, I am on the verge of suicide (foolish act though it be) but probably inevitable; it is only a question of a few months—according to the replies I am awaiting, replies back with money. Your friend Talboum is due to pay me 800 francs in June I think, which is next month. I suspect he will not pay and will go on merrily drinking his morning coffee without any thought for the fate of his creditor. What matter the death of an artist! Think of all this, Morice, and remember that actions speak louder than words.

Meanwhile, very sorrowfully yours,
PAUL GAUGUIN.

163.

TO CHARLES MORICE.   Tahiti, about 15 January, 1897.

Fragment.

France has sent here a ship *Le Duguay Trouin,* in addition to 150 men from Nouméa, brought by *l'Aube,* warship belonging to that station. All this to subjugate the Windward Islands, alleged to be in revolt. When Tahiti was annexed, they refused to accept the annexation. Then one fine day, the Negro Lascascase, Governor of Tahiti, wanted to play pranks and cover himself with glory. The natives, who are both acute and intelligent, countermined his operations. Landing troops were received with rifle shots and driven back to their boats. Last year in 1895 the delegate Chené came to Tahiti, having promised the French Governor to put down the rebels by mere persuasion. This cost the Colony a hundred thousand francs. Chené retired completely discomfited by barbarian diplomacy. At present all soldiers that could be collected, plus Tahitian volunteers engaged here, are at Raietou. After an ultimatum sent on the 25th, hostilities commenced on the 1st January, 1897. Little has happened in a fortnight, as the natives can hide in the mountains for a long time. You could make a nice informative article (the idea strikes me as original) of an interview by P. Gauguin with a native before action . . . And if you manage to get such an article in a paper send me a few copies. I should like to show some of the nitwits around here that I have still a few kicks left in me . . . Speaking of the hospital, I have just tried to get in for treatment. The officials insulted me as much as they could, and after great exertion, in return for a payment of 5 francs a day, they handed, what do you think, an admission ticket marked " Native "! Needless to say that, although in great agony, I declined to go in and be put among soldiers and servants. Besides, here as in France, there is a section which regards me as a rebel, and, as everywhere, but here more than elsewhere, a man who is hard up is handled very roughly. Of course, I am only referring to Europeans in Papeete, because in my own corner the natives are always very good and very respectful to me. . . . .

PAUL GAUGUIN.

164.

TO WILLIAM MOLARD.   Tahiti, August, 1897.

My dear Molard,

I would have written you last month on receipt of your letter but (it is a big but) I was physically incapacitated from doing so. I was suffering from a double inflammation of the conjunctiva, from which I have not yet completely recovered. Alas, my health is worse than ever.

After experiencing a real improvement, the disease returned with fury over a very wide surface, I am at the present time prostrate twenty hours out of the twenty-four and have little sleep. I have not painted for two months. I have received no letter from Chaudet for 5 months and not a penny, all credit has been cut off, while I have debts amounting to 1,500 francs, and, in spite of austerity, I do not know how I am going to live. In France people owe me 2.700 francs, plus a balance of about 300 francs for pictures sold by

Vollard,[1] all exhibition accounts made up and purchases made by Daniel. I receive nothing, it is enough to drive one mad. By the way (without blaming you) Talboum must not be left in peace on the strength of his promises, for 800 francs is more than 6 months' living expenses. I have not his address, else I would have written him a stinging letter. Look here then, seriously. Either he gives you four notes of two hundred francs each at monthly intervals, or else he is a scamp who won't pay his debts—and stubbornly—you are waiting for the crisis of my anguish to pass. I confess to my shame that on receipt of a short letter from my wife announcing the bad news[2] my eyes were dry, and I have not answered. Why answer? The emotions I felt were those of anger, of rage, something like the delirium of the patient who is tortured and who clamours for fresh suffering.

Ever since my infancy misfortune has pursued me. Never any luck, never any joy. Everyone always against me, and I exclaim : God Almighty, if You exist, I charge You with injustice and spitefulness. Yes, on the news of my poor Aline's death I doubted everything, I gave a defiant laugh. What use are virtue, work, courage, intelligence ?

Crime alone is logical and rational.

Then I feel vitality waning, fierce anger stimulates no longer, and I give way to base thoughts: Ah, these long sleepless nights, how ageing they are ! It is to-day that I feel grief for Aline's death—the torpor has passed. And my disease gets the upper hand. Worry and distress which are of an essentially nervous nature have now got the better of my body and in the long run abundant peace of mind is the only cure.

But when shall I get it ?

Kindest regards to all,

PAUL   GAUGUIN.

Thanks for the Stockholm exhibition, although I consider it more solemn than productive.

---

[1] Ambroise Vollard, famous picture dealer and publisher.
[2] Mette had just informed her husband of their daughter Aline's death, of infectious pneumonia. Gauguin wrote shortly after to Monfreid: "This news made no impression on me, so long habituated to suffering: then, each day as reflection supervened, the wound deepened, and at this moment I am quite cast down." For this daughter, whom he adored, Gauguin had written *Copybook for Aline* in 1893.

Gauguin, painted wood sculpture   1890

It is a rendezvous of elegant sharpers fom all nations, varnished, painted, smiling. Besides, the King of Sweden is an amateur and protector of the Arts . . . His opinion carries weight. What do you think that a prim and shabby poet has to do with such a business. What I should have liked is an intelligent correspondent over there to show my canvases to customers and make them understand them.

165.

TO HIS WIFE. Undated.

Tahiti, August, 1897.

I am looking over the shoulders of a friend who is writing:
Madam,

I asked you that the children should write me on the 7th June, my birthday, " My dear Papa " and a signature. And you answered me : " You have no money, do not expect it."

I will not say, " God keep you," but, less incredibly, " May your conscience sleep to prevent you welcoming death as a deliverance."[1]

Your husband.

And this same friend writes me : " I have just lost my daughter I no longer love God. Like my mother, she was called Aline. We all live in our own way. Some love exalts even into the sepulchre. Others—I do not know. And her tomb is over there with flowers—it is only an illusion. Her tomb is here near me; my tears are her flowers; they are living things.

166.

TO CHARLES MORICE. Tahiti, November, 1897.
(Fragment).

It is probable that I shall not see the book[2] printed, my days being numbered. God has at last heard my beseeching voice,

---

[1] After receipt of this letter Mette Gauguin desisted from correspondence with her husband

[2] Charles Morice for long laid claim to the idea of *Noa-Noa*, but it seems pretty clear to-day that the first idea of this work belonged to the painter. In certain editions the prefatory pages; *Memory and Imagination*, the first chapter *Dreams* and the *Poems* belong to Charles Morice. In his Tahitian solicitude Gauguin re-wrote *Noa-Noa* as he was illustrating it. The manuscript published in facsimile under the editorship of Herr Meier-Graefe of Berlin, was offered by Daniel de Monfreid to the Musée du Louvre.

not for a change, but for total deliverance: my heart, always beating too fast, buffeted by reiterated shocks, has become very diseased. And this disease makes me cough and spit blood every day. The body resists, but it is bound to collapse. And this would be better than my killing myself, to which I was being driven by the lack of food and of the means to procure it . . .

P.S.—If I can find the strength, I will re-copy and send you an essay I have composed recently (I have not painted for six months) on Art, the Catholic Church and the modern spirit.

It is perhaps the best expression I have ever given to my philosophical point of view.

I remember what you said about Renan in your book. Here is what I think of him.

Ernest Renan lost his faith and confessed as much. Was this confession a deliberate excuse for reaching the goal of his ambition, the Academy? putting his conspicuous talents at the service of himself, of his secular ambition.

It was his great learning, it seems, that prevented him from believing any longer in the Church, so he left it—the stamp of the seminary being obliterated forever. This we are bound to believe, for did he not write the *Life of Jesus*? Which provoked a scandal, a cry of indignation from the whole Catholic world, and Pio Nono, so arbitrary was he, at first would not believe it.

If we examine this so-called rebellion, we find it to be no more than a boyish prank, very much on a par with modern beliefs, and in this sense Leo XIII would have approved it. The fabulous garments in which the Church had arrayed Jesus had made the stupid multitude very lukewarm towards him, and the man Jesus of Renan, a new and illogical figure, was bound to impart to the faithful a fresh outburst of faith without in any way diminishing the prestige of the Church.

And all men reaching their last stage of perfectibility through wisdom would become Buddhists. And all the texts of the Gospel, if properly and not literally understood, portray Jesus, together with his Apostles, as children of God—of course, in the spiritual and not in the material or literal sense. Only the elect comprehend this, whereas the multitude want something different, and Renan deliberately provided them with it. This the Church realized later on and she forgave him his prank. I am quite convinced that she powerfully assisted Ernest Renan *to* become what he in fact became.

"See how we bring them up!" she might say. "Here is another one who has left the fold."

Whereas a Renan who would have placed his learning, his commanding intelligence, his talents, at the service of a great cause, the true cause of God, that is to say, wisdom and the good of mankind, this Renan became a secular apostle, unincumbered by priestly robes, fighting the Church as one acquainted with her iniquities and her life (it was he who told her : "In my searching examination of the texts I lost my faith," in the mouth of a man like Renan, this meant *faith in the Church*, since the texts interpreted by those who understand can only inspire faith in divine wisdom), this Renan, taking Jesus himself as pattern, could have been a man dangerous to the Church. Now the Church never forgives.

And Renan would have lived a martyr, perhaps in obscurity, but Renan preferred worldly life, the pleasures of an honest citizen, remaining, in spite of all, an *obedient seminarist*.

A sceptic? Perhaps. A rebel? No.

And . . . Without being recreant to himself, he who becomes a sceptic cannot submit, cannot tacitly make common cause with imposture. It is a pity.   .   .   .   .

167.

TO WILLIAM MOLARD.   Tahiti, March, 1898.

My dear **Molard,**

I thank you for your New Year's wishes, in spite of the scanty hope of seeing my position improve, a position which deteriorates more and more, thanks to the ill will, I would even say the bad faith of my debtors. It must be confessed that the fate allotted by society to me as an artist is cruel, Leclercq will no longer sell my canvases in Norway, and in this connection I know nothing of the result of the Exhibition in Sweden. I know full well it is nil in the pecuniary sense, but as to any moral effect you do not breathe a word. Don't mention Talboum to me again, I have resigned myself to my loss.

I see according to your letter that you go on working bravely; will our good Roinard[1] succeed with his play, at least will he

---

[1] F. R. Roinard, styled Napoleon Roinard, eccentric poet and man of letters, Bohemian companion of Jehan Rictus and Julien Leclercq.

succeed in getting it played with his system of subscriptions which I read about in the *Mercure*? If I were in Paris, I believe I could have helped him with his orchestra, thanks to Schnecklud the violoncello player, and then with the choir to which he belonged. But as you say one can manage with a piano and a harmonium.

I smiled at your faith in the Captain's message and still more at the treatment of Schuffenecker, who has tried every kind of medicine, and who in the last resort would undergo treatment at Charenton. He must be annoyed by my silence, but I confess it is impossible for me to reply to the few silly letters he has sent me, letters in which he speaks of nothing but his troubles with money and art, which he finds so barren and so ungrateful. Whereas I would have been so happy, he says, if I had not been so wayward and improvident.

By mere chance, as I do not read the newspapers, I heard that Strindberg had left in a balloon for the North Pole, and that no news had been received from the three explorers for three months. I hope at all events that he will return without any bones broken.

Do not lose sight of the fact, my dear Molard, in spite of your preoccupations, that I left you a special power of attorney for the publication of *Noa-Noa*, which is always hanging fire with Morice. Keep this in mind, as otherwise, with this rascal the money will slip through his fingers.

Give my best wishes to Ida and all my friends.

Cordially yours,

PAUL GAUGUIN.

168.

TO DR. GOUZER.[1]   Tahiti, 15 March, 1898.

Dear Doctor,

I was already far away when your letter arrived. It was very good of you to think of writing, to remind me of some pleasant moments passed on board the *Duguay-Trouin*, and I would have

---

[1] Doctor on board the *Duguay-Trouin*, Gouzer made the painter's acquaintance during a call at Tahiti. Appreciating the artist, he bought a canvas from him for one hundred francs, and Gauguin gratefully offered him two drawings.

liked to reply sooner, but not having your address I was unable to do so.

Daniel, to whom I write regularly every month, has just repaired this omission. Is not Daniel a fine fellow as well as a real artist? Since I have known him I have never found anything but loyalty and affectionate devotion. I am glad that you have not only made his acquaintance, but also entered into permanent relationship with a man like Daniel. When one lives long in the same narrow circle—however elevated it may be—one often develops false and one-sided ideas about people, and it is good sometimes to refresh oneself by contact with a different type of mind.

Or else, like me, to live alone in silence—and this is to suffer much. Fortunately, I am rapidly breaking up, and I can see at no distant date the end for which I long so ardently at this moment so as not to be forced to anticipate it—my state might even improve —constraining me to be patient, and my wish is not to abandon my post.

For this reason I cannot contemplate returning to France, as you advise me, even if I had the money for the journey. Every day—my last important works testify to it—I perceive that I have not said everything about Tahiti, that there is much more to say, whereas in France, given my present aversion, my brain would perhaps become sterile; the cold shatters me physically as well as morally, everything grows ugly in my eyes.

It is true that with me on the spot, the struggle would be easier from a propagandist point of view, and that I could do more commercial painting; all of them considerations that I cannot contemplate without horror and revulsion. It would be unworthy of me and of the career that I have followed, not unworthily, I hope.

It would be a bad end to such a good start. But I should live, you say. Why live at the expense of losing the reasons for living?

No, it is altogether out of the question.

Moreover, the martyr is often necessary to every revolution— my work considered as an immediate and pictorial result, has little significance compared with its final and moral result: the emancipation of painting henceforth of all impediments, of this accursed

tissue woven by the schools, the academies, and specially the mediocrities.

Look what may be dared to-day compared with the timidity
of ten years ago. Practical jokers may take advantage of it as they
like; what matters—there are others, and a whole constellation of
signatures at this very moment. My name may and must disappear,
what matters.

Shall we meet again? I wonder. Meanwhile,

Yours sincerely,
PAUL GAUGUIN.

169.

TO AN UNKNOWN CORRESPONDENT.

Tahiti, February, 1899.
(A fragment)

I read very few books now, however, when I do read, without
fear of ill effects, I read more than the cover of the book, more
than the title of the chapter, more than all the lines. I read between
the lines.

I would not dream of shielding Barjau. Believe me, I have
done no more than pass the time of day to this gentleman. It is
the same with him as with many others.

I know how Morice progresses and *how he works*. This
wretched trade of " earning one's daily bread."

I know it too well and I do not blame him, but I regret it.
This terrible social order, which elevates pigmies to the detriment
of great men, but we must submit to it, and it is our calvary. But
there may be a few who pause on the road if their deserved success
should become easy.

To end up, we are in agreement about Morice. The book
Noa-Noa is another matter. I beg of you to believe that I have a
modicum of the experience and instinct of the civilized, savage
though I be. The narrator need not disappear behind the poet. A
book is what it is . . . incomplete—good . . . however—if by a few
stories one says all that one has to say or hint at, it is much. Verses
are expected from Morice, I know, but if there should be many in
this book, all the simplicity of the narrator would disappear and

the flavour of *Noa-Noa* would lose its origin. Then do not be afraid of those who are waiting jealously and not those who wait as friends saying Yes, Morice has talent, but he lacks the creative spirit and without Gauguin he would not have any ideas; and I am sure that this will be said if there are many. Whereas few put things in their proper place and announce the fine sequence that you know is all ready in his papers..

The publication of his volume immediately after being well introduced by *Noa-Noa* would be worth much more.

I have made a great point of all this because I am absolutely sure I am right. Do not believe for a second that it is a question of self-esteem which prompts me, to the point that if Morice wants to publish the poems inspired by *Noa-Noa* without the recitals or any collaboration, I give him full permission, happy to make this sacrifice for my friend.

Let us say together to the little manuscript.

Sleep, 'tis now night.

Believe me, Madam,

Yours sincerely,
PAUL GAUGUIN.

170.

TO ANDRE FONTAINAS. Tahiti, March, 1899.

Un grand sommeil noir
Tombe sur ma vie
Dormez, tout espoir
Dormez, toute envie.
VERLAINE.

Mercure de France, January number, two interesting articles on Rembrandt. Vollard Gallery. The latter refers to me: despite your reluctance, you have tried to study the art or rather the work of an artist who does not move you, and to discuss him with fairness. A rare thing in ordinary criticism.

I have always held that it was a painter's duty never to reply to criticism, however harmful—specially that, or however laudatory, which is often inspired by friendship.

Without departing from my usual reserve, I am smitten with a mad longing to write you, a caprice if you will—and, as with all passions, something difficult to resist. It is by no means a reply, because it is personal, but a simple discussion of art, which your article has invited, nay, prompted.

Well, we painter chaps, those of us condemned to poverty, accept the worries of material existence without complaining, but we suffer from them in so far as they are an impediment to work. What an amount of time is lost in seeking our daily bread, in sordid labourer's tasks, defective studios and a thousand other obstacles. Hence so many discouragements, with resulting impotence, storms and rages. All considerations which must readily occur to you, and to which I refer only to convince both of us that you are right to point out all the defects. Violence, monotony of tones, arbitrary colours, etc. Yes, all this must and does exist. Sometimes, however, deliberately, these repetitions of tones, monotonous harmonies, in the musical sense of colour, do they not bear an analogy to those Eastern recitatives, chanted by shrill voices, accompanied by vibrant notes which are contiguous to and enrich them by opposition, Beethoven makes frequent use of them (if I understand him aright)—in the Pathetic Sonata, for example. Delocroix with his repeated harmonies of chestnut and dull violets, a sombre cloak suggesting the drama. You often go to the Louvre: think of what I say, look closely at Cimabue. Think also of the musical part which colour will henceforth play in modern painting. Colour which is vibration the same as music is, reaches to what is most general and therefore vaguest in nature: its interior force.

Hear, near my hut, in complete silence, I dream of violent harmonies in the natural scents which intoxicate me.

A delight distilled from some indescribable sacred horror which I glimpse of far off things. The odour of an antique joy which I am breathing in the present. Animal shapes of a statuesque rigidity: indescribably antique, august, and religious in the rhythm of their gesture, in their singular immobility. In the dreaming eyes is the overcast surface of an unfathomable enigma.

And comes the night when all things are at rest. My eyes close in order to see without comprehending the dream in the infinite space stretching out before me, and I have the sensation of the melancholy progress of my hopes.

Praising certain pictures that I regarded as unimportant, you exclaim—ah! if Gauguin were always like that. But I do not want to be always like that.

In the large panel that Gauguin exhibited, there is nothing that reveals to us the meaning of the allegory. Well, my dream cannot be apprehended, it requires no allegory; being a musical poem, it needs no libretto (quotation from Mallarmé). " Accordingly immaterial and superlative, the essential quality of a work consists precisely in what is not expressed: what follows implicitly is line without colours or words, it is not materially constituted of them."

Hear also Mallarmé in front of my Tahitian pictures: " It is extraordinary that so much mystery can be put into so much splendour."

Returning to the panel: the idol is there not as a literary explanation, but as a statue, less statue perhaps than the animal shapes; less animal, too, embodying my dream, in front of my hut with nature entire, reigning in our primitive soul, imaginary consolation for our sufferings in what they suggest of the hazy and incomprehensible before the mystery of our origin and our future.

And all this is chanting mournfully in my soul and my surroundings, as I paint and dream at the same time, without apprehensible allegory in my reach—perhaps due to want of literary education.

On awakening, my dream ended, I say to myself: whence come we, what are we, where are we going? A reflection which is no part of the canvas, put in language spoken quite earnestly on the wall which frames not a title, but a signature.

You see I have failed to understand the value of words—abstract or concrete—in the dictionary, I cannot grasp them any better in painting. I have tried in suggestive ornament to translate my dream without any resort to literary methods, with all the simplicity possible of my craft, a difficult task. Accuse me if you like of having failed in this, but not of having attempted it, advising me to change my aim and toil after other ideas, already admitted and consecrated. Puvis de Chavannes is the supreme example of this. To be sure, Puvis overwhelms me with his talent and the experience that I lack; I admire him all the more and as much as you but for different reasons. (Do not be offended as you begin to go into this matter more deeply.) Each has his age.

The State does right in not commissioning me to decorate any public building, as such decoration would clash with the ideas of the majority, and I should have done wrong in accepting such a commission with no alternative but to cheat or to do a violence to my own feelings.

At my exhibition at Durand-Ruel's a young man asked Degas to explain my pictures, as he did not understand them. Degas smiled and told him one of La Fontaine's Fables—"Don't you see," he said, " Gauguin is the lean wolf without a collar."

Here we have a struggle lasting fifteen years to emancipate us from the School, and all the mass of prescriptions, without which it is supposed there can be no health, no honour, and no money. Drawing, colour, composition and sincerity anterior to nature? How do I know? Only yesterday some mathematician imposed on us immutable lights and colours.

The danger is past. Yes, we are free, and yet I glimpse a danger on the horizon; I should like to discuss it with you. This long and tedious letter is written practically for this purpose. The serious criticism of to-day, however full of good intentions and well informed tends to impose on us a method of thinking and of dreaming, and this would be a fresh servitude. Preoccupied with what concerns it, its special domain, i.e., literature, it loses sight of what concerns us, i.e., painting. If such were the case, I would quote proudly Mallarmé's dictum.

A critic: a gentleman who meddles with what does not concern him.

In his memory, may I offer you these few features sketched in a moment, vague remembrance of a loved pleasant face looking intently into the shadows—not a present, but an appeal to the indulgence which I need for my madness and my savagery.

Yours sincerely,
PAUL GAUGUIN.

171.

TO MAURICE DENIS.   Undated, Tahiti, June, 1899.
Sir,

In reply to your letter, I regret it is not in my power to answer Yes. To be sure, it would be interesting to see, after an interval of 10 years, a gathering of the artists who frequented the Café

Volpini and with them the young fellows I admire, but my personality of ten years ago is of no interest to-day. At that time I wanted to dare everything, to liberate, as it were, the new generation, and then labour to improve my talents. The first part of my programme has borne fruit, to-day you are free to dare everything, and, what is more, nobody is astonished.

The second part, alas, has been less fortunate. Now I am an old fogey, the pupil of many in your exhibition; *in my absence,* this would become far too obvious. Much has been written on this subject and everybody knows that I have actually pillaged my master, Emilc Bernard, so that no painting or carving is left to him. He has had this printed. Do not believe that the thirty or so canvases that I gave him and that he sold to Vollard were mine? They are a frightful plagiarism of Bernard's.

There is another reason, which happens to be the true one.

My work is finished; my friend Daniel, in an effort to relieve my poverty a little, has exhibited the attempts I have been able to make these last three years, but without any result in money.

Being very ill and obliged to earn a little bread by doing work which is anything but intellectual, I no longer paint, except Sundays and holidays. I am not therefore in a position to supply you with recent specimens, which, moreover, could not be properly framed, and would not be sufficiently in the movement. My Papuan art would have no meaning by the side of the symbolists, the idealists; I am sure that your exhibition will be very successful. Nearly all of you having means, a numerous clientèle and powerful friends, it would be astonishing if each of you could not reap the legitimate fruit of your talent and your discoveries. I fear you may be exposed to a little ridicule over the Rosicrucians, athough this may be a wonderful advertisement, believing that Art has no business in this house of Peladan[1].

Yours sincerely,

PAUL GAUGUIN.

[1] Joseph-Aimé Peladan changed his Christian names for that of Josephin, and later called himself Sar Peladan. Born at Lyons in 1858, he died in Paris in 1928. Reviver of the Rosicrucian movement, founded in 1888 by Stanislas de Guata, and author of the *Vice suprême.*

172.

TO ANDRE FONTAINAS.　　　　　　　　Tahiti, August, 1899.

Dear Sir,

I think that whatever misunderstanding might have existed between us has now been cleared up; I can hardly recall the terms of my letter.

However, what really prompted me to write you, as far as I can remember, could not for a single moment be held as an intention to classify you as a professional critic—one of those for whom criticism is often a form of blackmail. Good God, no; it was not on this account that I wrote you, as I write only to those I esteem. And if I said (see my letter) critics, that is, people who meddle in what does not concern them, it was to designate the whole tribe, which in every age, according to the reigning taste, says to the painters, " You shall think on these lines, else you will be at our mercy."

With respect to this tribe, I see from your letter that you have pluckily cast yourself overboard so as not to leave one of your colleagues enslaved to a party. Certainly, your intention was very laudable and I admire it, but I do not quite believe that admiration any more than hate has a great influence, inasmuch as the idiotic readers are not worth the effort of bothering about them. It would then be for the artists !

If you praise or deprecate Falguière[1], what difference does it make to his Balzac? As for me they said that my art is coarse, Papuan art. I do not know whether they were right and were therefore justified in saying so; what does it matter, as I could not change overnight either for the better or the worse. My much more frightful work, critically speaking, classes me either as a horror or as a glory. Some friends say that I have a strong and virile soul, while others, above all the younger ones, suffer severely from these base criticisms and sometimes succumb. I am sorry for them. Puvis de Chavannes remarked to me one day, quite flabbergasted by reading an adverse criticism, " But cannot they understand? The picture is very simple." (It was his *Poor Fishermen*.) I answered,

" And as to the others he will speak to them in parables, so that seeing they see not and hearing, they hear not."

---

[1] Alexandre Falguière, French sculptor (1831-1900).

You give me lively pleasure in confessing that you had wrongly believed that my compositions, like those of Puvis de Chavannes, originated from an idea, à priori, abstract, which I sought to vivify by plastic representation . . . and that my letter enlightened you a little.

Not wrongly, since I act conscientiously according to my intellectual nature. I act a little like the Bible, of which the doctrines (particularly regarding the Christ) are expressed in symbolical form presenting a double aspect; a form which first materialises the pure Idea to render it more palpable, affecting the guise of supernaturalism; which is the literal, superficial, allegorical and mysterious meaning of a parable; and then the second aspect which gives its spirit. And this is the meaning, no longer allegorical but figurative and explicit of that parable.

Having no other means of explaining my art than by my pictures, I find myself misunderstood up to the present time; and A. Delaroche, in a remarkable article entitled " From an aesthetic point of view," is the only writer who seems to have understood me in this description of one of my pictures:

" In a circus of strange colours, whether the waves be of diabolic or divine brewing one cannot tell—mysterious water spouts from the tainted lips of the Unknown."

But a truce to talk about myself, which I find very boring.

Of course I read you, as I am on the free list of the *Mercure*, owing to my extreme poverty, and I very much enjoy it, for I am a great reader of literature, not because it instructs me—my brain is refractory to instruction; but because in my solitude (O beata solitudo ! O sola beatutudo; say Saint Bernard) reading puts me into communication with others without mingling with the crowd, of which I have always been afraid. It is one of the blessings of my solitude. Ah, Mr. Fontainas, if instead of criticism under the heading of *Modern Art* you would sometimes write criticism under the title: Blessings of Solitude. . . we should then understand each other perfectly—or at least I would understand you better, for I am a reader and fond of good literature.

Just think of it, a dozen years ago I made a special journey to Saint Quentin to look at the works of La Tour all together seeing him badly hung in the Louvre. I guessed he looked quite different at Saint Quentin. In the Louvre I do not know why I put him beside Gainsborough. He is nothing of the sort looked at in the proper setting. La Tour is thoroughly French and a gentleman, for if there is one quality that I esteem in painting it is that. Of course I do not forget the distinction of the modelling.

It is not the heavy sword of a Bayard but rather the rapier of a marquess, not the club of a Michelangelo, but the stiletto of La Tour. The lines are as pure as Raphael's; the composition of the curves always harmonious and significant.

I had almost forgotten it until the *Mercure* came to hand to revive a pleasant memory, and also allow me to share in your feelings in front of the portrait of the *Singer*. In your welcome letter you recall names that are dear to me: Degas, Manet, for whom my admiration is unbounded. I also see again this fine portrait of Samary[1] which I saw formerly at the Fine Arts Exhibition of Portraits of the Century.

In this connection I may tell you a little story. At the time of that exhibition I was calling on an enemy of Manet, Renoir and the Impressionists; and this person was horrified. To distract his attention I showed him a large portrait: *Father and mother in a dining-room*. The signature was so small as to be invisible. " That's something like a painting," he exclaimed. " But that is by Manet himself." He was furious, and since that day we have been irreconcilable enemies.

So there are abundant reasons why I should want other articles from you by way of an amelioration of my solitude.

Excuse my symbols, parables and other futilities, and believe me,

Yours, etc.,
PAUL GAUGUIN.

173.

TO EMMANUEL BIBESCO.[2]   Undated, Tahiti, July, 1900.

Dear Sir,

First I fear that your Ingres sheets of paper won't be of much use. I am very exacting in the matter of paper. Then this specification of size intimidates me so that I can scarcely begin.

---

[1] Portrait of *Jeanne Samary* by Renoir.
[2] Emmanuel Bibesco, amateur in painting, who in March, 1900, suggested to Daniel de Monfreid to replace the dealer Vollard. He asked for 24 canvases a year to fetch 200 to 250 francs each.

Now every artist (if you regard me as such and not as a mere mechanism) can only do well what he feels, and what does size matter! I have made experiments of every kind in my life and in Brittany: I love experimenting; but if this picture must be a water-colour or a pastel, well, I lose all interest in it; you would be the loser as well, as it would be a dull thing to exhibit. Every amateur has his own taste: one like impressive work, another work sweet as sugar. I have on hand at this moment a series of experiments in drawing which has fairly pleased me, and of which I send you a tiny specimen; thick ink is used instead of pencil, that is all. You mention painted flowers, I do not really know which, despite the small number of them I have done: and this is owing to the fact (which you have no doubt noticed) of my not being a painter according to nature—to-day less than before. With me everything happens in my wild imagination. And when I am tired of drawing figures (my predilection) I begin on still life which I finish, more-over, without a model. Then this is not really the country of flowers. And you add (which seems contradictory) you will take everything that I do. Please be more explicit. Do you mean only flowers, or figures and landscapes. With delays of five months between sending a letter and receiving a reply we may go on discussing things for two years without reaching any result.

If you insist on questions of price " you say " it is because my painting is so different from others that nobody wants it. The dictum is hard it if is not a little exaggerated. I am a little sceptical about the matter. I have seen Claude Monets sold in 1875 at 30 francs each and I myself bought a Renoir for 30 francs. I have also had a collection of all the impressionists which I bought at a very low price. It is in Denmark at my brother-in-law's, the famous Brandès, who won't let go of it at any price. A dozen Cézannes among them.

And when I was in Paris I sold my own pictures from 2.000 francs to 500 francs the lowest. No, the truth is that it is the picture dealer who makes prices when he goes to work the right way. When he is himself convinced and especially when the painting is good. *Good painting always fetches its price.*

Then I have received a letter from Maurice Denis, who is very well informed on what goes on in Paris. He tells me that Degas and Rouart argue about my pictures and that in the auction room my pictures fetch a pretty good price. So much for your suggestion that nobody wants my work, a cold douch even for the man most hardened to every kind of discouragement.

Besides, I don't want to be mixed up in these things at all, and am in course of so arranging my life as to have less and less to do with painting, retiring as they say from the scene to do a little writing in Tahiti varied with a little work on my allotment. The proceeds remaining from my pictures in store in Paris will go to supplement my daily black bread. Next month I shall be sending by someone who is proceeding to France about 275 proofs of wood-cuts. 25 or 30 numbered proofs are pulled from each block and then the blocks are destroyed. Moreover, half have been used twice and only I can pull the proofs in this manner. I will give Daniel instructions. This ought to be a good business for a dealer owing to the limited edition. I would want 2.500 for the lot or 4.000 piece-meal, half in cash and the balance in three months.

Coming to the question of prices. The last prices you paid Daniel were really a surprise if not a misunderstanding. And if I had been there or informed I would have bluntly refused prices less than a half of those of ten years ago. They cannot therefore be regarded as a precedent. But Daniel thought he was acting for the best. I thought therefore that he had done well and that I could do no more than congratulate him. For people must be made of very superior clay indeed for no misunderstanding ever to arise between them.

And in spite of the fact that nobody wants my painting because it is different from that of others. What a strange and mad public it is that exacts from the painter the utmost originality and then only accepts him when he is like the others! By the way, I am like those who imitate me. And in spite of this you are still anxious to do business with me. And it is not convenient *at this distance*. And you inquire with whom you must fix up prices? You need no telling that if I were interested as a man of business, I would have earned much money by a little dexterity, exploiting the Brittany vein and similar things which deaden talent. But I should not thus have become what I am and what I want to continue to be: a great artist. Which is to tell you that in your dealings with me you must rely upon my word. I accept the low price: 200 francs on an average for all kinds of canvases which I am in the habit of making

Gauguin   Self portrait
Pencil drawing executed in the last years of the artist's life
(Mmle. Annie Joly-Segalen)

to a maximum of 25 a year. You are to send me at your cost canvases and colours (details from Daniel) then for drawings an average of 30 francs each, whatever size and whether water-colours or not. The few little drawings that Van Gogh sold for me at Goupil's brought an average of 60 francs. And the lowest price for paintings was 300 francs. Here then is my formal proposal. Being able to assure you, of which my loyal word as artist is the guarantee, that I will send you only Art and not mere merchandise done to earn money. Otherwise, there is no point in discussing the matter further.

I have always said—Van Gogh used to think so also—that a dealer could make much money with my pictures because (1) I am 51-years-old with one of the greatest reputations in France and abroad. And coming to painting very late, there have been very few pictures from my brush, the greater number of which are located in Denmark and in Sweden. Consequently, there is not in my case to be feared, as with the others, such an avalanche of pictures that they must be continually bought in. Even if my wife does keep the proceeds when she sells a picture, I sold long ago everything I did in Denmark. And from that quarter nothing comes to Paris. Thus for a dealer it is only a question of will and patience and not of large capital outlay as for Claude Monet. I reckon 300 canvases as the maximum number since I began to paint, of which one hundred do not count, being the work of a beginner. Of the balance fifty can be located abroad and a few in France with private persons who would not part with them. Thus the number left is very small. And moreover there is this to be considered that the price of 200 francs is the price of a beginner and not of a man who has a well established reputation. I think I have now replied fully to your letter.

Yours,
PAUL GAUGUIN.

174.

TO CHARLES MORICE. Tahiti, July, 1901.

My dear Morice,

After a long silence, a few words from me.

I confess that the publication of *Noa-Noa* at quite the wrong time has no interest for me to-day. Why send me a hundred copies—

here they become waste paper. I wrote you previously that Dela-grave, the son, would take the responsibiltiy of having it published with profits.

Another thing, and this is very important: I refer to the pur-chase of the big picture; but is not this one of your usual worked up enthusiasms which end in disappointment; it is difficult to find a Maecenas to-day.

Of course, the youth of to-day who are profiting owe all this to me.

They have plenty of talent; much more than I, who had not, like them, every facility for learning and working. But perhaps without me they would not exist; without me would the world accept them?

I am laid up to-day; beaten by poverty and especially the disease of a premature old age. That I shall have some respite to finish my work I dare not hope: in any event I am making a final effort by going next month to settle in Fatu-iva, a still almost cannibalistic island of the Marquisas. I believe that there, in savage surroundings, complete solitude will revive in me, before I die, a last spark of enthusiasm which will kindle my imagination and form the culminating point of my talent.

This big canvas so far as execution is concerned is very im-perfect; it was done in a month without any preparation and pre-liminary study; I wanted to die and in this state of despair I painted it at one go. I was in a hurry to sign it and then I took a large dose of arsenic. Too much probably; excruciating pangs but not death and since that time all my ramshackle frame which stood the shock has been aching.

Perhaps what this picture lacks in poise may be compensated by something inexplicable to him who has not suffered to the utmost and who does not know the author's state of mind.

Fontainas, who has always been very well meaning towards me, reproaches me for being unable to make my ideas understood, the abstract title being by no means reflected in concrete forms on the canvas, etc., and he quotes Puvis de Chavannes, always com-prehensible and knowing how to expound his ideas.

Puvis explains his idea, yes, but he does not paint it. He is

Greek whereas I am a savage, a wolf in the woods without a collar. Puvis will call a picture *Purity* and to explain it will paint a young virgin with a lily in her hand—a hackneyed symbol, but which is understood by all. Gauguin under the title *Purity* will paint a landscape with limpid streams; no taint of civilized man, perhaps an individual.

Without going into details there is a whole world between Puvis and me. Puvis as painter is a scholar and not a man of letters, while I myself am not a scholar but perhaps a man of letters.

Why, when they gather in front of a picture, will the critic seek for points of comparison with old ideas and other authors. Not finding there what he expected, he fails to understand and remains unmoved. Emotion first! understanding afterwards.

In this big picture:

Whither are we going?
Near the death of an old woman.
A strange stupid bird concludes.
What are we?

Day-to-day existence. The man of instinct wonders what all this means.

Whence come we?

Spring.
Child.
Common life.

The bird concludes the poem by comparing the inferior being with the intelligent being in this great whole which is the problem indicated by the title.

Behind a tree are two sinister figures, shrouded in garments of sombre colour, recording near the tree of science their note of anguish caused by this science itself, in comparison with the simple beings in a virgin nature, which might be the human idea of paradise, allowing everybody the happiness of living.

Explanatory attributes—known symbols would congeal the canvas into a melancholy reality, and the problem indicated would no longer be a poem.

In a few words I explain the picture to you. Few are required by a man of your intelligence. But for the public, why should my brush, free from all constraint, be obliged to open everybody's eyes.

Are the forms rudimentary ? They have to be.

Is the execution thereof far too simple ? It has to be.

Many people say that I cannot draw because I draw particular shapes. When will they understand that execution, drawing and colour (style) must harmonise with the poem ? My nudes are chaste without clothes. To what can this be due if not to certain shapes and colours which are remote from reality ?

To facilitate your subscription, I give you some names that you do not know and who are admirers of my works. The first is a multi-millionaire :

Fayet, curator of the Béziers Museum.

Bibesco, the son.

Revue Blanche, a whole group, Nathanson, Sérusier, Maurice Denis, who has many connections.

Roussel, whose doctor father is rich.

Leclanché, address from Portier.

Funny enough, Thaulow, the Norwegian painter and my ex-brother-in-law.

Rip-Roney, who has many connections.

I do not think we need stick out for the price of 10.000 francs which seems to me enormous for a living painter. It is above all the moral effect for the future that should be important.

If therefore no more than 5.000 francs can be raised, I think this would be sufficient.

You do not tell me in your letter the state of your business, your hopes or the health of your family.

> Yours,
> PAUL GAUGUIN.

When writing me and especially when sending money consult Vollard, who knows how to get money to me at the Marquisas. Perhaps it would be well to write to Eva Brandès, Editor of the newspaper *Politiken,* Copenhagen, and who is the critic's brother And in Denmark there are some amateurs of my pictures.

Write nothing to my wife.

175.

TO WILLIAM MOLARD.   [1]Atuana, 16 March, 1902.

My dear Molard,

I have only just received your letter dated October, in which you mention Leclercq is ill and strangely enough *last* month I received a letter announcing his death, which shows you the disorder in the stupid machine they call colonial administration.

As regards the Bauchy business, 300 francs, I consider you have been prudent to excess; I should have thought Vollard's receipt would have covered you for ever. Vollard will send me the money one of these days, if he has not already done so, but I have not yet received any intimation. You mention the despatch of canvases to Slévinski[2] at Pouldu, which amazes me, and I should like you to ascertain through your sources of information the meaning of this. If needs be, write to Slévinski, who is a perfect gentleman. But with all my canvases, which have been on tow, as it were, since I have been travelling, and then Chaudet's dirty trick of stealing from me, I have always some sharp practice to fear.

I see that you bid fair to make a reputation in music, which delights me even more than Judith's reception on the Champs de Mars.[3] " The infatuated *bloc* tells me nothing worth while."

In telling you that it lacked a plan did Colonne mean to tell you that it lacked flights ? People like that, I know, but you will perhaps say that in matters musical I am a Philistine; it is true, I always had a mania to carry over painting to music, which incapable of being understood scientifically becomes a little intelligible to me through the relations in which I place the two arts.

Kindest regards to all your circle, including the painteress of the Champs de Mars.

PAUL GAUGUIN.

1 During the summer of 1901, Gauguin sold his little Pounoaouia property in Tahiti in order to settle in La Dominique (Hive-Oa), Marquisas Islands.

2 Artist of Polish origin, who stayed in the Spring of 1894 in a villa at Pouldu, where he entertained Gauguin for some weeks.

3 Judith Arlberg, Molard's step-daughter, was exhibiting at the Independent's Gallery, then located in the Grande Serre de l'Alma, in the Cours la Reine.

176.

TO ANDRE FONTAINAS.   Atuana, September, 1902.

Dear Mr. Fontainas,

I send you this little manuscript, written in haste, with the sole object that, having read it (and approving it), you would get the *Mercure de France* to publish it for me.[1]

I do not apply directly to the *Mercure* for two reasons.

The first is that you are its art critic and that you might thereby impute to me an ill-will which does not exist.

The second is that the *Mercure* is sent me gratuitously. Being poor, silence might be the better course for me.

What I have written has no literary pretensions but expresses a deep conviction which I am anxious to make known. From some few lines written you previously to which you were good enough to reply, at the same time sending me your fine book, I have already hinted at the nature of my ideas on this subject.

Do not be surprised if to-day I return to the subject, besides I know—your love of beauty preserves you from it—that you are above these paltry things. If my manuscript is not published, I should be grateful if you would send it to my friend, G. Daniel, artist, Domaine de St. Clement, via Villefranche de Conflent, Eastern Pyrenees.

" Although Gauguin's drawing reminds one a little of Van Gogh's . . ."

As a matter of information, do you mind, merely to do me justice, re-reading some letters from Van Gogh to his brother, which were published in the *Mercure*?

" Gauguin's arrival at Arles is calculated to change my painting considerably . . . "

In his letter to Aurier: " I owe much to Gauguin."

If you have an opportunity, study Van Gogh's painting before and after my stay with him at Arles. Van Gogh, influenced by his neo-impressionist studies, always worked with strong contrasts of tone on a complementary yellow, on violet, etc. Whereas, later,

---

[1] On receipt of this manuscript entitled *Reflections of a Dauber*, André Fontainas handed it to Alfred Valette, Editor of the *Mercure de France*, who submitted it to the Publications Committee, of which the writer was not a member. Publication was not recommended as the article lacked topicality.

following my advice, and my instructions, he worked quite differently. He painted yellow suns on a yellow surface, etc., learned the orchestration of a pure tone by all the derivatives of this tone. Then in the landscape all the usual medley, the subjects of still life, a former necessity, was replaced by great harmonies of solid colours suggesting the total harmony of the picture, the literary or explanatory part, whatever you like to call it, taking a back seat in consequence.

He had to make a great effort to get his drawing to fit this new technique. That is all in the day's work, to be sure, but very necessary.

But as all this impelled him to make experiments in accordance with his intelligence and his fiery temperament, his originality and his personality could only gain in the process.

All this is *between ourselves*, to show you that I would not take anything away from Van Gogh, while reserving a little credit to myself; to show you also that the critic has everything *to see* and discern—that he is liable to err, however well-intentioned.

If when discussing such a noble nature as Van Gogh's I am forced to praise myself, me the artist with sealed lips, this does not apply to other things in Brittany; in particular to the young Bernard. He was then 19, very deft in adapting himself first to one thing and then to another, to-day the neo-impressionists, to-morrow the Florentines, etc.

After having confessed to Van Gogh and to all who were then in Brittany, as well as to me in a letter which I have carefully preserved; after having acknowledged his debt and drunk at my spring, he dares in my absence to charge me with having robbed him of all his experiment.

To-day we behold him a man exhibiting fine things, I thank heaven for it.

My work from the start until this day—as can be seen—is congruent with all the gradations which comprise an artist's education—about all this I have preserved silence and shall continue to do so being persuaded that truth does not emerge from argument but from the work that is done.

Moreover, my life in such remote parts sufficiently proves how little I seek transient glory—my pleasure is to see the display of talent by others.

And if I write all this to you it is because, valuing your respect,

I should not like my manuscript to be imperfectly understood by you, nor should I like you to detect therein merely a desire to talk about myself, no—only I am furious when I see a man like Pissarro maltreated, wondering whose turn it will be to-morrow.

When I am maltreated it is another thing, I am not in the least annoyed, as I reflect: I may be nobody after all.

In all candour,

Yours very sincerely,
PAUL GAUGUIN.

177.

TO ANDRE FONTAINAS.   Atuana, February, 1903.

Dear Mr. Fontainas,

Your friendly letter does not surprise me as regards the *Mercure's* refusal: I had an idea that this would happen. On the *Mercure* there are men like Mauclair[1] who must not be meddled with. It is that rather than the lack of topicality.

Perhaps it is just as well for the following reason. I have just written quite a miscellany[2] of childish recollections, the wherefore of my instincts, of my intellectual development: thus what I have seen and heard (with criticisms of men and things), my art, that of others, my admirations, as well as my hates. It is not in the least a literary work, but something quite different: civilized man and the barbarian face to face. Consequently, the style must be in harmony with the subject, undressed like the whole man, and frequently shocking. However, this comes easy to me—I am not a writer.

I will send you the manuscript by next mail: in reading it you will divine between the lines the personal and malicious pleasure which I should feel in getting the book published. I *want* it published, but not in any luxurious style. I do not look for many readers—merely a few.

But why do I apply to you, a man I do not know very well?

[1] Gauguin detested the art critic Mauclair, whom he had known at Mallarmé's receptions.

[2] This refers to the manuscript entitled *Before and After,* published for the first time in facsimile by Kurt Wolff at Leipzig, in 1918. This manuscript loaned by André Fontainas to Mette Gauguin was never returned to him.

Put it down to my strange nature, my instinct . . . even at a distance I bestow confidence irrationally.

It is thus a considerable business I entrust to you, a labour, a responsibility. I have written about it to one of my friends: allow me to introduce you to him as an accomplished gentleman and a talented artist too modest to blow his own trumpet:

Georges Daniel de Monfreid,

Domaine de St. Clement, à Corneilla de Conflent.

I wrote him on this matter telling him to sacrifice the whole proceeds from my first exhibition of Tahiti pictures at no matter what price, to raise the money for this edition.

If therefore you would undertake this business, and I do not think you would like to disappoint and deeply distress me, get back what I have written for the *Mercure* and insert it in whatever place in the book you consider suitable.

You can interview on my behalf Delagrave the son (of the Delagrave printing works) : this young man did his service on a warship bound for Tahiti and as he is in touch with all the publishers he very kindly offered to assist me if ever I wanted to publish anything.

The drawings are of the same nature as the style . . . very unusual, sometimes scaring.

I should be grateful if you would, whatever happens, retain as a remembrance of me in a corner somewhere, like a barbarian trinket, and not in your drawer full of wonders, the manuscript with the sketches. This is not meant as recompense, a *troki-troka.*

We natives of the Marquesas know nothing of them; all we know is that we sometimes hold out the hand in friendship. Our hand would never be gloved.

In your cordial letter you ask me : Why do we no longer see your works ? Do you despise yourself to this extent ?

No, I do not despise myself : on the contrary, but this is the state of affairs. For several years I have been afflicted with an eczema half way up the leg, and for the last year I have suffered so severely from it that any sustained work has been impossible. Sometimes I go for two months without touching a brush. In spite of this I send something from time to time to Vollard, for the wherewithal to buy bread and drugs. I believe Vollard hides all these things, doubtless to hold for a rise. But I think he would show you some canvases, if you were to ask him. If I can manage, if not to get cured, at least to suffer not quite so much, I should be only half ill, for my brain goes on working and I will resume work in an attempt to finish properly the work I have commenced.

Besides, this is the only reason which, in my most terrible moments, stays my hand from blowing out my brains. My faith in my work is unconquerable. You see, my dear Sir, that I do not despise myself. One thing I fear is that I may become blind . . . in that case, I should be vanquished.

Yours sincerely,
PAUL GAUGUIN.

178.

TO CHARLES MORICE.   Atuana, February, 1903.

I enclose duplicate of a memorandum addressed to the Inspector of Colonies. Here in the Marquesas, besides the atrocious sufferings caused by my disease, I have a terrible struggle to wage against the authorities and the police.[1] I implore you, using all the influence at your command, to stir up as much noise as possible in the Press. But no time must be lost.

Abominable things are happening here in the Marquesas—and I am about to be expelled for not grovelling to a gendarme, I am accused of instigating the natives to revolt because I tell them what are their rights.

A gendarme says to a native: *Bougre de couillon:* and the native, not knowing French, replies: *Toi couillon.* This native asks me what couillon means; I tell him and they question his right to be informed. Of course, the native is put in prison.

Here is a fine cause to take up, but be quick.

PAUL GAUGUIN.

179.

TO THE INSPECTORS OF COLONIES.

Gentlemen,

You have requested us, even pledged us to tell you in writing all that we know about the Colony, together with any observations that may occur to us. As regards myself personally, I refrain from

[1] The police reported Gauguin as an anarchist, a dangerous madman and an inveterate drunkard.

submitting to you the eternal conspectus of the financial, administrative or agricultural situation, etc. . . . these are serious questions which have been discussed for a long time and have this peculiarity, that the more they are agitated by abundant demands—accompanied even by violent polemics—the more they lead to an aggravation of all the specified evils and to the Colony's eventual ruin, with the consequent necessity for the ill-used colonist to find another island, less tyrannical and more fertile.

I would merely ask you to find out for yourselves all about the natives of the Marquesas and the behaviour of the police towards them, inasmuch as " for reasons of economy, justice is administered here once in about 18 months."

The Magistrate arrives then, in a hurry to dispose of the accumulation of arrears, knowing nothing about them . . . nothing of what the natives are like, nothing of the matters except what is contained in the file submitted by the gendarme. Seeing before him a tattooed face, he says to himself: " Here is a cannibal brigand," especially if the interested gendarme tells him so. The gendarme draws up a charge on a mere denunciation covering one or thirty persons, no matter how many, for dancing, singing and drinking—some of whom have drunk orange juice. The thirty persons are fined 100 francs each (here 100 francs is equivalent to 500 francs in any other country) making a total of 3.000 francs plus costs—the gendarme's share being one-third of the fine, 1.000 francs. This third has recently been abolished, and to get their own back the gendarmes have increased the number of their charges, no doubt to show that they are always doing and have done what they call their duty.

I must add that this sum of 3.000 francs plus costs exceeds the total yield of their valley for a year; not to mention that the valley does not belong to them at all (as there are other natives in this valley under similar penalties).

I would also add that fines of this severity were levied after the calamity of the cyclone which burned all the bread-fruit trees, which means that for six months the natives were deprived of their only food.

Is this human? Is it moral?

The Magistrate arrives then and elects to stay at the gendarmerie headquarters, not at the hotel, taking his meals there, mixing with nobody except the inspector who hands him the files with his own amplifications.

Another one, yet another one, all of 'em bandits, etc. . . . And the Inspector adds: "Look, your Honour, if we are not severe with these people, we shall all be assassinated." And the Magistrate is persuaded.

I fail to see what intelligence there is in this.

At the hearing the accused is questioned through an interpreter who is ignorant of the shades of meaning of the language, and especially of the language of judges, a language very difficult to translate into this primitive language, except with many circumlocutions. As, for instance, when an accused native is asked if he was drunk, he answers no, and the interpreter says: "He says he has never been drunk," and the Magistrate exclaims: "But he has already been condemned for drunkenness."

The native, very timid by nature in front of the European who appears to him so much wiser and his superior, remembering also the gunfire of former days, comes into Court terrified by the gendarme, by the judicial precedents, etc., and prefers to confess even when he is innocent, knowing that a denial of the charge will expose him to a punishment much more severe—the reign of terror.

Say there is a gendarme who has drawn up a charge against several natives who have been unwilling to send their children to Monseignor's school, a Jesuit school, registered in the Annual as a " free school."

Say also that the magistrate has condemned them. Is it legal ?

With regard to these natives, remember that there are gendarmes in the stations exercising an absolute power, whose word has the effect of law, under no immediate supervision, interested in lining their pockets, in living on the backs of the natives, however poor they may be. The gendarme lifts his eyebrows and the native gives him chickens, eggs, pigs, etc. If not, let him look out for a prosecution. The gendarme orders a native to lead him into his house to see if there is any drink there. The native obeys and if he has the misfortune to have hidden there a carved cocotree or other knick-knack, he is sure to be forced sooner or later to make a gift of this article; if he disobeys he is condemned to a fine of 100 francs, he and his wife also, who, moreover, never had a key in her possession. (Atuana judgment of 18/2/03.)

When by chance an *exceptional colonist,* who is a little independent and very energetic manages (in spite of the difficulties) to put a policeman in the dock, everybody is turned topsy-turvy; but the worst that can happen is a little lecture behind closed doors and a transfer to another post.

It can be stated that the policeman is coarse, ignorant, venal and ferocious in the discharge of his functions; very clever, however, in looking after himself.

So if he receives a flagon of wine, you can be sure that he can produce the receipted account. A captain of a whaler said to anybody who cared to listen :

" I have greased the palms of the policeman sufficiently to be able to smuggle . . . but I have forgotten those wonderful invoices —we shall have to run out to sea after the whales."

Here the policeman discharges all sorts of duties, notary, local tax collector, sheriff's officer, harbour master . . . all without any proof of qualifications or honesty.

It is to be observed, however, that he is nearly always married; without counting his numerous mistresses who yield themselves always out of fear of future prosecutions.

It is further to be observed that the wife, although of very low condition, can dispense with a servant, and she and her husband may pick and choose among a host of people, in rivalry one with the other, prisoners, male and female, prison warders, officer's servants of both sexes, at the expense of the taxpayers. (Inspector Charpillet, year 1902.)

But when it is a matter of crime or murder, the scene changes at once. The policeman, in fear of being hit by a stone, preserves absolute silence, taking the left-hand side instead of the right, questioning nobody, even warned by the colonists, and saying : " when the magistrate come, he will see about it."

Apart from crimes which are happily very rare, as the population is for the most part, very well behaved, nothing remains but minor infractions of the law, drinking offences. The natives, having no amusements or distractions, are limited entirely to the pleasure of forbidden fruit, that is, a little fermented liquor, supplied gratis by nature : orange, banana, or cocoanut juice; and for this he flees the centres to hide himself somewhere else—the game flees the hunter and of course it is the game which starts the business ! At such times the agricultural or merchant colonist may seek in vain for labourers. In this manner the native reverts to savagery and

begins to hate the European. If not the consequence of such conditions, at any rate statistics record much more mortality at the
present time. In all this the policeman finds what he expects. Man
hunting is the way of getting many things for nothing.

I therefore request the Inspectors to inquire seriously into the
question in order to demand from the authorities in France, from
the men who sit in the seats of justice and humanity, what I would
require of them.

1. To ensure that justice in the Marquisas should be both
respectable and respected, I urge that the magistrates hold no communication with the police except for strictly business purposes,
boarding and lodging away from them, and also mixing with disinterested persons of influence who are able to give them useful
information.

2. It is essential that a magistrate should not accept police
reports without carefully checking them, even seeking useful information from colonists, and above all they should not invoke the law
unless the gendarme has acted with strict propriety.

And to that end I urge, what is a very simple matter and no
more than strict honesty, that the regulations governing the conduct
of the police, with regard to arrests, the right to draw up charges
and the strict limits imposed thereon, should be affixed to the wall
of the police office attached to the Court; that any breach of these
regulations committed by a gendarme should be punished and
should suffice to quash any sentence.

3. I urge that the fines for drink offences, pending their
revision on more liberal lines, should be proportionate to the means
of individuals, as it is inhuman that a fine of 60.000 francs in addition to its taxes should be imposed on a district which yields no
more than 50.000 francs.

If you look into the figures for yourselves, you will find that I
have understated the facts. I urge also that the police report should
not be considered as evidence pending the time when it can be
checked, and when the native population (knowing the French
language) will be able to testify against a gendarme without being
terrorised, without also passing through the hands of an interpreter,
so much cautioned as to be at the complete disposal of the police
(his position depending on them) while he is as at present imperfectly acquainted with French. as anyone can verify.

If on the one hand yon enact special laws preventing the natives from drinking while Europeans and negroes may do so: if on the other hand their evidence given in Court is nullified, it is a mere mockery to tell them that they are French electors and to give them schools and other religious humbug.

This hypocritical proclamation of Liberty, Equality and Fraternity under the French flag takes on a singular irony with respect to men who are no more than tax fodder in the hands of a despotic gendarme.

And yet they are compelled to cry, " Long live the Governor. Long live the Republic." When the 14th July comes round there is 400 francs in the cash box to be distributed among them, whilst in addition to their direct and indirect taxes they will have paid thousands of francs in fines.

In short, what we urge is that justice should be justice: not in scurvy and empty words, but in actual fact, and to this end, you must send us efficient men who are animated by generous intentions, so that they can study the question on the spot, then act with energy . . . in the full light of day.

When by chance a Governor visits here it is to take photographs and if a chief should dare to speak to him, asking for a wrong to be righted, the answer takes the form of abuse.

This then is what I have to tell you, if you should indeed be interested, unless you would say, with Pangloss . . . All is for the best in the best of possible worlds.

> February, 1903,
> Atuana,
> PAUL GAUGUIN, Painter.

180.

TO WILLIAM MOLARD.   Papeete, 30 March, 1903.

My dear Molard,
In haste, as our mails are like the coming and going of omnibuses.

All my congratulations on your daughter being provided for no doubt in accordance with your wishes.

> Yours,
> PAUL GAUGUIN.

181.

TO CHARLES MORICE.   Atuana, April, 1903.

My dear Morice,

    As something foreseen in my report on the police force of the
Marquesas which I sent you, I have just been caught in a snare
by the police, and I have been condemned all the same.[1] It spells
my ruin and appealing may make no difference, but at all events,
I must provide against all contingencies. If I lose an appeal, I will
take the case to the Paris Court of Appeal. I believe that Delzant[2]
is pretty good, and you must now find out who is the best advocate
for me in this Court of Appeal, if I have to go there.

    You see how right I was when I told you in my previous letter
to act quickly and with energy. If we win, the struggle will have
been glorious and I shall have done a great work in the Marquesas.
Many iniquities will have been abolished, and that will have been
worth all the suffering endured.

    I am down but not yet vanquished. Is the Indian who smiles
under torture vanquished ? Emphatically the savage is better than
we are. You were mistaken in saying that I was wrong to call myself
a savage. This is nevertheless true : I am a savage. And civilised
people have an inkling of this, for in my works there is nothing
that surprises or upsets if it is not this " savage in spite of myself."
This is why it is inimitable. A man's work is the explanation of that
man. And in it there are two kinds of beauty, one which comes
from instinct and the other which comes from study. To be sure the
combination of the two with the modifications it brings about yields
a great richness of a very complicated nature which the art critic
should be assiduous to discover. You are an art critic to-day; allow
me, not to lead you, but to advise you to open your eyes to what I
have just told you in a few rather mysterious lines. The great virtuosity of Raphael does not baffle me and does not prevent me for a
moment feeling, nay even comprehending his fundamental element,

---

[1] Gauguin who had long supported the natives against the authorities, had
levelled certain accusations against a gendarme named Guichenay, and
which were subsequently found to be true in part. But on the 23rd March,
1903, he was sentenced to three months' imprisonment and a thousand
francs fine. " I have just fallen victim to a frightful snare," he wrote to
Daniel de Monfreid. " It spells my ruin and the complete destruction of
my health."

[2] Delzant, advocate at the Paris Court of Appeal.

Gauguin "War and Peace" Carved wood

which is the instinct for the beautiful. Raphael was born with this sense of the beautiful. Everything else with him is only modification. In art we have just passed through a very long period of bewilderment caused by physics, mechanical chemistry and the study of nature. Artists having lost all their savagery, no longer having instinct, one might even say imagination, have gone wandering into all sorts of paths to find the productive elements which they lack the force to create, and consequently, are no longer active except in disorderly crowds, feeling afraid and lost when they are alone. This is why one must not prescribe solitude to everybody, for stamina is necessary to support it and act alone. All I have learned from others has impeded me. I can therefore say : nobody has taught me anything; it is true that I know very little ! but I prefer this little which is my very own. And who can say if this very little, exploited by others, may not become a big thing. How many centuries are needed to create an *appearance* of movement.

Yours ever,
PAUL GAUGUIN.

182.

TO PASTOR VERNIER.[1]   Beginning April, 1903.

Dear Mr. Vernier,

    Would it be troubling you if I asked for a consultation, as my eyesight is getting worse and worse ? I am ill. I can no longer walk.

P. G.

---

[1] Pastor Vernier, Protestant missionary, whom Gauguin esteemed and consulted from time to time about the sufferings he endured. Utterly exhausted, the artist died on Thursday, 8th May, 1903, at about 11 o'clock in the morning, of a heart attack. His last letter addressed to Daniel de Monfreid ended thus: " All these worries are killing me."

APPENDIX.

I.

THE naturalist writer Huysmans published "Modern Art" in 1883. In the pages devoted to the 1881 Exhibition of the Independents, he spoke of Gauguin's contribution in warm terms. " M. Gauguin is represented by a very characteristic canvas and one that reveals the undisputable talent of a modern painter. It is called *Study of a Nude.* In the foreground, a woman profile view, seated on a sofa engaged in mending her chemise; behind her the floor recedes, covered with a violet carpet up to the wall, on which is hung an Algerian curtain. The flesh is glaring; it is no longer the flat, smooth poreless skin of Millet, that skin uniformly dipped in a rose vat and passed under a warm iron by all painters. It is an epidermis, red blood pulsing beneath it and nerves that twitch. I am delighted to hail a painter who has felt like me, imperious disgust for the mannequins, with smooth, rosy breasts, small and hard bellies, mannequins overweighted by a so-called good taste, drawn according to recipes learnt in copying plaster work."

But Gauguin distrusted Huysmans, who only judged his painting according to naturalist theories. The year following, in fact, Huysmans reproached him with having made no progress.

" As to his *Interior of a Studio,* the colours are scurvy and heavy." Gauguin never forgave a disciple of Zola the expression " scurvy colour."

If Gauguin disliked art critics whom he accused of not understanding painting, he made an exception in favour of Albert Aurier, and towards the end of his life was very gracious to André Fontainas.

Albert Aurier, young symbolist writer, was born at Chateauroux in 1865, and contributed to the *Plume,* the *Decadent,* and the *Modernist,* to which Gauguin contributed articles; then becoming art critic of the *Mercure de France,* he published in that periodical some studies of Van Gogh,.Carrière, Monet, Pissarro and finally, symbolism in painting Paul Gauguin.

In connection with this important article, Emile Bernard, who was one of Aurier's best friends, wrote him the following letter: " My dear Aurier,

" I write you to discuss some fresh matters regarding which your co-operation would be an immense help.

" Gauguin and I want to go to Madagascar, and, for this purpose, need money. I cannot hope for any being too young and immature to sell pictures, but Gauguin who agrees to be responsible for me and who has greater chances, having passed through his apprenticeship stage, has written me to remind you, not for reasons of advertisement or of self-glorification, but for the interest that it might inspire in the public for our common life, to remind you of your projected articles about him.

" This could only be a very small matter for you, seeing that Gauguin's talent has already made an impression on you, to anticipate a little that which you intend to write.

" I will give you whatever notes and letters I can find, and you know where to see the canvases and are familiar with his ideas from his *Moderniste* articles. If you could publish this in the next *Mercure* it would be in the nick of time, or better still in the *Revue Independante,* which is better known.

" You have done Vincent, Pissarro, Raffaelli; I don't know whether the latter are included in the isolationist group, but Gauguin, the most isolated of all, deserves, it seems to me, to be placed in front of the latter.

BERNARD.

This article, the publication of which Emile Bernard urged so insistently, was one of the causes of his rupture with Gauguin.

II.

Gauguin sometimes made notes for the composition of certain canvases. Among the papers of Albert Aurier were found two visiting cards of : *Paul Gauguin, artiste peintre,* showing traces of a pencil sketch.

In the back of the first card are the words:

Christ   Special agony of the betrayal
                               applying to Jesus to-day and
                                      to-morrow
                                 small explanatory group
                                the whole sober harmony
                                  sombre colours and
                                    red—supernatural

The second visiting card contains rough notes for the composition of the Breton Calvary (1889) which is now in the Brussels Museum of Fine Art.

On the back   Calvary
                                  cold stone
                         of the soil — Breton   idea
                         of the sculptor who explains
                         religion through his Breton
                         soul with Breton costumes—
                         Breton local colour

passive sheep
and on the right

                         All in a Breton landscape
                             i.e., Breton poetry
                         point of departure (colour
                         brings the circle into heavenly
                         harmony
                                etc. . . . sad to do
                         In opposition (the human shape)
                                 poverty, etc.

III.

Mette Gauguin maintained friendly relations with Emile Schuffenecker, whose character and kindness she appreciated and whom she knew to be equally unhappy. She never missed calling on him on each of her visits to Paris and often wrote to him.

Of this important correspondence which has been almost entirely destroyed, I deem it necessary to publish three letters in which Mette Gauguin reveals to Schuffenecker her real feelings about her husband.

LETTER FROM METTE GAUGUIN TO
EMILE SCHUFFENECKER.   Wimmelskaftet, 47.
                                   (Copenhagen), 6 May, 1891.

My dear friend,

Pardon me for having let three months pass before answering
your very affectionate letter which I received in a whirlwind of
lessons and work, which may perhaps excuse me in your eyes; I
have had much to do this winter, fortunately, and I am a little tired,
but satisfied to be able still to carry the burden that Paul so wantonly
laid on me.

Dear friend, read the enclosed letter, and add the address. I
have forgotten the number of the house : I write him so rarely and
I think of him even more rarely; but I consider that when I learn
he has money,[1] it is my duty to remind him that he has five children
and that the work I do is not enough to maintain them all. Ah ! if
I did not have such devoted friends, what would become of me !
God in heaven ! But my heart is filled with bitterness at the thought
that Paul could be so criminally egoistic, and never have I heard of
or seen such a thing. And yet I do myself an injustice to complain.
I am happier here in a different way than in Paris. Only my children
will one day blush for their father and that is hard for them.

Everybody is well, the huge Emil seems to be working at the
Polytechnic School. Aline is taller than I and very elegant, a young
person extremely proper. Clovis works in his shop, returning in the
evening, grimy like a real blacksmith, washes himself, devours his
meal and is perfectly happy, for the little wretch detests study and
school. Baby Jean is immensely like me—both inside and out—he is
keen to be a naval officer, and it is about this matter that I am
asking Paul to help me, which would be the least he could do. Pola
is pretty, a pretty little Spaniard and very intelligent; they are all
happy, but I cannot avoid thinking with some apprehension about
their future, if I should be taken from them—and I am getting
old, my hair is almost white, and my strength is no longer what it
was.

Kiss the children, remember me to your wife, and *au revoir*—
when ? I confess I am not attracted to Paris, I suffered there too
much ! But you could come to Copenhagen; I am not going into the

---

[1] Mette Gauguin had just learnt that her husband had received 9.860 francs,
the proceeds of the sale of the 23rd February previously at the hotel
Drout, with which he left for Tahiti.

country this year because of Clovis who cannot leave his workshop. Here is a long letter, reply to me. Tell me if you think I was wrong in approaching Paul. True I am 20,000 miles away from him, but this does not alter the fact that he is the father of five children, whose future haunts me.

Yours very sincerely,

METTE GAUGUIN.

LETTER FROM METTE GAUGUIN TO
EMILE SCHUFFENECKER. (Copenhagen) 15 September, 1893.

My dear Schuff,

I have not replied to your letter of the 25th August in which you informed me of Paul's arrival, which in fact happened sooner than, we, Daniel and I, thought. And so he has returned ! according to his letter, just as he was when he departed, relying on the most monstrously brutal egoism, which for me is phenomenal and incomprehensible.

No, Schuff, from him nothing can be expected ! He never thinks of anything but himself and his welfare; he prostrates himself in complete admiration before his own magnificence. That his children have to be fed through his wife's friends is a matter of perfect indifference to him, he does not want to be told of it! *Dame,* he does not know it ! Yes, this time, I am furious. You probably know what has happened ? Eight days after he arrived our uncle died in Orleans, very conveniently for Paul, who will inherit 15.000 francs. Paul wrote to me to know if I could send him some money; unfortunately the few hundred crowns that I had collected (I sold some old pictures that were exhibited) have been spent on different things unforeseen or rather foreseen Emil's leaving school, clothes for this giant, etc., and I had *dame,* nothing; a matter he is magnanimous enough to pass over in silence, now he is within reach of uncle's little legacy. We know, you and I, that he left for his little trip to Tahiti with *all* the proceeds of his sale, and I said nothing; this time he does not even mention giving me a part of the 15.000 francs, and I must be allowed to say something to him about that. Besides he asks me to find the money for a little trip to Paris ! ! ! I am more than ever constrained to stay, I cannot leave alone five big creatures, for whom I *alone* am responsible! If he wants to see us, he knows where to find us ! For my part I am not running about the world like one demented! Perhaps, dear friend, you will find me cold, severe, venal, as Paul used to say, but candidly all these affectations are enough to make one tired ! I have been very worried about Emil's future, I mentioned it to Paul, who tells me that we should not worry ourselves about anything, the boy being big enough to make his own way. Yes, he is pretty big, but not to make his own way, if we desire to see him placed in a suitable position in society. Fortunately my friend, the Countess de Malthe, thinks differently from his father. She will continue to support him after he has taken his degree and to-morrow we are going to decide where he will finish his studies to become a civil engineer. When I see the kindness of others compared with the egoism of Paul, I do not know whether to laugh or cry. I do neither the one nor the other, I have too much to do to try to make these children useful citizens. Aline is home from boarding school; she is quite charming, and does her best to help me to look after her brothers; the children are good looking and healthy. Paul, the youngest, will soon be 10 years old. Perhaps, Schuff, the worst is over, and one day I shall have a reward for my work other than the mere satisfaction of duty done, which, between ourselves, is not very satisfying. But can you understand a father who feels nothing, nothing, nothing ! I believe he would see us all die without being unduly agitated. What happiness if I could have been able to live surrounded by my family and cherished with no other worry save the care for the morrow, and that other, very poignant indeed, of lacking affection for him who is everybody's father.

However, I have written you because I wanted to relieve my heart. Tell me if you find me unjust. No, don't tell me that, for I fear I cannot alter my opinion ! My summer has done me good, but I confess that at this moment I feel furious ! Kiss Jean, good health to Paul, whom you ought to send to me. I believe it would do him good to breathe the calm and honesty of this adorable and blessed little country, where I have found peace, and my splendid boys would be excellent friends for him.

Your old friend,

METTE GAUGUIN.

Do not show this to a living soul, promise me !

LETTER FROM METTE GAUGUIN TO
EMILE SCHUFFENECKER.   (Copenhagen) 11 June, 1900.

Dear friend,

Two lines only to acquaint you with the cruel calamity that has just befallen me. My poor Clovis has died at 21; you know that three years ago he had an accident resulting in a stiff hip. It was thought that an operation might remedy his condition and 12 days after the operation he died of blood poisoning. For blows of this kind there can be only bitter tears and I bewail for the second time the loss of one of my big children; alas ! two of those for whom I have worked and hoped have left me, leaving a frightful void in my heart and in my life. I am alone at present with the two youngest, Jean and Paul. Emil left the day before yesterday for Bogota, he did not want to finish his studies—another very bitter pill for me—but perhaps it will be the making of him out there ? He knows enough to get a job as a Civil engineer; he really is able to work, I am sure he will be able to make a livelihood.

Dear friend, give me Paul's address if you have it. It seems to me that he must be written to although it goes much against the grain, for his ferocious egoism revolts me every time I think of it.

I have borne heavy burdens, I have suffered all these distresses, all these worries *alone*. Or would you send him this letter ? Do what you like and believe me always yours very sincerely,

                    METTE GAUGUIN.

But Schuffenecker, shocked by Gauguin's attitude towards her, never wrote him again and Gauguin on his part never forgave his old colleague of Bertin's Bank the friendship, always disinterested, which he bore towards his wife. This is evidenced by some of the painter's letter to Daniel de Monfreid.

CHRONOLOGY OF LIFE OF PAUL GAUGUIN.

1848. June 7, birth of Paul Gauguin, 56, rue Notre-Dame-de-Lorette, Paris. His father: Clovis Gauguin, native of Orleans and journalist, contributed to the *National.* His mother :. Aline-Marie Chazal, daughter of Flora Tristan, of Peruvian origin, Saint Simonian writer.

1851. After Louis Bonaparte's coup d'etat, Clovis Gauguin lost his position. Departure of the family (two children, Paul and Marie) for Peru. The father died on the way from aneurysm. He was buried at Fort Famine (Straits of Magallan) Stay of four years in Lima

1855. Return to France to settle estate questions. Madame Aline Gauguin and her children reside with Uncle Isidore Gauguin, 7, rue Endelle, Orleans.

1859. Paul enters Petite Seminaire.

1865. Joins the mercantile marine and embarks on the *Luzzitano.* Voyage from Havre to Rio de Janiero, where he discovers the wealth of exotic landscapes.

1868. National Navy. Registers at Havre on 26th February. Embarks on the *Jérome Napoléon.*

1871. Discharged on 23rd April. Becomes a clerk to the exchange broker Bertin, rue Lafitte, where he makes the acquaintance of Emile Schuffenecker.

1872. Gauguin's financial position is excellent.

1873. Marriage with a young Dane : Mette Sophie Gad, on 22nd November at the Town Hall of the 9th Arrondissement. Religious ceremony at the Lutheran Church, Rue Chauchat.

1874. In June, Gauguin is often with Pissarro and at the Colarossi Academy. September, birth of Emil.

1876. 25th December, birth of Aline. Gauguin who has been painting for two years on Sundays, exhibits for the first time at the Salon.

1877. Moves to Rue des Foureaux, where he makes the acquaintance of the sculptor, Bouillot.

1879. Under the influence of Pissarro, who really initiated him into painting. Gauguin makes a collection of impressionist canvases. Birth of Clovis.

1880. Takes a more active interest in painting. Moves to 8, Rue Carcel, where he stays until the beginning of 1883. Takes part in the Exhibition of the Independents and in the 5th Impressionist Exhibition, 10, Rue des Pyramides.
WORKS: les Pommiers de l'Ermitage, les Maraichers de Vaugirard.

1881. J. K. Huysmans in his article of the 1881 Exhibition of the Independents, refers to Gauguins, *Study in the Nude*: " I do not hesitate to assert that among contemporary painters who have worked in the nude, none has so far uttered so vehement a note in the real, and I do not except Courbert from such painters."

1882. In March, 7th Impressionist Exhibition, 251, Rue Saint Honore, in which Gauguin took part, after long discussions among Pissarro, Degas, Renoir and Claude Monet, who did not want to exhibit with the " first upstart dauber."
WORKS: Peniches sur la Seine, le Petit Ruisseau.

1883. In January, without warning either his wife or his friends, Gauguin forsook the Bourse. " At last I can paint every day," he exclaimed. Pola born in December.

1884. To reduce his living expenses Gauguin leaves Paris for Rouen. He leaves for Denmark in early November.
WORKS: Portrait de Paul Gauguin au Chevalet, la Mere de l'artiste.

1885. In the first months of this year Gauguin represented in Denmark the tilt manufacturers, Messrs Dillies & Co., of Roubaix. Unpleasantness with his wife's family: " I hate the Danes," he declared. In June, he returned to Paris with his son Clovis and lodges in the cul-de-sac Frémin. Three weeks' stay in England. On 13th October rents a lodging, 10, rue Cail.

1886. 8th Exhibition of impressionist painting, rue Lafitte from the 15th May to the 15th June. In June, after placing his Clovis in a boarding school at Antony, he goes to Pont-Aven for the first time and stays in the Gloanac pension. First meeting with Emile Bernard in August. Return to

Paris in November; meets Van Gogh. Spends December in hospital.

WORKS: Nature morte au profil, Chaumiere a Pont-Aven.

1887.   On 10th April, in company of Charles Laval, leaves Saint Nazaire for Panama and Martinique.

WORKS: Paysages de la Martinique.

1888.   On returning to France penniless, Gauguin stays with Emile Schuffenecker, 29, rue Boulard. In August at Pont-Aven fresh meeting with Emile Bernard. Birth of " the synthesis." First oneman show at Boussod and Valadon. Beginning of October paints the *Talisman* for Serurier, on 22nd of same month rejoins Vincent Van Gogh at Arles, where he remains until the 25th December, on which day Vincent attacked him with a razor.

WORKS: le Vision apres le sermon, les Lavandieres, le Cabaretiere, Arles.

1889.   Gauguin rents until March a studio at 25, Avenue Montsouris. Universal Exhibition. Visits the Javanese Village. Schuffenecker organizes an Exhibition of the impressionist and synthetic group at the café des Arts kept by Volpini. Crowd flock to the café, derisive success, Maurice Denis, Paul Serusier, Pierre Bonnard leave perplexed. Gauguin returns to Pont-Aven in April and spends the winter at the Marie Henry Inn, Pouldu.

WORKS: le Christ jaune, la Famille du peintre Schuffenecker, le Belle, Angele, Portriat charge de Paul Gauguin. Bonjour, M. Gauguin, bois sculpte: Soyez amoureuses, vous serez heureuses.

1890.   On 28th January asks for shelter at Schuffenecker's rue Durand Clay, then takes a room at a hotel in the rue Delambre. Then to Pouldu until 7th November. Mette Gauguin remains permanently in Copenhagen with her children.

WORKS: le Calvaire breton, Portrait d'enfants.

1891.   On 23rd February auction at the Drouot Hotel, banquet on 23rd March. Leaves for Tahiti on 4th April, arrives at Papeete on 8th June. Takes up his abode 30 miles from town.

WORKS: Portrait de Mlle. Vaite Goupil, Te Tiare Farani, Je vous salue Marie " Ia Orana Maria."

1892.   Year of intensive work, painting, carving. Health bad but he writes and illustrates Noa-Noa.'

WORKS: Matamoe, Joyeusetes: "Arearea," Pastorales tahitiennes.

1893. 3rd August, arrives at Marseilles. 4th November, Exhibition at Durand-Ruel's. He rents a studio, 4, Rue Vercingetorix, where he lives with Annah the Javanese. Holds big receptions every week. At the end of December receives his share of his Uncle Isidore's estate.

WORKS: Annah la Javanaise, Paul Gauguin a la palette, Paul Gauguin a l'idole, l'Esprit des morts veille: "Manao Tupapau."

1894. In January visits Bruges. From April to December stays at Pont-Aven and La Pouldu. At Concarneau with sailors, who break his ankle. Returns in December to Paris, where he discovers that Annah has carried off most of the articles that decorated his studio.

WORKS: les Blanchisseuses, Bretonnes sur la route.

1895. Disgusted with the life he is leading in Paris, Gauguin decided to return to Tahiti. On 18th February new auction at the Drouot Hotel, more disastrous than the preceeding. A few days later he quits France for ever. In spite of the disagreements which have arisen between him and his wife, he still corresponds with her.

1896. Tahiti. Crisis of despair: *I fall on my knees and cast aside all pride. I am nothing if not a failure.*

WORKS: Poemes barbares, la Femme au Mangos: "Te Aru Vahine," Portrait de Paul Gauguin a l'ami Daniel.

1898. On 11th February, scorned by the Europeans, without money and exhausted, in a state of feverish excitement, he attempts suicide. Removal to hospital. To support life, works in the office of Public Works and Survey of Lands. In December, Ambroise Vollard shows interest in him.

WORKS: D'ou venons-nous? Que sommes-nous? Ou allons-nous? Faa Iheihe.

1899. In June publishes *Wasps*, a satirical journal, and in August launches the *Smile*.

WORKS: les Seins aux fleurs rouges.

1900. His sufferings at their height Gauguin abandons painting from March to November. End of December enters hospital (12 francs a day).

1901. Life in Tahiti becoming too dear, Gauguin sells his hut and transports himself to Atuana, a village in La Dominique (Hiva-Oa), Marquesas Islands. He calls his new abode The House of the Reveller.

Work: Et l'or de leur corps.

1902. Gauguin lost no opportunity of championing the cause of the natives, and, of course, quarrelled with the Bishop and the Authorities. He disliked the police, whom he accused of smuggling. He is now receiving next to no money from France. His poverty is extreme, and heart disease is gaining on him. His legs covered with eczema cannot be cured, syphilis ravaging his once so powerful body.

WORKS : Adam et Eve, Tahitiennes dans la case l'Appel.

1903. Prosecuted for slander by the policeman Guichenay, Gauguin is condemned on 31st March to 3 months' imprisonment and 1,000 francs fine. He appeals and would certainly have won his case, but could not raise money to go to Tahiti. On 8th May about 11 in the morning, Paul Gauguin dies. Fastened to his easel is an unfinished canvas : Breton Village Under the Snow.